The Crib, the Cross, and the Crown

The Crib, the Cross, and the Crown

Reflections on the Stories of
the First Christmas and Easter

MICHAEL HOOTON
Foreword by Dianne Tidball

RESOURCE *Publications* · Eugene, Oregon

THE CRIB, THE CROSS, AND THE CROWN
Reflections on the Stories of the First Christmas and Easter

Copyright © 2016 Michael Hooton. All rights reserved. Except for brief quotations in critical publications or reviews, no part of this book may be reproduced in any manner without prior written permission from the publisher. Write: Permissions, Wipf and Stock Publishers, 199 W. 8th Ave., Suite 3, Eugene, OR 97401.

Resource Publications
An Imprint of Wipf and Stock Publishers
199 W. 8th Ave., Suite 3
Eugene, OR 97401

www.wipfandstock.com

PAPERBACK ISBN: 978-1-4982-8295-6
HARDCOVER ISBN: 978-1-4982-8297-0
EBOOK ISBN: 978-1-4982-8296-3

Manufactured in the U.S.A.   06/01/16

Scripture quotations are taken from the HOLY BIBLE, NEW INTERNATIONAL VERSION ®, Copyright © 1973, 1978, 1984 by International Bible Society. Used by permission of Zondervan. All rights reserved.

Contents

Foreword by Dianne Tidball | vii
Abbreviations | viii
Preface | ix

1 The Incarnate Word | 1

2 The Promised Messiah | 12

3 The Baby of Bethlehem | 38

4 The King and Judge | 59

5 The Teacher, Lord, and Prophet | 73

6 The Passover Lamb | 98

7 The Leader and High Priest | 115

8 The Suffering Servant | 135

9 The Crucified Savior | 150

10 The Risen Christ | 168

Bibliography | 201

Foreword

The well-worn paths of the Christmas and Easter stories come to us through Michael's writing with fresh insights, great wisdom and contemporary understanding. This is a clearly written book, detailed and well argued, with a pastor's application and a reality about life today. There are witty and amusing illustrations supporting a thoughtful and rigorous approach to the Biblical texts which has been informed by wide knowledge and careful reflection.

For preachers who face the Christian seasons with foreboding about presenting "the message of Christmas and Easter again," this offers a resource which is both clear in explanation and practical in application. With some tricky concepts which are difficult to present, the author gives helpful approaches such as Jesus' second coming being "close" signifying, not a chronological time table, but more spiritual imminence.

I particularly liked the thoughts about communion having perspectives of looking backward, forward, around, inward and outward, and things such as the priestly prayer as a pattern for our praying.

From Haydn to Harry Potter, Michael uses every possible illustration to bring new ways of grasping the Good News of salvation in Christ. His writing is intellectually accessible and credible, and spiritually satisfying. It seems as if this small but comprehensive book has surveyed the whole Gospel, and the whole of discipleship, through the lens of the Biblical narratives of Jesus' birth, death and resurrection.

Dianne Tidball
Vice-President of the Baptist Union of Great Britain

Abbreviations

NBD *New Bible Dictionary*, edited by I. H. Marshall et al. Leicester, UK: Inter-Varsity Press, third edition, 1996.

NIDNTT *The New International Dictionary of New Testament Theology*, edited by Colin Brown. English edition, 4 vols. Grand Rapids, Michigan: Regency Reference Library, Zondervan, 1975–78.

ODQ *The Oxford Dictionary of Quotations*, edited by Angela Partington. Oxford University Press/London: Book Club Associates, fourth edition, 1992.

PDQ *The Penguin Dictionary of Quotations*, compiled and edited by J.M. and M.J. Cohen. Harmondsworth, Middlesex, UK: Penguin, 1960.

SOED The *Shorter Oxford English Dictionary*, revised and edited by C. T. Onions, 2 vols. Oxford University Press/London: Book Club Associates, 1983.

Preface

"The beginning of the Gospel about Jesus Christ . . ." (Mark 1:1)

Aristotle said in his *Poetics* that a good story or plot was one which has a beginning, a middle, and an end. The story of Jesus as given in the four Gospels, which, as a famous Hollywood epic reminds us, is "the greatest story ever told," might be said to have a beginning (the birth story), a middle (the public ministry), and an end (the final week in Jerusalem leading to the cross and resurrection).

This book however falls short of Aristotle's ideal: I intend to leave out the middle, and discuss the account of Jesus' birth, and the events of the last week climaxing in the cross. I trust that no one will assume that that is because I regard the public ministry of Jesus as unimportant. There is a good reason—in addition to the obvious practical one of keeping this book to a manageable length—why writing about the birth and the death of Christ makes sense. It is the truth of the incarnation and the facts and significance of the death and resurrection that are the focus of the doctrines at the heart of the Christian faith. The great credal statements of the church do not normally mention the life and public ministry of Jesus: the *Apostles' Creed* moves straight from "He was conceived by the power of the Holy Spirit and born of the virgin Mary" to "He suffered under Pontius Pilate, was crucified, died, and was buried." The life and teaching of Jesus are a vital pattern for Christian discipleship; but it is the fact of who Jesus *is*—the Word who became flesh—and of what he *did* in his death and resurrection that are at the heart of the faith we profess and the Gospel we proclaim to the world.

The most obvious and basic fact about the "beginning" and the "end" parts of the Gospels is that they record events which happened once for all in history. The whole of our Christian faith rests, not on ideas or ideals, but on historical facts. The word "Gospel" means "good news," and "news" is about what has happened; the Gospel is not good ideas, useful teaching, or positive values, but the story of what God did when he sent his Son into the world and when Jesus died and rose again. But enshrined within those historical events are key truths: that Jesus is the Son of God incarnate, and that his death was an atoning sacrifice for our sins. Paul writes that "God sent his Son, born of a woman . . . to redeem those under law . . . " (Galatians 4:4–5): the essential Christian doctrines of *incarnation* and *redemption* are at the heart of the great historical facts that Christ was born and that he died on the cross. James 2:26 says that "the body without the spirit is dead"; and if our faith is to be a truly *living* faith it has to be the "body" of historical events animated by the "spirit" of the doctrinal truths which alone lend those events their unique significance. The stories without the truths of the incarnation and the atonement are not a living Gospel but merely a historical carcass; on the other hand the doctrines of salvation are not "disembodied" truths, but are encountered in the historical person of Jesus, the Word who became flesh.

This book is offered as a modest contribution to exploring and celebrating both the facts about Jesus' birth and death, and the truths that are incarnate in those facts. Its purpose is, first, to enable Christians to explore what the accounts of Jesus' birth and of his death and resurrection show us about who he is; and second, to think through the implications of those monumental events for our own lives and faith. It makes no claim to be a verse-by-verse commentary; but it does offer reflections on the central themes that are found in the four Gospels' presentation of the "beginning" and the "end" sections of the story of Jesus.

That is why there are in the chapters that follow a large number of references to texts in the Gospels; where it seemed appropriate I have often quoted the actual words of the Bible, but I have invariably added the reference in brackets. These references are intended to encourage the reader continually to go back to the Bible itself, just as the people of Berea "examined the Scriptures every day to see if what Paul said was true" (Acts 17:11). In the 1980 *Alternative Service Book* of the Church of England, a "collect" (or prayer) for the second Sunday in advent includes the words, "Help us so to hear [the words of Scripture], to read, mark, learn, and inwardly digest them, that . . . we may embrace, and for ever hold fast the hope of everlasting life." It is the Bible itself that is the food that nourishes our faith; the most that this book, or any other, can do is to help Christians who desire to "hold fast the hope of everlasting life" to be able to "inwardly digest" more of what is in it.

Where parallel verses or passages in different Gospels are listed, I have used the common convention of separating them by slanting parallel lines:

so "Mark 14:14//Luke 22:11" means that those two verses are Mark's and Luke's record of the same saying, even if the actual wording may occasionally differ slightly.

I am very grateful to Dianne Tidball, for her gracious and generous foreword; and to Andy Blurton, who helped in the preparation of the final manuscript.

Unless otherwise stated, Scripture quotations are taken from the *New International Version* (International Bible Society, 1973, 1978, 1984); I have used the 1996 edition (Zondervan, Grand Rapids, Michigan).

1

The Incarnate Word

"In the beginning..." (John 1:1)

The outline of Jesus' life in our Gospels starts with two complementary prologues, those of Luke (1:1–4) and John (1:1–18). Luke's prologue gives an assurance that his account of the Gospel is accurate and reliable; John's reveals Jesus as the eternal Word of God, who became a human being.

Without even reading beyond these two brief introductions, the Gospel writers have already presented us with the great mystery that lies at the heart of our Christian faith and of our understanding of Jesus: that he is both fully God and fully man. Luke stresses *the human side* of Jesus. He has researched the life of Jesus carefully—as he says, "I myself have carefully investigated everything from the beginning"—and in his Gospel he is offering the results of his study. There is a human side to the person of Jesus. He was a man who appeared in history, who can be investigated, studied and thought about; and a man about whom people can have a variety of ideas.

And that is what many Christians, very understandably, find difficult; we can be distressed or angered by the frequent airing of "new" and often quite bizarre theories about Jesus, which sometimes attract a level of attention in the popular media that falls only a little way short of the insatiable appetite for the latest gossip that is pandered to in the celebrity magazines. A hundred years ago, debate about alternative views of Jesus was confined largely to academic theological circles; in our day, it reaches a much wider public through popular paperbacks and, in particular, TV documentaries. So, for example, in April 2010, a series on the "Discovery Channel" entitled *Who Was Jesus?* presented a picture of Jesus as a pacifist political opponent of the Roman occupation of Jerusalem. In August 2008, Channel Five offered *Secrets of the Jesus Tomb*, claiming to have discovered the tomb belonging to Jesus' family, including his son, one "Judas," fathered, it is claimed, through a relationship with Mary Magdalen. In February 2007, Channel Four broadcast a program with the title, *Did Jesus Die?*, which not only re-hashed the (long-since discredited) claim that the explanation for the resurrection story is that Jesus never actually died on the cross, but added to it the suggestion that a wandering preacher named Jus Asaf, who was active in Kashmir in the middle of the first century, was in fact Jesus, presumably having made a fresh start following the near-disastrous end to the first stage of his career in Palestine. In December 2005, two magicians, Barry Jones and Stuart MacLeod, appeared on a Channel Four program entitled *The Magic of Jesus*, performing as magic tricks their own versions of a number of the miracles ascribed to Jesus in the Gospels, suggesting that Jesus was a kind of first-century "Dynamo." And in March 2001, the front cover of *Radio Times* depicted a computer-generated face, based on a two-thousand-year-old skull, under the heading "Is this the face of Jesus?"; it heralded a new series entitled *Son of God*, presented by the BBC Middle East correspondent Jeremy Bowen, who admitted to having started out skeptical about the historical accuracy of the stories about Jesus. One of the notable aspects of the series was the attempt to "fill out" the hidden years in Jesus' life between the ages of twelve and thirty.

It should be said that not all these and the many other television programs about Jesus that I could have listed were necessarily negative about or hostile to the Jesus of Christian faith. Some were; others were fairly neutral; some, like Mr Bowen's *Son of God* series, were in fact quite sympathetic to the Jesus of biblical history. But all were essentially secular; they presented a merely human view of Jesus as a historical character about whom there can be debate and discussion, and around whom there developed theories which later became part of traditional Christian theology.

It is that treatment of Jesus that makes our evangelical hackles rise. And there are many Christians who see this modern fascination with alternative views of Jesus as a serious impediment to the cause of Christian mission in our society.

Maybe. Or maybe not. Because Luke's prologue suggests that the situation in which we find ourselves today is not very different from that prevailing in the first century, when Luke wrote his Gospel. True, they were spared Channel Four and the internet. But there were in the days of the biblical Gospel writers a variety of other competing ideas about Jesus vying for the attention of a public as hungry for the latest religious ideas as our own society is for the latest gossip or controversy. In fact, as Luke himself tells us in Acts 17:21, people in the Greek society into which the Gospel was first preached "spent their time doing nothing but talking about and listening to the latest ideas," which could easily be a description of our own twenty-first-century western world; all we would need to add, alongside "talking about" and "listening to," would be "and surfing the net in pursuit of."

"Many have undertaken to draw up an account" of the story of Jesus, says Luke; and we can be sure that he was not referring merely to Matthew, Mark and John. Luke is not of course saying that all or even most of the "many" were offering versions of the story of Jesus that were inaccurate; he simply says that lots of people are talking about Jesus, and so he wants to present a proper and "orderly account" of Jesus, one that can substantiate the other stories where they are right, and correct them where they are misleading. We know that a number of apocryphal stories about Jesus started to circulate very early in the history of the church, and that one of the reasons for the four biblical Gospels being written was to present an authentic and reliable account of the truth about Jesus. Even within the ministry of Jesus himself, people were expressing a variety of ideas about him, some of them distinctly unflattering: he was seen as an ordinary man ("Isn't this the carpenter?," Mark 6:3), as an immoral *bon viveur* ("Here is a glutton and a drunkard . . . ," Matthew 11:19), as mentally unstable ("He is out of his mind!," Mark 3:21), as a political activist (" . . . one who was inciting the people to rebellion," Luke 23:14), as a foreign impostor ("Aren't we right in saying that you are a Samaritan . . . ?," John 8:48), and as a tool of Satan ("You are demon-possessed," John 7:20).

That is the context into which the apostles first proclaimed Jesus as Lord and Savior. "Many [had] undertaken to draw up" their accounts of Jesus, and many more would continue to do so over the years to come. Those accounts would contain everything from the sublime to the ridiculous; some would be sympathetic to Jesus, some wildly inaccurate, some well-meaning but misleading or inadequate, some downright heretical. And if Luke were writing in our age, he might well have started his Gospel by saying "Many have undertaken to present TV programs offering ideas about the things that have been fulfilled among us . . . "

The general impression that we get from the New Testament is that the apostles' response to the multiplicity of religious views in their society—including the variety of wrong, misleading, silly or even blasphemous ideas about Jesus—was not to huff and puff about them, not to inveigh against them, not to bemoan the fact that they made the task of Christian evangelism so much more complicated, but simply to tell people the truth about

Jesus. Luke admits that many have presented their ideas about Jesus, but he says nothing about the degree to which he agrees or disagrees with any or all of them. He merely says that he is going to tell the story of Jesus as it happened.

It is worth saying that this fact significantly counters the frequent assumption that the life and ministry of Jesus was that of a simple preacher whose message could be summed up as one of moral and social teaching, and that the Gospel writers then embroidered this by adding all sorts of supernatural detail in order to make their Jesus a more "charismatic" and "divine" character. In fact, says Luke, the opposite is true. He has been at pains to strip away all the fanciful and legendary additions to and distortions of the story of Jesus, and give us the plain, unvarnished facts.

So how should the Christian church respond to the fact that we live in a society awash with theories about Jesus that are at best less than the whole truth and at worst a blatant rejection of the truth? Luke's prologue would suggest, simply by telling people about the real Jesus. In the church's evangelistic witness, two minutes spent sharing the truth about Jesus is more potentially fruitful than two hours explaining why other people are wrong. Jesus himself said that "the truth will set you free" (John 8:32); he did *not* say that denouncing those who don't speak the truth will set you free.

Luke presents us with a Jesus who is a man in history, who has been and can be investigated. Moreover, Luke's approach to his task of putting together his Gospel was, in a sense, very human: "I myself have carefully investigated everything . . . it seemed good also to me to write an orderly account . . . " That suggests a number of lessons for us.

1. Luke had done his homework. He had researched his subject, or, as he puts it, "investigated": the word used means literally "to follow" or "accompany," but it is never used in the New Testament in the sense of literally "following" Jesus in the way his disciples did, that is, accompanying him on his travels; Paul uses it in 1 Timothy 4:6 when he says that Timothy was "brought up in the truths of the faith and of the good teaching that you have *followed*," and Luke is here using it in the same sense, as a reference to his long and detailed study of the facts about Jesus, which has made him, humanly speaking, competent now to write his Gospel account.

2. Luke undertook this research "carefully." He was thorough; his was no Gospel sketched on the back of an envelope, but the result of a long and painstaking process of hard work.

3. He was at pains to produce "an orderly account": the same word is used in Acts 11:4, "Peter . . . explained everything to them *precisely as*

it had happened." Luke worked hard to put his Gospel together in the best and most helpful way, so as to convey accurately the true story of Jesus.

4. The whole of Luke's prologue is in the conventional style of the preface to a literary work in the ancient world. It is addressed to "Theophilus," presumably Luke's literary patron, to whom his two-volume work is dedicated, and Acts 1:1 gives a similar dedication of Luke's second volume. This Theophilus is addressed as "most excellent," the normal polite address to a socially prominent dignitary; and Luke's preface, as was customary, summarizes the purpose of, and the background to the writing of, his book. In other words, Luke's Gospel presents itself as a "normal" work of literature, one that could take its rightful place alongside other (secular) volumes of history; and, as one commentator has put it, "By writing in this fashion . . . Luke was claiming a place for Christianity on the stage of world history."[1]

5. Finally, he wrote his Gospel as a result of a personal decision and judgment that it was the right and proper thing to do: "it seemed good . . . to me." Later, at a vital turning point in the history of the early church, the leaders in Jerusalem would make decisions in the same way; in Acts 15:22 we are told that "the apostles and elders . . . *decided* to choose some of their own men and send them to Antioch . . .": the phrase is literally "it seemed good to the apostles and elders." They did it because it seemed to them the necessary and appropriate thing to do. Luke wrote his Gospel for the same reason.

Humanly speaking, that is. Please allow me here a moment of personal *credo*. I believe that the whole Bible, from Genesis to Revelation, is the inspired, infallible and eternal Word of God. I am convinced that the words of Scripture are the words that God himself has given us. I take quite literally the Bible's own description of itself as "God-breathed" (2 Timothy 3:16).

But it was still written down by people. Sometimes, no doubt, those human authors were very conscious that the Spirit of God was breathing through them and using them to be the channels of God's Word; certainly Jeremiah 20:9 suggests something of the sort ("His word is in my heart like a fire, a fire shut up in my bones. I am weary of holding it in; indeed I cannot"). At other times, it seems, the composition of biblical books seemed to their authors to be a human work; and Luke's prologue says that quite explicitly. Yet Luke's Gospel is as much part of God's inspired Word as Jeremiah. The Spirit of God worked through Luke's careful study and detailed preparation just as he had worked through Jeremiah's fire in his bones.

1. Marshall, *Luke*, 40.

That does not detract from or deny the human process of research and composition that Luke's prologue describes. But the Spirit who first inspired Luke to see it as "good" to decide to write a Gospel, and who guided him through his background preparation, also saw to it that the words that Luke penned were not just "orderly," but were also "God-breathed."

And that brings us to the other Gospel prologue, that of John. If Luke's prologue shows us the human Jesus, John's reveals *the heavenly Jesus*. "In the beginning was the Word, and the Word was with God, and the Word was God" (verse 1). As so often in John, simple, everyday, and mainly single-syllable words—language that seldom becomes any more complex than "the cat sat on the mat"—encapsulates the most sublime, eternal, heavenly mysteries. "In the beginning" immediately takes us right back to the start of Genesis and the work of creation; and John tells us that the one whom he calls "the Word" was there, co-operating with God in his creative work: "Through him all things were made; without him nothing was made that has been made" (verse 3). There is a mystery about the relationship between the Word and God: "the Word was *with* God, and the Word *was* God" (verse 1). John tries neither to explain nor to expand on this remarkable paradox; he simply states the fact that Jesus is at the same time one who relates to God ("was with God") and one who shares the being and nature of God ("was God"), in words that a child of six can understand, but with theological implications that are beyond the ability of the most learned professor fully to grasp.

John 1:1 is in fact one of about nine places in the New Testament where the title "God" is explicitly used of Jesus; others are John 1:18, John 20:28, Acts 20:28, Romans 9:5, Titus 2:13, Hebrews 1:8, 2 Peter 1:1, and 1 John 5:20. Many people will know that the Jehovah's Witnesses, in their desire to deny the deity of Christ, have adapted the wording of most of these in their *New World Translation of the Scriptures*, where John 1:1 is rendered " . . . and the word was *a god*," on the grounds that the Greek has no definite article in front of the noun *theòs* ("God"). It is true that there is no definite article there; but—with apologies for the grammatical technicalities here—neither are there any definite articles in front of *theòs* in verses 6 ("a man sent from God"), 12 ("children of God"), 13 ("born of God") or 18 ("No one has ever seen God"), yet the *New World Translation* translates each of these, rightly, as "God." The word *theòs*, it is true, is more often than not used with the definite article,[2] but it is used many times in the New Testament without

---

2. English speakers may find this strange, but it is quite normal in biblical Greek to put the definite article in front of proper names: more often than not, where our English Bibles say, for example, "And Peter said . . . ," the Greek is literally, "And *the* Peter said . . ." However odd that may sound to us, it is perfectly normal in Greek; so there is nothing

the article—including eighteen times in John's Gospel—and it always clearly means, and is translated as, "God"; and there are a number of occasions, including two others in John—3:2, "we know you are a teacher who has come from *God* [no article], for no one could perform the miraculous signs you are doing if *[the] God* were not with him"; and 13:3, "Jesus knew . . . that he had come from *God* [no article] and was returning to *[the] God*"— where, as in 1:1, the word *theòs* is used twice in quick succession, once with and once without the article, but where both obviously mean "God." Most importantly, the whole point of John's statement ("was *with* God . . . and *was* God") is that it is a mysterious paradox; to change the translation of the second *theòs*, making it mean something less that "God," removes the glorious mystery of how the Word can at the same time be *with* God and can also himself *be* God, which is precisely what John's language is intended to convey. "The Word was God" is the right translation of John's phrase.

So John presents Jesus as the eternal Word of God, who became a human being. There is mystery about the person of Jesus which ultimately goes beyond all our human understanding.

John's prologue stresses the divine mystery of Jesus in two other ways. First, with regard to salvation. "To all who received him, to those who believed in his name, he gave the right to become children of God—children born not of natural descent, nor of human decision or a husband's will, but born of God" (verses 12-13). How we can become God's children is beyond all human ability, not only to achieve, but even fully to understand, as Nicodemus was later to find out (John 3:4,9); we can do nothing make ourselves God's children, or to deserve the status of being his children. It is Jesus alone who can enable us to become children of God. The word translated "the *right* to become children of God" is more correctly the "authority"; Jesus, who was later to say that "all authority in heaven and on earth has been given to me" (Matthew 28:18), and who accomplished all his great miracles because of the authority he had as the Son of God, has the unique authority to perform the greatest and most mysterious miracle of all and make us children of God.

And second, with regard to revelation. "No one has ever seen God, but God the One and Only, who is at the Father's side, has made him known" (verse 18). God is invisible, beyond our ability to see or know. But Jesus reveals him. In Christ, the Unknowable can be known, the Invisible can be seen, the Incomprehensible can be understood. Jesus makes the

---

strange about "God" being, literally, "*the* God." The same is true, incidentally, in some modern European languages: it is normal for example in Portuguese, where "Bernado" would usually be *o Bernado* (= "the Bernado"). So a Portuguese speaker would find this New Testament Greek convention less surprising than we English speakers do.

transcendent and ever-glorious God real to us, in terms that we can grasp, that our mortal humanity can cope with. *How* this happens is probably beyond all human ability to explain in words—Jesus is truly, as Charles Wesley put it, "our God contracted to a span, incomprehensibly made man"[3]—yet it is the testimony of every believer *that* it happens.

Which is part of the reason why John describes Jesus as "the Word." John uses this title for Jesus here, in verses 1 and 14, and again in his first letter (1 John 1:1) and in Revelation 19:13. Whole libraries have been devoted to expounding the significance of the term "the Word of God"; so I am merely scratching the surface if I here offer the following summary of its main implications.[4]

1. It means that Jesus is God revealing himself to us. A person's "words" show what the person is really like on the inside; and Jesus is God expressing himself to us in human form. The main thread that runs through John 1:1–18 is that of "revealing" or "making known." Jesus is "the light of men" (verse 4); John the Baptist points to Jesus as the true light (verse 7–8); Jesus is the light "that gives light to every man" (verse 9); through him we see the glory of God (verses 14,18); Jesus makes God known (verse 18). If people want to know what God is really like, they need to look at Jesus. He is, as Donald Soper once said, "the human photograph of God."[5]

2. "The Word" means the message; the phrase "to preach the word" is used many times in the New Testament to mean to proclaim the message about God's Kingdom and Christian faith. The message of Christianity is Christ himself. Jesus is not just the bringer of the message, he is the content of the message. Our message is not the teaching of Christ, or a theology of Christ, but the Person of Christ himself. Evangelism means simply telling people about Jesus.

---

3. From Wesley's hymn, the first line of which is "Let earth and heav'n combine, angels and men agree." It is a pity that this hymn is not better known or more widely sung these days; it is a remarkable statement about God the Son becoming flesh to save us.

4. *Lógos* ("word") was a term used by Greek philosophers, especially those of the Stoic school, in the sense of "the essential principle of reason and rationality that pervades the universe"; it is of course the word from which we get our English word "logic." Because of this, many people have suggested that, in calling Jesus the *lógos*, John means that he is the embodiment of divine reason. Whilst there is no doubt at least some truth in that, it is far more likely that the background to John's use of the title *lógos* is to be found in the Old Testament doctrine of the Word of God; that understanding of "the Word" is more personal than philosophical, which is far more in keeping with the spirit of the Scriptures.

5. Rolph, *Does Pornography Matter?*, 41.

3. In the Old Testament "the Word of the Lord" is not just verbal information or instruction. It is the power of God himself active in the world. By his Word, God created the universe (Psalm 33:6). By his Word, he governs the world (Psalm 147:15,18). By his Word, he sustains our lives (Deuteronomy 8:3). The Hebrew term translated "word" (*dābār*) can also be translated as "deed," "action," or "event": it is in particular the word that is used in the phrase that occurs many times in the books of 1 and 2 Kings, "As for the other *events* of X's reign, are they not written in . . . "[6] Calling Jesus "the Word of God" means that it was through Christ that God made and governs the world. In Jesus, the dynamic power and energy of God is active to accomplish his purposes.

4. To call Jesus "the Word of God" stresses that he is true and reliable. God's Word is absolute truth (John 17:17)—and Jesus is absolutely true. He is "full of grace and truth" (John 1:14,17).

5. Calling Jesus "the Word" reminds us, finally, of what is perhaps the most vital and distinctive fact about the Christian faith, which is that truth is not propositional but personal; it is found, not in reflecting on theories but in relating to Jesus. Christianity is about not about abstract ideas, but about truth as it encounters us in the person of the Christ who lived as a flesh-and-blood man in history. This is affirmed very clearly at the beginning of John's first letter: he speaks of the Word of life as that "which we have heard, which we have seen with our eyes, which we have looked on and our hands have touched" (1 John 1:1). We do not discover the truth by meditation, by contemplation, by study, by analysis. We find God's truth by responding to the historical person of Jesus, as we encounter him in the Gospels, and relating to him by his Spirit.

So the Gospel starts with these two complementary prologues. Luke shows us the human Jesus, the man who can be investigated like any other historical character. One of the most helpful things we can ever do for those whom we want to see become Christians is simply to give them a copy of a

---

6. In Goethe's *Faust* there is a scene in which Faust tries his hand at some Bible translation, starting with John's Gospel. The opening phrase, "In the beginning was the word," troubles him; he tries a number of other terms, and eventually hits on "In the beginning was the deed." Goethe's point is that "mere" words are not what Faust, the man of dynamic energy, the man who wants to experience all of life, is interested in; he wants actions, deeds. Goethe was a great poet, but his theology leaves something to be desired: unlike in western thinking, the Bible does not see the word of God as mere information, as the communication of facts, but as active, dynamic, energetic. The Word *does* things.

Gospel. Let them look for themselves at the person of Jesus, as Luke invited Theophilus to do. The same Spirit who inspired the writing of these historical records can also breathe through them, so that a contemporary reader can "know the certainty of the things" he reads about Jesus.

John shows us the divine Jesus, the Jesus whose very being is a mystery, yet who comes to us in flesh and blood. John reminds us that no human being can come to know or understand God except as Jesus reveals him by his Spirit. He alone is the light that can shine in the darkness.

These two prologues present us, not only with the paradox of Jesus as the man who is God, but also with the paradox of how we too can present Jesus to the world. Luke, as we said, worked hard in preparing his Gospel. He did his homework. He undertook painstaking research. Those of us who wish to communicate the Gospel have no excuse to do less. There is unfortunately in today's church a form of what I can only call pseudo-spirituality that seems to regard such work as a denial of the ministry of the Holy Spirit. The very idea that, for example, sermons should be carefully prepared means to those who hold such views that the preacher is operating solely in the flesh. What Spirit-filled preachers are to do is simply stand up, and expect the Spirit to give them there and then what to say. And there are those independently-minded and self-appointed "evangelists," who are equally dismissive of any suggestion that they might benefit from training in how to share the Gospel; training, they seem to think, is merely the secular substitute for the gifting of the Spirit.

Luke knocks all such nonsense on the head. One of Luke's great themes is the Holy Spirit; yet he also worked hard and carefully to plan and prepare his Gospel. I fear that the confident claim (which I have actually heard; I am not tilting at windmills!) that "I don't prepare messages; the Spirit will just give them to me when I need them" is an indication, not of inspiration, but of laziness. One of the most abused promises of Scripture, in this regard, is Matthew 10:19–20, where Jesus says to his disciples, "Do not worry about what to say or how to say it. At that time you will be given what to say, for it will not be you speaking, but the Spirit of your Father speaking through you." The words immediately preceding these—"But when they arrest you"—show clearly that Jesus is not referring to "normal" preaching or evangelism; he is referring to what he assures the disciples will happen, that they might, at any time, be "brought before governors and kings" (verse 18), and forced to answer questions about why they have been speaking about Jesus. In such circumstances, when they are put on the spot, so to speak, God's Spirit will guide them in how to respond to their accusers. To wrest that wonderful promise, which has again and again been fulfilled in the history of the persecuted church, and make it a reassurance to lazy preachers that they can get by without preparation, is a hideous distortion of the Bible. Unfortunately, there are those who will very happily take refuge behind Jesus' promise of the Spirit's inspiration, not because they are suffering persecution, but simply because they find that actually having to prepare messages to preach is too much like hard work.

Not for Luke, it wasn't. This Spirit-inspired missionary worked hard to get his Gospel ready before presenting it. He knew that the Holy Spirit could and did inspire and guide careful preparation, as well as, where necessary, spontaneous utterance.

And yet we also have John. And his prologue reminds us of the complementary truth, that all the hard work (which we dare not shirk) and all the careful preparation in the world will never *in itself* enable people to see and receive the truth about God. Only the One who reveals spiritual truth can do that. John himself can record the things in his Gospel only because God has supernaturally revealed them (verses 14,18); and we can understand the Gospel only because God supernaturally enables it to be revealed to our spirits. So it is the preacher's responsibility to plan and put together the best possible presentation that he or she can; and it is good for anyone who wants to share their faith to submit themselves to proper training and the discipline of practicing the best ways of communicating the good news. But in all such preparation, we must always remember that no sermon or witness will ever achieve its purpose unless the Spirit uses it to open spiritually blinded eyes and to reveal Jesus to spiritually dead hearts. As the nineteenth-century American Presbyterian preacher James Henley Thornwell said, "Effective sermons are the offspring of study, of discipline, of prayer, and especially of the unction of the Holy Ghost."[7] By the grace of God, that unction (or, as we would say today, anointing) is freely available, when the discipline and the prayer go hand in hand.

---

7. Quoted in Blanchard, *Gathered Gold*, 239.

2

The Promised Messiah

"Prepare the way for the Lord" (Mark 1:3)

Before we come to the story of Jesus himself, Matthew and, in particular, Luke give us the story of how God started to prepare people for the fact that the Christ was about to be born. So we have the birth of John the Baptist announced to his father Zechariah by the angel Gabriel (Luke 1:5–25);[1] the visit of Gabriel to Mary to tell her that she has been chosen as the one who will bear the child who will be "great, and will be called the Son of the Most High" (Luke 1:26–38); the dilemma faced by Joseph, when he discovers that his fiancée is pregnant, and his vision of the angel who tells him how the child has been conceived by a miracle through the Holy Spirit (Matthew 1:18–25); the visit of Mary to Elizabeth, John the Baptist's mother, who is now well advanced in her pregnancy (Luke 1:39–56); and finally the birth

---

1. One detail in Gabriel's announcement to Zechariah is that (verse 15) "he [the future Baptist] is never to take wine or other fermented drink." The background to this perhaps puzzling requirement is found in Numbers 6:1–4, where God gives his Old Testament people regulations for those who, whilst not being priests, wished for a specific period of time to consecrate themselves to special service for God. Such people were known as "Nazirites"—the word means "consecrated ones"—and one of the particular distinguishing marks of a Nazirite was abstinence from all alcohol for the duration of his special vow. Whilst he did not enter into conventional priestly service, John the Baptist, in the spirit of a Nazirite, was to be specially consecrated to the service of God all his life. Incidentally, the term Nazirite has nothing to do with the place-name Nazareth: the two words are unconnected, but just sound similar.

of John the Baptist, and the prophetic words spoken over him by his father (Luke 1:57–80).

These stories show how God brought the centuries-long process of preparing his people for the coming of Christ to its climax. Jesus did not simply arrive in human history "out of the blue"; God had planned and prepared for his coming. Those preparations are now in their final phase. Matthew 1 and Luke 1 are the overture: the curtain is about to go up for the grand opera itself. And just as an orchestral overture will often contain tunes that will later recur in the opera to follow, so this "overture" presents us with a number of themes that reflect important truths that we will find in the coming ministry of Jesus.

Natural and Supernatural

These sections combine spiritual and "supernatural" things with a down-to-earth reality. They are all about very natural and normal human things. We have here *ordinary human hopes*. A young working-class village girl called Mary is looking forward to getting married. At the time our story begins, Mary is "betrothed" (Matthew 1:18, Luke 1:27; the NIV translates as "pledged to be married"). In Jewish society, betrothal was more than our "engagement"; it was the legally binding first stage of marriage, and was marked in a formal and public ceremony, after which the betrothed couple were referred to as "husband" and "wife"—hence Matthew 1:19, "Joseph her *husband*"—although they did not live together or begin to have sexual relations until after the second ceremony of formal marriage, which usually took place about a year later. To break off a betrothal required a legal divorce. Part of the reason for this formal betrothal was to offer security to girls who were too young to marry, but who, in a society where it was not uncommon for fathers to pass away before their children had reached maturity, could find themselves vulnerable and unprotected if they did not happen to have older brothers to take care of them. Even before they were formally married, Joseph, in the event of Mary's father's death, would have the legal responsibility to provide for his betrothed.[2]

---

2. Part of the importance of this is that the New Testament uses the picture of betrothal to describe the status of Christians in this present life. In 2 Corinthians 11:2, Paul says that "I promised you to one husband, to Christ," and the word translated "promised" is literally "betrothed." Our relationship with Christ now is not casual or unofficial. We stand in a proper and secure relationship with Jesus, to which he has formally committed himself—we are the "betrothed" of Christ. Heaven is often spoken of as a marriage-ceremony, when our present spiritual union with Christ, our betrothal, will be perfected and consummated.

We have *ordinary family disappointments*. An elderly couple, Zechariah and Elizabeth, have had to come to terms with the pain of being childless, in a society in which childlessness was felt to be something of a social stigma. When Elizabeth does eventually become pregnant, she thanks God that he has "taken away my disgrace among the people" (Luke 1:25).

We have *ordinary moral dilemmas*. Joseph hears that his bride-to-be, Mary, is pregnant. What is he to do? He knows perfectly well that he is not responsible for her condition, so he draws the only conclusion that he can possibly draw—she has obviously been with another man. Hence his dilemma. On the one hand he is "a righteous man" (Matthew 1:19), and the rules of righteous conduct clearly require that he divorce his betrothed, and refuse to have any further contact with her. On the other hand, he loves her; he knows that a public divorce will cause her humiliation which, however much she might (he assumes) deserve it, he is unwilling to put her through. So he resolves "to divorce her quietly." This, incidentally, involved some risk to his own reputation. A formal divorce would give him the opportunity to declare before the world that he was not the father of the expected child; Mary would be branded as immoral, but his own good name as a man who did the right thing would be secure. By forgoing that process, he would probably be assumed to be the father of Mary's child: in other words, a man who had abandoned his moral principles, because he couldn't be bothered to wait until the wedding day. Yet he is willing to live with that social disgrace in order to protect Mary as much as he could. It is probably because of the painful cost involved in his decision that he spent some time, and no doubt several sleepless nights, "considering" (Matthew 1:20) what he should do—wrestling with the problem of what was best for himself and for Mary.

In most modern presentations of the birth story the focus is on Mary; Joseph often remains a fairly nondescript figure in the background. Yet Matthew chooses to focus on him; and the reason may be that Joseph's dilemma and decision are a remarkable illustration of how God sent his Son to save us. Joseph is "a righteous man"; and God is the righteous God. But Joseph is also a gracious man, who is willing, at considerable cost to himself, to shield Mary from the consequences of what he has to assume is her sin: the fact that, as he will find out later, Mary has actually done nothing wrong does not make his decision any less a striking example of grace. Joseph chooses to act in a way that will mean that he, and not Mary, will take the blame for what has happened; and God sent his Son not only into the world but specifically to the cross precisely in order that he, the righteous one, might take the blame and suffer the punishment for our sins. Joseph's dilemma is a smaller version of God's dilemma. We often say, rightly, that the cross is God's solution to our problem, but it is first and foremost God's solution to his own problem: the problem of how he, as the righteous God, can, without compromising his righteousness, love and accept sinful people. Joseph faced the same question: how could he *both* do the righteous thing *and* spare Mary?; and although he could not have known it at the time, his solution prefigured God's far greater solution to the far greater problem of human sin.

We have *ordinary religious practice*. Zechariah is a priest (Luke 1:5), and he is chosen "to go into the temple of the Lord and burn incense" (verse 9). This—the burning of incense at the times of morning and evening sacrifice—was a daily ritual in the temple, and it was one of the many priestly duties that were assigned by lot; but because it was regarded as one of the most significant, and because of the large number of priests, no priest was allowed to perform this ritual more than once in his lifetime. Today is Zechariah's turn. So on the one hand, this is a very special and privileged occasion for him; he would no doubt think of it as the greatest day in his professional life, as it was indeed to turn out to be, though for reasons quite different from those he might have expected. But on the other hand, it is a regular and familiar religious routine. These sacrifices, and the burning of incense, had been the normal practice amongst the Jewish people for centuries. So Zechariah faithfully goes into the temple to carry out his duty. So far, so conventional.

And we have *ordinary life experiences*. There is the basic fact of pregnancy and childbirth; what could be more down-to-earth than that? When Gabriel speaks to Mary, Elizabeth is in her sixth month. She has the experience, when Mary is visiting her, of feeling the baby kicking hard in her womb (Luke 1:41). A few months later "she gave birth to a son" (verse 57); and there is even, though of course without any comic intent on the part of Luke, the familiar issue, which has led to many an extended discussion between expectant couples, of having to choose a name for the baby, when different people have different ideas on the subject (verses 59–63).

This is clearly and recognizably the normal human world, a world full of the typical joys and sorrows, the ups and downs of human relationships and responsibilities—the themes of every soap opera in our own day.

But in the midst of this very human reality there is also the heavenly and the spiritual. Angels appear and speak to people; there are dreams and visions of God. There are miracles: a barren woman past child-bearing age becomes pregnant; Zechariah loses the power of speech and then is miraculously healed. People are filled with the Holy Spirit and prophesy (Luke 1:41–42,67). Most remarkable of all, a virgin becomes pregnant by the power of the Holy Spirit.

Christianity is like that: it doesn't take us out of the ordinary and the human—but the reality of God's heavenly, spiritual life impacts us in the midst of the ordinary business of human life. Through the ages, there have been those who have understood spirituality to mean having nothing more to do with the ordinary issues of life. Perhaps the most famous and extreme example of the early ascetic movement was the fifth-century mystic Simon Stylites, who was so determined to focus all his time and his life on communing with God, without any distractions from other people, that he lived for thirty-seven years on a rough platform on top of a tall thin pillar, having found the more conventional hermit's cave insufficiently removed from society. It is frankly hard to see any connection whatever between that kind of bizarre asceticism and the world of Luke 1. Yet it is into the world of Luke 1 that Jesus came. And whilst contemporary ideas of "avoiding the world" would rarely take quite such eccentric forms as those favored by Simon Stylites, there are still some groups and individuals within the Christian tradition that will see their commitment to live the life of a spiritual disciple as requiring a complete renunciation of such mundane distractions as having bank accounts or pension plans, pursuing hobbies or sporting activities, visiting theaters, cinemas or concert halls, going to birthday parties or wedding receptions, voting in political elections, belonging to trade unions, and even of having marriages and families.

There may be some who feel a personal call from God to such extreme separation from conventional society; and certainly, singleness can be, as the apostle Paul said (1 Corinthians 7:7) a specific call from God for some, and can be the context in which people can devote themselves even more fully to the service of God (verses 32–35). But it is only by disregarding or twisting Scripture to a hideous degree that anyone can claim that complete non-involvement in human society should be the Christian norm. Mary, Zechariah and Elizabeth were not taken out of their social and family settings in order to meet with God on some spiritual desert island; rather, God came to them where they were, in the midst of their relationship issues, their family challenges, their day-to-day duties; his coming transformed the people they were, but it did not transport them out of those human contexts—rather, it led them to live with a new purpose within them. And the Jesus whom we follow is the Jesus who went to a wedding reception (and performed a miracle there), the Jesus who spent time with children, the sick, the morally and socially marginalized (and brought them a touch of the grace of heaven), the Jesus who went to dinner parties with tax collectors (and offered them the forgiveness that could change their lives).

We live in the real world of Luke 1. But then there is the other side. Into that real world God sends his angel to bring heavenly good news and his Holy Spirit to work miracles; and in that real world people see visions and speak prophecies. And just as there have been those for whom spirituality has meant no contact with the real world, so there are, sadly, all too many for whom "religion" is a purely conventional and social formality, without any actual experience of the spiritual world; whose faith and religious practice is as normal, as conventional, as traditional and, in every sense of the word, as "established" as Zechariah's priestly duties. He is commended as a good and genuinely devoted man (Luke 1:6), and his priestly work was no doubt carried out with exemplary fidelity and care; and there are many who in a similar way will faithfully say their prayers, go to church, seek to live a good and righteous life. I have no wish to belittle or dismiss such devotion. But if that is all there is—if that is the sum of what being a Christian means—then Luke 1 and Matthew 1 suggest that something is missing.

The coming of Jesus means that the heavenly Kingdom of God impacts us in the midst of our human ordinariness. We see that in the introduction to the Gospels in four ways.

Experience

There is, first, the direct experience of God. Heaven, the spiritual realm where God reigns and in which the angels operate, is revealed to Zechariah whilst he is going about his conventional religious duties; to Mary whilst she is (we assume) going about her ordinary life in Nazareth; to Joseph whilst he is wrestling with the problem of how to react to the shocking news that Mary is pregnant, and wondering what the right thing to do might be. To people who live, and will continue to live, in that world of everyday religious devotions, domestic duties and challenging decisions, there comes the revelation of another world, a world of heavenly glory, a world of spiritual power, the world of God's Kingdom. And their experience of God's glory, though it is supernatural, is not vague or "mystical." Zechariah's experience of the angel Gabriel is as real to him as his priestly duties were; Mary's encounter with Gabriel is as real to her as her birth pains would later be. Almost certainly they believed in the existence of that spiritual world before our stories start; but now they have seen it, tasted it, been touched by it, and they will be changed by it.

That is Christian life. Jesus makes it possible for us, not only to believe in God, but to encounter God; not just to believe in heaven, but to be touched by the reality of heaven; not just to believe in salvation, but to live a saved life; not just to believe that God is good, but to "taste and see that the Lord is good" (Psalm 34:8). And we take that touch of heaven with us back into our life in the world of domestic, professional and social responsibilities, joys and sorrows.

Communication

Experience leads to communication. Angels are sent, not to give Zechariah and Mary angelic experiences for their own sake, but with messages; in a dream God reveals to Joseph what is actually happening to Mary and shows him how he should respond to it. God speaks personally to people.

He still does. Of course he can speak, as Hebrews 1:1 says, in various ways. Historically, he has spoken once for all in Christ. For us who live after the time of Christ's earthly ministry, he speaks above all in Scripture. The Bible is not only one of the ways in which God speaks, not even just the most important way in which God speaks, but is the way by which all other claims to have heard from God need to be tested; Scripture is not only the supreme form of revelation, but the benchmark by which to assess the authenticity or otherwise of all other secondary forms of revelation.

Our world is skeptical about anyone who claims to have heard God speaking to them. To quote the old wisecrack, "If a man says he talks to God, they call him a saint. If he says that God talks to him, they call him a schizophrenic." And it is often assumed that to hear God speaking necessarily means to be eccentric, if not actually mentally unstable. Sadly, I have known a number of genuine Christian believers who, if they think that they are hearing God speak to them, ask with some concern if they might not be "going a bit mad."

No, they're not. Of course, that does not mean that any and every claim to have "heard from God" has to be accepted without question; we are told in the Scriptures to "test the spirits to see whether they are from God" (1 John 4:1), and it is possible for someone to think they are being led by God when in fact it is their own imagination that is misleading them. But the fact that fallible human beings can sometimes mistake their own thoughts for the prompting of the Spirit does not mean that there can never be a real experience of hearing from God; part of Christian maturity is learning to discern the voice of God, and to distinguish it from whatever other "voices" there may be within and around us. These chapters in Matthew and Luke, and for that matter the whole Bible, show us that God does indeed speak to his people. The only surprising thing about that is why we should find it surprising. Human beings are made in the image of God, which means that all that makes us distinctively human is a reflection of the nature and character of God: and one of the most distinctively human things about us is our ability to speak. Does that not suggest that God himself is the God who speaks? When we believe in Jesus, we become children of God—and why would any good father not want to communicate with his children?

Here, in the introduction to the story of Jesus, we see examples of God speaking to his people to confirm to them the reality of Jesus, who he is and how he will come, and to guide them in how they can serve the outworking of his good purposes. That the children of God hear their Father speaking to them to similar ends today is part of what Watchman Nee called *The Normal Christian Life*. Zechariah, Joseph and Mary were normal people; and when God spoke to them, they did not cease to be normal—they became normal people through whom God was able to work in remarkable ways.

Miracles

There are also miracles. A barren woman past child-bearing age conceives; a man robbed of his power of speech has it suddenly and supernaturally restored. It has been suggested that what happened to Zechariah in Luke 1:20–22 was that he suffered a stroke. Maybe. But I see no value in trying to give a natural explanation for events which the Bible explicitly says are acts of God: too often that implies that, whilst people in the first century thought that it was God who brought about things like Zechariah's loss of speech, we now know how to account for them scientifically. That is not only arrogant but also betrays a lack of understanding of how the processes of nature can be used or over-ruled by God for his own specific purposes. Whatever the medical diagnosis might have been, the text of Scripture is quite clear that Zechariah's loss of speech was inflicted by God as a temporary punishment for his lack of faith (verse 20). That does *not* mean that every medical problem must be seen as divine punishment. Many medical conditions are simply medical conditions, but some might also be linked to a spiritual problem: for example, Jesus treats the deaf and dumb man in Mark 7:31–35 as a man with a medical affliction who needed to be healed, whereas he recognizes that the condition of the dumb man in Matthew 9:32–33 was linked with a spiritual problem caused by a demonic spirit. In the case of Zechariah, even if his loss of speech is ascribed to a stroke, that must not be taken to mean that strokes are punishments from God. It simply means that, in this particular instance, God was disciplining Zechariah. And the restoration of his speech in verse 64 is just as clearly to be understood as a miracle from God: the use of the passive verb ("His mouth *was opened*") means that Zechariah did not simply recover, but that God restored his speech; and the fact that this happened "immediately" (that is, in an instant) rules out any natural explanation, such as a gradual recovery from a stroke. God healed him.

Miracles will of course be a major strand of the ministry of Jesus. The most important thing to learn from these stories that pave the way for the birth of Christ is that miracles are never arbitrary; God does not work miracles merely to prove points or to demonstrate his power. God's miracles all serve the coming and the advance of his Kingdom. In the purposes of God, it was time for the forerunner of the Messiah to be born; and as John the Baptist will have a special ministry, he has a special birth. Later in Jesus' ministry, there were those who asked him to perform a miracle in order to convince them to believe in him (Matthew 12:38, 16:1, John 6:30); he always refused. And those who want God to "do a miracle" to satisfy their intellectual curiosity or skepticism will be similarly disappointed. Miracles are signs of and instruments in the advance of God's Kingdom.

But they are, again, part of normal Christian life, not in the silly sense of "six miracles a day before breakfast," but in the spirit of these miracles in Luke 1. For what is happening here is that God is, by his spiritual power, enabling people to do that which they could never do by their own human means. Zechariah and Elizabeth could not have children—they had proved that over many years. Mary certainly could not, so long as she remained a virgin, conceive a child. But God enabled them to do what they could not do in the course of nature.

In the same way none of us can, in the course of nature, or in our own human strength, attain the spiritual life of God's Kingdom, do the works of Jesus, touch other lives with the healing, the grace and the renewing power of God. We can no more produce the works of God's spiritual Kingdom than Elizabeth could produce a baby. But she did, because God worked in her. And we who believe in Jesus can also produce the fruit of righteousness, as the power of God works in us. That is what miracles are about.

Prophecies

And finally, there are prophecies.[3] There had been no prophetic ministry in Israel for about four hundred years. As the old Christmas carol[4] put it, "And

---

3. The basic meaning of "prophecy" in the Bible is not, as is sometimes assumed, foretelling the future; it is simply receiving and passing on messages from God. Whilst there can be a predictive element in some prophecy, it is never simply giving objective information about what is to come; it is always about God revealing the moral and spiritual character of what he is doing or is about to do, or his spiritual and heavenly perspective on events on earth.

4. "Earth was waiting, spent and restless," by Walter Chalmers Smith (1824–1908).

the oracles were silent, and the prophets all were dead." Then, in anticipation of the coming of Jesus, people in Luke 1 start once again to be filled with the Holy Spirit and to prophesy: Elizabeth (verses 41–45), Mary (verses 46–55), Zechariah (verses 67–79). Here are initial examples of the gifts of the Holy Spirit that, from Pentecost onwards, will characterize the church of Jesus Christ.

Mary's prophecy, the so-called *Magnificat*, is in the style of an Old Testament psalm of praise about God coming to rescue the poor. That is deeply significant: God is speaking again in the same way that he spoke in the past. The canon of Scripture is not yet closed. God has more to say, arising out of and consistent with what he said in the past, but with a new focus. Zechariah's prophecy specifies what that focus will be: it is a remarkable description of how Jesus will save us, and what John's task as a witness to Christ will be. And though, with the completion of the New Testament, the canon of Scripture now *is* definitively closed, God can and does still move his people, by his Spirit, to speak for him, with an effect that goes beyond human words.

These, then, are the four ways in which the heavenly and the supernatural is seen to operate within the context of the ordinary lives of ordinary people. Because Jesus is coming—and, we can now say, has come—God's believing people can experience him, hear from him, do works for him, and speak out for him, whilst continuing to be ordinary people living in the everyday and normal world.

The Virgin Birth

Though it is part of the same theme of God working supernaturally and miraculously in the context of the normal and the everyday, it is worth devoting a separate section to consider the virgin birth—or, more correctly, the virgin conception.

The Bible clearly teaches that Mary was an unmarried virgin when she became pregnant. In Luke 1:34, "I am a virgin" is literally "I know not a man." To "know" is of course a well-known biblical euphemism for sexual relations; Mary is unambiguously saying that she is not now, nor has she ever been, living on terms of sexual intimacy with any man. Matthew 1:18, "before they came together she was found to be with child," means before Joseph and Mary were fully married and before they had sexual relations for the first time. In verses 22–23 Matthew says that Mary's becoming pregnant was in fulfillment of Isaiah 7:14, "The virgin will be with child and will give birth to a son"; and whilst the debate continues about the Hebrew word *'almāh*, and whether, whilst it certainly includes the sense of virgin, it is necessarily restricted to only that sense, there is no doubt whatever about the meaning of the Greek word which Matthew uses to translate Isaiah: *parthénos*[5] means in Greek exactly what "virgin" means in English, and that is the term he uses of Mary.[6] Then in verse 25, "He [= Joseph] had no union with her until she gave birth to a son," is again, literally, "he did not know her," that is, he had no sexual relations with Mary until after Jesus had been born. By a miracle of God the fetus that developed in her womb and was born as the baby Jesus was created supernaturally, without any human father.

That traditional and fundamental Christian doctrine has in our day been, understandably, regarded with some skepticism,[7] and is often treated as a beautiful symbol, though not (of course!) to be taken seriously. A proper appreciation of the significance of the virgin conception is not helped by misunderstanding it, as though it were first and foremost saying something special about who Mary is, rather than about who Jesus is, or as if it were casting moral aspersions on the normal process of human reproduction. And the virgin birth is perhaps most frequently thought of as a familiar literary allusion, a part of traditional religious mythology.

The Bible says it happened. And some understanding of *why* it happened is important to our understanding of who Jesus is. What follows is a brief summary of some points that we can learn from the virgin conception of Jesus, and why the virgin birth is important to a biblical understanding of the person of Christ.

The Uniqueness of Christ

It speaks of the unique character of the child to be born. In the Old Testament, special people often had special births, for example Isaac (Genesis 15:2-6, 21:1-5), Samson (Judges 13), Samuel (1 Samuel 1); and at the start

---

5. From which, incidentally, the name of the Parthenon is derived. The Parthenon was a temple dedicated to the Greek goddess Athene, who, in Greek mythology, was the only one of Zeus' daughters who had no human mother, which gave rise to her other name, *Parthénos*, the virgin. Hence the name of her temple.

6. Oswald Becker and Colin Brown compare the evolution of the meaning of *parthénos*, which they define as "maiden, virgin," to that of the German word *Jungfrau*: originally it meant (literally) simply "young woman," but then came to have the more specific meaning of "one who has not yet been touched by a man." (*NIDNTT*, vol. 3, 1071.)

7. And sometimes with something worse than skepticism. C. S. Lewis said that he once received an anonymous postcard informing him that he should be publicly flogged, because he had said that he believed in the virgin birth. (Lewis, *First and Second Things*, 122.)

of the New Testament, the same is true of John the Baptist (Luke 1:5–25). Jesus' birth was not just special, it was unique, because Jesus himself is unique.

It is often objected that to talk about the uniqueness of Jesus ignores the fact that every religious leader, indeed every person, is unique: yes, Jesus is unique, but so is Mohammed, so is the Dalai Lama, so for that matter are Mr Bones the butcher and Mrs Bun the baker's wife. That is true; but it misses the point. By speaking of the fact that Jesus is unique, we are not just saying that he is different from other people or that he has distinctive characteristics; that is certainly true to a greater or lesser degree of everybody. But the uniqueness of Jesus means that he is in his essential being and nature in a different "category" from the whole human race. He is uniquely different, not as Oliver Twist is different from David Copperfield or as Little Dorrit is different from Fagin, but as any or all of them are different from Charles Dickens. Dickens exists at a different level of reality from that of any of the characters in his books: he is part of what we might call the real, historical human world, whereas all his characters inhabit the fictional world of the novel. In an analogous way, Jesus inhabits the real eternal world of the Godhead; all people, with all their differences, are the characters in his created world, of which he is the author. That is the miracle of the incarnation: that the author of life stepped down into his own creation, and lived as a character in that created world of human history.

The Miraculous Nature of Christ

It shows that Jesus was a wholly supernatural person. Jesus did not just perform miracles—Jesus himself *is* a miracle. So biological questions about how the virgin conception could happen are beside the point: God worked a unique miracle in bringing Jesus into the world. And because of the virgin birth, no merely human explanation of or theory about Jesus will do. There is a widespread tendency in our day to focus on the common humanity of Jesus. That is real and true, but it is not the whole of who Jesus is. Jesus does not just do supernatural things; any believer, in principle, can work miracles: in the Old Testament, for example, Elisha worked a number of miracles which are similar in character to the works of Jesus, including healings, raising the dead, and feeding a crowd with a small amount of food which was miraculously multiplied (e.g. 2 Kings 4:18–37, 4:42–44, 5:1–14), but those works do not show that Elisha is anything other than a man through whom God did his own divine works. The Gospels, and the virgin birth in particular, show that Jesus is not just another and even greater Elisha; his very nature is supernatural. In Jesus, we do not see a believer reaching up and laying hold on the power of God; we see God the eternal Son reaching down and choosing to live as part of this human world. The only Jesus in the Bible is a miraculous and supernatural Jesus, not just a Jesus who does miraculous and supernatural things. There is a world of difference between the two.

The above comment that biological objections are "beside the point" requires some justification. Miracles are often objected to on scientific grounds ("We know things like that can't happen!"), and none more so than the virgin birth, so this is as good a place as any for a brief comment about the place of scientific criteria in assessing the miracles of Jesus. No responsible Christian would say that there is no place for scientific thinking, method and enterprise. But two of the fundamental premises of Christian faith are: first, that God, having created the world, has built into it certain normal patterns which govern its operation (the "laws of nature"), and second, that God can, if and when he chooses, act in ways that go beyond those laws.

The phrase "go beyond" is important. It is often said that miracles "break" the laws of nature. That is not true. Miracles may be described as natural events without natural causes. All "normal" events take place as part of a chain of cause and effect, according to the laws that God has written into his universe. A miracle is an event that is, in a real sense, natural: the birth of Jesus was a normal human birth, preceded by a normal period of gestation and labor, and accompanied by normal birth pains. But instead of arising in the normal way from the cause that is part of the natural order—sexual reproduction—this birth is brought about independently of the normal chain of cause-effect. God does it in a different way, by his own direct intervention, for his own purposes. That does not invalidate the laws of nature, nor the proper study of them. It merely says that the laws of nature are not all that exist in the universe. God, who put those laws in place, can act in ways that go beyond them without invalidating them.

Every school has a time-table, according to which, for example, year nine will normally be doing biology after lunch on Tuesday. But the head teacher who devised the time-table can, for special and appropriate educational reasons, adapt it, so that next week year nine will not be doing biology on Tuesday, but will be attending a one-off lecture from a local poet. That does not invalidate or abolish the time-table, or biology; and the larger purpose of promoting the pupils' education, which is after all the whole purpose for which the time-table was put together in the first place, has not been damaged, but rather enhanced. The time-table is still the pattern by which the normal school week unfolds, and biology will always have its place within it. But the one in authority over the time-table can sometimes adapt how it applies.

God is the head teacher of the universe. The "time-table"—the laws of nature—does not exist by chance; it exists because he put it in place. It is quite proper for the scientist to study and learn from the natural order. But he can only claim that nothing can ever happen outside the norms of the time-table if he has forgotten, or if he does not believe, that the school is governed, not by a self-existent time-table, but by the head teacher who devised it.

So to say that the virgin conception is impossible because it cannot occur within the course of nature is a fallacy. A miracle is by definition an event whose causes lie outside the normal cause-and-effect patterns of nature, which are what the scientist studies. Of course biology cannot account for the virgin birth; but then, neither can it account for irregular French verbs or the date of the Battle of Hastings, which most biologists would admit are also valid and real parts of the school time-table—of the world we can study. But when it comes to theology, it sometimes seems that different criteria apply, as though some of the biology teachers in the school have forgotten that biology, though a real and valuable part of the curriculum, is not the whole of the time-table.

The Incarnation of Christ

The virgin birth points to the fact that Jesus is God who became a human being. The technical term for this is "incarnation," which means literally "becoming flesh"; it is based in particular on the wording of John 1:14, which says "And the Word became flesh."[8] In conjunction with verse 1, the meaning is clear, however hard it is to grasp the nature of the physical processes involved: "The Word was God . . . and the Word became flesh." God became a human being. In Luke 1:35, Gabriel says to Mary that, because it is by a miracle of the Holy Spirit that she will conceive, "the holy one to be born will be called the Son of God." A human father would mean a human baby. But Jesus had no human father: he was brought into the world by God himself. Jesus is literally "God incarnate," God who came to us as a human being.

This does not, however, mean that the Holy Spirit "stood in" for Joseph, and became a kind of surrogate father, by supplying the male chromosomes which a father would normally supply. Jesus was not "half man"

---

8. In the New Testament "flesh" refers, not specifically to the physical body, but to ordinary human life, as distinct from the spiritual life of God. For that reason a number of versions of the Bible translate John 1:14, quite rightly, as "the Word became a human being."

(from Mary) and "half God" (from the Holy Spirit). Such a being would not be a true incarnation, but a hybrid—and, as P. T. Forsyth so memorably put it, "No half-god could redeem the soul which it took a whole God to create."[9] Jesus was no hybrid demi-god; he was 100 percent human and 100 percent divine. What God did through his Spirit was to create a brand new fully human person, who did not derive his humanity from his parents, but was created as a whole human person by God. Then that human person was united with and became one with the person of God the Son. The fact that we struggle to understand that does not mean it could not happen; God is, after all, far bigger than our minds, so it should not surprise us that he can do things that our minds cannot fully comprehend.

The New Humanity of Christ

Following on from that, the virgin birth shows that Jesus marks the beginning of a brand new start for the human race. When God first made human beings, he started by creating one man, Adam (Genesis 2:7, Acts 17:26). Adam's humanity was not derived from other people, but was created new by God. Since Adam, all people have derived their humanity from their parents, and from the whole stock of the human race going back to Adam. That human stock is of course tainted by sin—it is corrupted. When God had created Adam, he made him, as he said, "in our image, in our likeness" (Genesis 1:26). Man's sin tainted that image; and so when in Genesis 5:3 we read that "Adam . . . had a son in *his* own likeness, in *his* own image," it clearly means that his son, and all of the ensuing human race, bore the tainted image of Adam rather than the perfect image of God.[10] But Jesus does not come from that corrupt human stock. In creating the human person of Jesus, God makes a fresh beginning. As he began by creating Adam himself, so he created the human life of Jesus himself. Jesus is the start of a brand new humanity. And that new human nature is not transmitted by sexual reproduction, but by "spiritual reproduction"—by our being born again of the Spirit of Jesus (John 3:3–8). That is why Paul refers to Jesus as another "Adam" (1 Corinthians 15:22,45–49).

It is significant, in connection with this, that the language of Luke 1:35 recalls Genesis 1:2, which describes the Spirit as "hovering" like a

---

9. Forsyth, *Person and Place*, 86.

10. That does not mean that human beings are no longer "in the image of God"; James 3:9 clearly says that they are. That image is tainted, but it is not simply abolished; and that, as James 3 points out, has important implications for how we treat all people, including the good, the bad and the ugly.

mother-bird over the beginning of creation. The same Spirit will now "hover" or "brood" over Mary. Jesus is the start of a new creation.

The Human Experience of Christ

The virgin conception shows that God has entered into our human experience from the very moment of conception. God himself has gone through everything that belongs to our humanity, including nine months in the womb. That should be a great comfort to us; God himself knows what it is like to be human—he has been through what we go through. But it is also a challenge. In particular, it has very serious implications for the whole debate about abortion. If God himself came and identified with an unborn fetus in the womb—if God regarded the process of his Son becoming a human being as having to start in the womb—then we cannot treat unborn children as less than fully human.

The Pre-existence of Christ

An important aspect of the New Testament doctrine of Christ is his "pre-existence"; that is, the fact that he did not begin to exist at the moment of his conception, but had always existed from all eternity as the Son of God. Whilst the virgin conception does not strictly speaking prove Jesus' pre-existence, it is consistent with it. In our case, our conception was the moment at which we began to exist as people.[11] But Christ has always been the Son of God in heaven (John 1:1–2, 17:5). The virgin conception involved Jesus taking a new form, as a human being: "the Word *became* flesh" (John 1:14). We need to understand the two natures that are combined in Christ. His human nature as the man Jesus began to exist when he was created new by God in Mary's womb. But his divine nature is eternal; he has always been God the Son in heaven. Strictly speaking, the name "Jesus" refers to his human personality. To refer to his eternal divine nature, we ought to speak of Christ as the "Son of God."

---

11. The idea has occasionally been suggested that human souls are "pre-existent," and that when a new person is conceived, a newly-formed body is united with a pre-existent soul. That view was taught by the sometimes controversial theologian Origen (*c.* 185–254), but it was never accepted as part of orthodox Christian faith—William Shedd said that the theory of the pre-existence of souls "may be said to rise and set with Origen" (*Christian Doctrine*, vol. 2, 8)—and is best regarded as a mystical and aberrant theory which has no basis in Scripture.

It is significant in this respect to note the tenses of some of the verbs in John's prologue. In our English translations, both verse 1 and verse 6 traditionally contained the word "was": "In the beginning *was* the word . . . there *was* a man who was sent from God; his name was John"—the NIV translates the latter verse as "there *came* a man." In verse 1, speaking of the eternal Word of God, the verb is in the "timeless" past tense: the Word "always was," as Hebrews 7:3 says, "without beginning of days or end of life." In verse 6, the verb is not the simple verb "to be" (= "to exist"), but the Greek verb *ginomai*, which can mean to come into existence, to begin to exist, to become; and it is in the tense which means "at one particular time in the past." There was a moment when John the Baptist began to exist, and the same is true for all of us. But there was no moment at which the Son of God "began to exist": he always was. What is said in Psalm 90:2 of God (the Trinity) is equally true of the Son in particular: "from everlasting to everlasting you are God." But there was a moment at which that eternal Son became flesh.

The Salvation of Christ

Finally, the virgin birth is a picture or pattern of how we become Christians. Joseph could not himself produce a child who would be the Son of God—any child fathered by Joseph would simply be a human child, however special in other respects, and would inherit the flawed human nature of Adam. In the same way, none of us can produce spiritual, eternal life in ourselves—all we can produce, even at our best, is human good works. The Holy Spirit needs to reproduce the eternal life of Jesus in us: we need to be born again of the Spirit (John 3:3–8). Just as the Spirit of God produced in the womb of Mary the physical life of Jesus, so the same Spirit reproduces in us the spiritual life of Jesus.

Before moving on from the virgin conception, and in the interests of—forgive the pun—avoiding *mis*conceptions, we should distinguish the biblical account of the virgin birth from some of the non-biblical theories that have been tacked onto it in the Catholic tradition. That tradition maintains, first, that Mary remained a virgin all her life. That is not what the Bible says, and it seriously distorts the significance of the virgin conception, which, as we said, is not about Mary in herself, but is about Jesus; and it certainly does not mean that there would be anything improper or inappropriate in Joseph and Mary, as a married couple, enjoying a normal marital relationship, including sexual intimacy. Nothing in the Bible militates against the assumption that, after Jesus was born, Joseph and Mary went on to have normal marital relations, and to have other children; and much supports it.

- The most natural way of understanding Matthew 1:25 ("he had no union with her until she gave birth to a son") is that Joseph had no sexual relations with Mary *until after* Jesus was born; the two-word phrase translated "until" (Greek: *héōs hoû*) is used, apart from here in Matthew 1:25, twelve times in the New Testament,[12] and in every case the obvious and (usually) explicit sense is that of a changed situation: at a particular point something happened (or will happen) which until that point had not happened (or will not happen). If the claim is made that Matthew does not say explicitly that Joseph and Mary began to have sexual relations after the birth of Jesus, it is nonetheless the case that, if he does not mean that, he is using "until" in a way that is different from all its other uses in the New Testament.

- Luke 2:7 calls Jesus Mary's "firstborn," and again, the most obvious sense of that phrase is that she later went on to have other children.

- The other children of Joseph and Mary are named in Matthew 13:55–56//Mark 6:3. Catholics who wish to maintain the "permanent virginity" of Mary usually account for the list of Jesus' siblings by saying that they could be the children of Joseph by a former marriage, a theory for which there is not only no shred of evidence, but which conflicts with the most obvious way of understanding the words of Scripture, and has to be dismissed as a purely hypothetical theory invoked to make the words of the Bible compatible with an extra-biblical dogma that some people are unwilling to question. It is true that the Hebrew or Aramaic words for "brother" could have a wider range of meanings, including "half-brother" or even "cousin," but the Greek word *adelphós*, which Matthew and Mark use in the verses mentioned above, means the same as our English word "brother," and, as David Hill points out, "texts of Paul, of Acts, and of John also mention Jesus' brothers in Greek to Greek-speaking readers, and it is likely that they meant the term *adelphós* to be understood as 'brother' in the accepted sense of the word."[13]

Second, the Catholic tradition sees this alleged "permanent virginity" of Mary as a necessary aspect of the equally unbiblical doctrine that she

---

12. Matthew 13:33//Luke 13:21, Matthew 17:9, 18:34, Luke 15:8, 22:18, 24:49, Acts 23:12,14, 23:21, 25:21, 2 Peter 1:19.

13. Hill, *Matthew*, 222. Hill does not identify the specific texts he is referring to, but examples are Acts 1:14, 1 Corinthians 9:5, and John 7:3,5.

was without sin. That involves two errors. One is that the Bible does not support any notion that Mary was sinless; she herself, in the *Magnificat*, calls God "my Savior" (Luke 2:47)—and only sinful people need a Savior. Whilst there is no doubt that Mary was a good and devoted character, it is contrary to the plain teaching of the Bible to suggest that she was without sin: "All have sinned and fall short of the glory of God" (Romans 3:23). It is the Lord Jesus himself who alone is without sin (1 John 3:5); so for Catholicism to claim sinlessness for Mary separates her from the rest of fallen humanity, and ascribes to her a spiritual standing analogous to that of the Lord himself. The New Testament sees Mary as a model of devoted and obedient discipleship—"I am the Lord's servant" (Luke 1:38)—rather than as a model of the Savior.[14] Moreover, for a married woman to have sexual relations with her husband would not in itself involve any corruption or sin. Though the Bible will not allow the idea that Mary was without sin, her living in normal marital relations with Joseph would in no way be wrong; the Catholic idea that chastity is somehow morally purer than marriage implies that marriage, and the sexual union of a married couple, is a necessary evil, or an unfortunate compromise in the life of anyone whose desire is to be clean in the eyes of God. It is not so. Marriage and marital love are affirmed in the Bible to be positive and right, and as part of God's good gifts in creation.

Paul's comments in 1 Corinthians 7, where he says that, whilst marriage is good, it is even better to remain single, have often led to accusations of his being "anti-women" or "anti-marriage." That seems harsh, bearing in mind that Paul's central theme in this chapter is that, contrary to the mistaken idea that being married is somehow "unspiritual," normal marital relations are entirely compatible with living a holy and spiritual life. In saying that those who, like himself, remain single are making a better choice, he does not mean "better" in the moral or spiritual sense of "right or wrong": he gives two quite practical reasons why singleness, especially in the social context in which he is writing ("because of the present crisis," verse 26), has some advantages. First, the single person has a greater degree of freedom from domestic responsibilities to be able to devote him- or herself to Christian service (verses 32–35); and second, in an age when being a Christian would increasingly bring "troubles" (verse 28), including severe persecution, family life would inevitably bring extra concerns and pressures. Those who are offended by Paul's apparent relegation of marriage to a status of, at

---

14. The frequently misquoted and misapplied words of the angel Gabriel to Mary, traditionally rendered in the Catholic tradition as "Hail, Mary, full of grace," do *not* mean that Mary is in herself a source of grace; they mean that God has shown grace to her. Hence the correct NIV translation, "Greetings, you who are highly favored" (Luke 1:28). Mary does not bestow grace, she receives it, as we all do in one way or another.

best, secondary importance are missing a lesson that our society is paying a very heavy price for failing to heed. Contrary to popular romantic mythology, true fulfillment and security is found, not in any human relationship, however good and precious, but in Christ. But to use that perfectly correct principle to claim that marital relations are in any way inappropriate or improper, or that singleness is in itself morally and spiritually superior to marriage, is a terrible *non sequitur*.

As part of teaching about marriage, Paul says in 1 Corinthians 7:28, speaking to the unmarried, "But if you do marry, you have not sinned," and part of his reason for saying something that to most people is a statement of the obvious is that there seems to have been an idea circulating in Corinth that there is something inherently wrong or improper about marital relations, and that it is therefore better for a Christian couple to conduct their marriage on purely platonic lines. Paul says, in effect, that that is nonsense. Whatever good reasons there may be for this or that individual to choose to remain single, marriage and family life are the norm, and there is nothing in any sense wrong in marital love. That is as true of Joseph and Mary as of any other married couple.

Jesus' Genealogy

This chapter on the introduction to the story of Jesus is perhaps the best place to make some comments about the two genealogies of Jesus, in Matthew 1:1–17 and Luke 3:23–38.

There are lots of "genealogies" in the Old Testament—long lists of names that we find it very hard to read through. Some people are rather put off to find that the New Testament begins with yet another genealogy. But that is because the New Testament grows out of the Old; it does not do away with or replace the Old. Just as Jesus' genealogy shows that Jesus' coming "grew out of" the Old Testament promises, so the new life and faith that he brings grows out of the Old Testament preparation.

Matthew in particular includes his genealogy in order to show that Jesus is descended from King David. One of the titles of the promised Messiah was "Son of David," and Matthew is showing that Jesus fulfills that qualification. Later in his Gospel, Matthew uses "Son of David" as a title for the Messiah eight times. But in 22:41–45, Jesus also says that he is more than just a descendant of David—he is also Lord.

The names in the two genealogies are significantly different. There may be a number of reasons for this—one reason that has been suggested is that Matthew might be giving the list of names of those who were kings of the

Jews, or who would have been if there had still been a monarchy in Israel after the exile in Babylon, whereas Luke is recording a straight father-son sequence—but the simplest and most likely reason is that such a genealogy did not necessarily include every generation. It is characteristic of Hebrew style to use the word "father" to mean, not merely one's immediate parent, but more generally "ancestor"; Jacob refers to Abraham as his "father" in Genesis 32:9, though he was technically his grandfather, and even more strikingly 1 Kings 15:11 refers to David as the father of King Asa, whereas he was actually his great-great-grandfather. Matthew's genealogy, unlike that of Luke, actually uses the verb *gennáō*, traditionally translated "to beget" ("Abraham begat Isaac, Isaac begat Jacob"). But the same point applies: "to beget" did not have to refer solely to someone's immediate parent, but could be used generally of forefathers. The famous line from the apocryphal book of *Ecclesiasticus*, a Jewish writing from the second century BC, "Let us now praise famous men, and our fathers that begat us," is a call to learn from the early patriarchs of the Jewish nation: later verses in the same chapter refer to Enoch and Noah as examples of the "fathers that begat us." This shows that "begat" (translated in the NIV as "[was] the father of") does not in Jewish usage have to refer to the immediately following generation. So whatever may be the reason for the particular selection of names in these genealogies, when Matthew says (verse 17) that there are fourteen generations in each part of his genealogy, he does not have to mean that only fourteen ever lived; he could well be saying, "Of all the generations . . . [here are] fourteen from Abraham to David . . ."[15] That does not invalidate the genealogy—if I say that the M1 runs from London to Dunstable to Milton Keynes to Northampton, I am not "wrong" simply because I did not mention that it also passes *en route* via Harpenden, Redbourne, Steppingley and Newport Pagnall—and certainly not in Hebrew eyes.

Both genealogies use number symbolism. They both revolve around the number seven. This always symbolizes the full and finished work of God (based on the seven days of creation). Matthew stresses (1:17) that his genealogy is arranged in three groups of fourteen; Luke's genealogy contains seventy-seven names (with Admin inserted after Amminadab in verse 33, as in the NIV footnote), and these fall into eleven groups of seven, with particularly significant names coming at the beginning and/or end of each

---

15. Indeed, when we compare Matthew's list of names with some of the Old Testament genealogies, we see some actual omissions, demonstrating that Matthew has not been concerned to list every generation. For example, in verse 8 Matthew moves straight from Jehoram to Uzziah, whilst 1 Chronicles 3:11–12, which gives a more complete line of succession, lists Ahaziah, Joash and Amaziah as coming between the two: note that "Azariah" in 1 Chronicles 3:12 is another name for Uzziah.

group (e.g. Enoch, Abraham, David, Jacob/Joseph). Whatever may be the historical basis for this arrangement, it shows that the writers are convinced that God sent his Son "when the time had fully come" (Galatians 4:4), when the time of preparation for his coming was perfectly complete.

Matthew's arrangement of his genealogy in groups of fourteen names may also, as William Barclay points out, have a symbolic significance, in addition to being a multiple of the significant number seven, bearing in mind that his purpose is to stress that Jesus is the son of David. In the ancient world letters, and therefore words, always had numerical values (A = 1, B = 2, etc.), and the numerical values of the letters in the Hebrew name "David" (DWD) are 4+6+4 = 14; as well as stating his point, Matthew is also symbolizing it.[16]

Matthew, unusually, includes the names of four women in his genealogy (plus, at the end, Mary, the mother of Jesus). All those he mentions are, in some sense, outcasts, the poor, victims. Tamar (verse 3) was the victim of incestuous rape (Genesis 38); Rahab (verse 5) was a prostitute (Joshua 2); Ruth (verse 5) was a Moabite, in other words, a member of a nation that was a long-standing enemy of Israel (Ruth 1:4); and Bathsheba ("Uriah's wife," verse 6) was seduced by David, and her husband was murdered. Jesus comes from a line of victims, foreigners, and outcasts—which reminds us that he comes in order to help and save victims, foreigners and outcasts.

Finally, the presence in the Gospels of a genealogy of Jesus seems to many people to be at variance with the doctrine of the virgin conception; if Joseph was not the natural father of Jesus, what is the point of a genealogy, tracing his ancestry through Joseph? The point is that the genealogy establishes Jesus' legal status, not his biological conception. Since Joseph was Jesus' adoptive father, Jesus inherited from him the status of being a descendant of Abraham and David. In Hebrew thinking "father" did not imply biological fatherhood so much as "protector" and "nurturer," a fact summed up in Psalm 68:5, which describes the Lord as "a father to the fatherless." In that sense, Joseph was indeed Jesus' "father"; though it is significant that both New Testament genealogies are careful to stress that he was not in fact Jesus' physical progenitor: Matthew, after thirty-nine repetitions of "[was] the father of . . . " (traditionally: "begat"), drops the term when he comes to Jesus, and concludes instead with "Joseph, *the husband of Mary, of whom was born* Jesus," whilst Luke, whose genealogy starts from Jesus and then traces back to Adam, begins "he was the son, *so it was thought*, of Joseph, the son of . . . " So, because Joseph was Jesus' adoptive father, Jesus is regarded as having the status of a descendant of David, because adoptive children had

---

16. Barclay, W., *Matthew*, 2–3.

exactly the same social status as natural-born children in Jewish society. But Joseph was not Jesus' biological father.

The same balance that we saw in Luke's and John's prologues is seen again in the virgin conception of Jesus on the one hand and the genealogies on the other. The virgin conception speaks of his uniqueness as God the eternal Son; the genealogies make the complementary point that in becoming flesh, the Son of God became a real part of human history. They show us from the outset that God's work to save us is rooted in historical events that happened at a particular time and in a particular place. Christian faith rests on a basis of historical fact: Christ died, was buried and rose again. The unbeliever may ignore the facts of history, or mock them, or dismiss them, or challenge them, or disbelieve them—but he cannot change them. When Pilate was put under pressure to alter his wording of the charge above Jesus on the cross ("King of the Jews"), he said, "What I have written, I have written" (John 19:22). With even more assurance we can say, what God has done, he has done.

The historical basis of our faith is, on the one hand, a source of great reassurance to the Christian believer: it means that our salvation rests on a solid foundation. It does not depend on a theory, or an ideology, or a vague and abstract concept; it depends on a historical event which has happened, and which nothing can change. But in our day there is also a new challenge for our mission. We live in an age that is skeptical about history, and especially about ancient history. It is generally doubted by most people that anything that happened centuries ago can have any relevance for us today. It may be interesting for those who are interested in exploring the past, but it is nothing to do with those of us who want to live in the present.

Sadly, the church has all too often seemed to concur, by changing the way in which we speak of the message of the Kingdom. Instead of preaching the fact that Christ died and rose again, the "Gospel" can often be presented as a promise about how God can become real in your life today, what he can do for you here and now. So what we offer ceases to be a historical work of atonement, and becomes instead a psychological prop or a spiritual "feel good factor." If people don't care about what happened in history, let's not tell them what God has done in history—let's tell them instead how he can make them feel today. That will interest them.

It may well; but it won't redeem them. Jesus told us to make disciples of all nations, not to dangle carrots before all nations. We need to have more confidence in the power of the Gospel story. To tell people what Jesus did does not have to mean giving them dry facts, a kind of historical lecture. We need neither to apologize for the fact that our Gospel is first and foremost about what happened in history, nor to find ways of adapting the story of

Jesus so that it panders to the prejudices of twenty-first-century Britain. In the spirit of 1 Corinthians 15:1–4, we can simply tell people that Jesus died for them and rose again, because it is by holding on to that message that, as verse 2 says, people are saved. The Gospel is still the power of God for salvation, even if it works at a level that is different from the mind-set of our contemporary culture. We do not necessarily need to explain to people *how* an event two thousand years ago can impact their lives today; it is enough to tell them about Jesus, and leave it to the Holy Spirit to do all the impacting that is necessary. I have absolutely no idea how electricity works; my understanding is more or less on a par with that of the man who, when asked how it was that the same electricity that made his fridge cold also made his cooker warm, replied that he supposed it was because they were on opposite sides of the kitchen. But my ignorance about how electricity works does not mean that I have to sit in the dark; I can turn the light on just as well as any qualified electrician. And the fact that modern man may not understand how something that happened in Jesus' day can flood his life today with spiritual light does not mean that he has to continue living in the dark. We do not have to give lectures about how electricity works to the man in the dark; we just need to show him where the light switch is. And we do not need to convince the modern western unbeliever that history is relevant after all; we can simply tell him the story of Jesus and his cross, and point him to faith as the light switch.

Jesus' Background

There is one more point of interest with which we conclude this chapter on the introduction to the story of Jesus. The New Testament teaches that Jesus came to bring about a new covenant between God and his people. A "covenant" is a binding relationship between two parties, in which each pledges himself to the other; God had created a covenant relationship with his people Israel when he rescued them from Egypt, and the phrase that sums up the character of that relationship is "I will be your God, and you will be my people" (Leviticus 26:12). In Jeremiah 31:31 God promises that he will one day bring about a "new covenant": he will raise the nature of his people's relationship with himself to a whole new level; and all four Gospel writers agree that Jesus is the one who brings about that new covenant relationship, and therefore brings the greater fullness of which the Old Testament is the foreshadowing. But they place the background to Jesus' coming at different stages of the Old Testament, and so emphasize different aspects of how Jesus is "making everything new" (Revelation 21:5). As always, these are not clashes but complementary truths.

Mark (1:1–3) starts his Gospel by speaking of Jesus as the one who fulfills the Old Testament prophecies about the coming of God's Kingdom. He quotes from the prophets Malachi and Isaiah, focusing especially on Isaiah's prophecy of the restoration of the old kingdom of Judah, following the period of exile in Babylon. Later, in Jesus' ministry, the nature of the Kingdom that he brings will start to become clearer; it will not be, as many Jews hoped, merely a political reinstatement of the monarchy and a liberation from Roman occupation. Jesus brings a different kind of Kingdom, one that is "not of this world" (John 18:36). Jesus is *the start of a whole new Kingdom*.

Matthew (1:1–17) goes further back. His genealogy, as we have seen, traces the line of Jesus back further than the prophets, to Abraham, the founder of the Jewish people, Israel. Israel was the people of God under the old covenant. Jesus comes to create a new people, a new community, of which Old Testament Israel was both the model and the seed-bed, but of which it does not set the parameters. In choosing his twelve disciples, Jesus was symbolically creating the nucleus of that new Israel: the twelve disciples are a new covenant parallel to the twelve sons of Jacob who were the founding ancestors of the twelve tribes of Israel. Jesus is *the start of a whole new Israel*.

Luke (3:23–38) starts even further back. His genealogy goes back, not just to Abraham, but to Adam, the first man, and the start of the human race. Jesus, as we said in discussing the virgin conception, brings a new start for the human race as a whole; he is *the start of a whole new humanity*.

And finally John (1:1–5) goes back further still to before creation itself. "In the beginning was the Word"; and the Word becomes flesh in order to come and make a new beginning. Paul says that what Jesus brings is "new creation" (2 Corinthians 5:17); and he says moreover that the present creation is groaning as if in labor pains, waiting for that new creation to come fully to birth (Romans 8:22). One day, the new creation will be completed, the old heavens will disappear, and the elements will be destroyed by fire (2 Peter 3:10); all the stars will be dissolved, and the sky rolled up like a scroll (Isaiah 34:4). Then there will be a new heaven and a new earth (Revelation 21:1). Jesus came, not just to save human beings, but to begin a whole new creation. Any Christian can quite properly rejoice and say that "Jesus saved me!"; but he should also remember that the Gospel of Jesus is big enough to save the cosmos. Jesus is *the start of a whole new creation*.

In our day we need to be very careful that we do not lose that bigger vision of Christ and what he does; we can so focus on the personal Christ, the Jesus who ministers to this widow, to that child, to this individual sick person, that we forget the cosmic Christ, the one who will renew all things. It is a much-used, maybe even an over-used image, but in sending his Son into the world, God is tossing a pebble into the middle of the pond of creation; and the ripples from that small beginning will spread over the whole pond. Human philosophies and ideologies all tend towards one of two foci: either individualism or collectivism. Individualism tends to be stressed more in democratic and "free market" societies: the individual matters more than the collective—at its most extreme that was expressed in Margaret Thatcher's infamous quotation, "There is no such thing as society."[17] The collective tends to be stressed in, amongst others, communist regimes: what matters is the bigger picture, typically the state, and the duty of the individual is to surrender his or her personal needs and preferences to the greater good. The Gospel of Jesus embraces and perfectly addresses both the individual and the "bigger picture": Jesus comes to people as individuals and shares his salvation and eternal life with them; *and* he is bringing about a new people of God, a new community of faith, ultimately a whole new heavens and new earth. Whichever end of the spectrum we might tend towards, the Jesus of the Gospels offers the necessary balancing corrective.

---

17. In an interview for *Womens Own* magazine, October 1987. Quoted in *ODQ*, 691.

3

The Baby of Bethlehem

"The time came for the baby to be born" (Luke 2:6)

Only Matthew and Luke tell the story of the birth of Jesus. Mark's Gospel starts with Jesus beginning his ministry at the age of thirty. John's Gospel speaks of the mystery of how Jesus was from eternity God who became a human being; but he then goes straight on to the witness of John the Baptist and the beginnings of Jesus' ministry as an adult.

What is more, the actual birth itself is hardly mentioned; it is referred to briefly in half a verse in Luke 2:7. The Bible has nothing whatever of the popular "stable scenes" that we know from nativity plays and Christmas cards. In fact, the Bible does not say that Jesus was born in a stable; and this is just one of a number of traditional and sentimental images that we now associate with the birth of Jesus that go way beyond what the Bible actually says. At the risk of appearing negative or a kill-joy, it is worth peeling away some of the popular nativity-scene myths, and establishing what the Bible actually says happened. There is, as we have said, no mention of a stable, nor of animals surrounding the manger. Neither is there any mention of an inn. The word traditionally translated as "inn" is simply the word for a lodging place or even a guest room; it is the same word that is used in Luke 22:11//Mark 14:14, where Jesus asks, "Where is the *guest room*, where I may eat the Passover with my disciples?" And the word translated "room" does not have to mean specifically a room which is part of a house, a chamber; it is the quite general word for a "place" or "space," just as someone might say, "I don't have *room* on my drive to park a car." A more accurate way of translating the familiar "no room at the inn" would be to say that no one had sufficient spare space in any of their rooms to put Mary and Joseph up.[1] The manger does not imply a stable, or the presence of animals; it simply means that Joseph and Mary made use of an animal's feeding-trough for a crib (2:7). Where Jesus was actually born is not stated, and whilst it may be interesting to speculate—was Jesus born outside in the street?, or in a field?, or was it in fact amongst animals?, or was it, as a tradition dating back to the second century says, in a cave?—we need to recognize that this is speculation, not biblical fact. It is what the Bible actually says that is God's true Word to us.

One of the traditions that came to be added to the Christmas story is of course the date. The celebration of the birth of Jesus on 25th December has nothing to do with the biblical story; the date seems to have been chosen in the fourth century AD as a Christian counterpart to a pagan Roman festival, either the winter solstice, or a festival of the sun. The Bible itself says nothing about the date or season in which the birth occurred; the only hint is that shepherds keeping flocks out of doors overnight (Luke 2:8) was most common between April and November. There is of course no reason why we should not use the arbitrary date of 25th December as a special focus for celebrating the incarnation, nor, in my view, enjoy a holiday festivity. Many Christmas carols contain lines like "Christ is born today," but to object to them on the grounds that it probably wasn't actually "today" would demonstrate a somewhat Scrooge-like mentality. Let us by all means enjoy all the popular festive traditions (trees, mince pies, etc.)—and I am even happy to go along with "ox and ass before him bow,"[2] a bit of poetical license that belongs to a Disney version of Christmas rather than to the biblical history—but let us always remember that what matters, and what we celebrate in worship, is that the Word became flesh.

Whilst we are speaking of the date of the birth, it is worth pointing out that, according to our present reckoning of calendar years, Jesus cannot have born in the year AD 0. Herod died in 4 BC, so Jesus must have been born some years before that: the usual estimate is some time between 5 and 7 BC. That has nothing to do with the accuracy of the biblical history. When the sixth-century monk Dionysius Exiguus invented the division of history into years BC and AD, he tried to calculate the year of the birth of Jesus, and simply got it wrong by a few years. But his calculation of AD 0 has remained

---

1. Raymond Brown summarizes verse 7 as "Jesus . . . was laid in a manger because of the lack of space at the lodgings." (Brown, *Birth of the Messiah*, 418.)

2. From the traditional carol, "Good Christian men, rejoice," which incidentally also contains the line "Christ is born today."

the basis for all modern calendars; hence the anomaly that Christ was born a few years before Christ!

The Human Reality of Jesus' Birth

The emphasis in the Bible is not on the physical birth scene itself, but on two other things in particular. First, we see again what we saw in Luke 1, the presence of the supernatural in the midst of the ordinary, the spiritual world of God's Kingdom impacting the everyday human world, a world that has an alarming amount in common with our own. There is the human reality of *poverty*—Joseph and Mary could not find anywhere to stay, and they have to improvise by borrowing an animal's feeding-trough to use as a crib. Whilst the traditional image of the stable is not what the Bible describes, there is no doubt that we are dealing here with a level of need, with homelessness in fact, that will be only too familiar from many of our inner cities and council estates. Then there is *political dictatorship*—Caesar can pass a law forcing people to travel miles to register for a poll tax; and Herod can kill all the children in a town in an attempt to destroy Jesus, whom he sees as a threat to his own position as king. Living as we do in a world of totalitarian regimes and ethnic cleansing, the Bible here reads like an extract from a contemporary newspaper. And there is the basic reality of *childbirth*, in, to put it mildly, less than ideal conditions.

But into that all-too-human world comes the supernatural and heavenly: angels are heard praising God (Luke 2:13–14), God speaks to Joseph in dreams (Matthew 2:13,19,22), the Wise Men are supernaturally guided (Matthew 2:12), the Holy Spirit speaks to and through people like Simeon (Luke 2:25–35).

From the very beginning, indeed even before he was, in his human nature, properly conscious of what was happening around him, Jesus is seen to be born into a life which identifies with the poor, the oppressed, the socially marginalized. The teenage girl who gives birth to a baby in what we euphemistically call "cardboard city" under a railway bridge can find in the Jesus of the Gospels one with whom she can identify, and who can say to her, "That's where I came from, too." The refugee fleeing political oppression with his small children can find in the Jesus who, as a baby, had to be taken by his family to Egypt or face being slaughtered in his own country, one who has himself been through exactly the same experience. Though in terms of his essential nature as the eternal Son of God, and in moral character, Jesus stands infinitely higher than even the best of us, in terms of his experience of human life, he stands alongside, not just humanity in general, but the neediest and humblest of people. He came among us as one who experienced what it means to be the victim of social rejection and political cruelty—he identified with the oppressed and the victims of life; he stood in their shoes, or, more accurately, he walked barefoot with them.

Yet even in that world of pain and poverty, God's intervention makes a difference—not always, as many would insist he should, by abolishing the pain and poverty, but by touching the people who live in it with his heavenly reality. The shepherds, having found the infant Jesus, went back to being shepherds, to their life as a group of people who were regarded as socially inferior;[3] but they went back "glorifying and praising God" (Luke 2:20), as people who had experienced something completely wonderful which had changed them forever. Joseph and Mary were frequently on the move because of threats to Jesus' life; but God always intervened to warn and preserve them (Matthew 2:13,22). In the story of the infant Jesus we see a striking instance of the promise of the twenty-third Psalm: "Even though I walk through the valley of the shadow of death, I will fear no evil, for you are with me; your rod and your staff, they comfort me." In this sinful world, the way of service for God will sometimes take us through the valley of the shadow, as it did for Jesus; but his protecting presence will never leave us nor forsake us.

The second theme in the birth narratives is the things that are said about Jesus, and the prophecies of what he will accomplish. The angels announce (Luke 2:10–11) "good news of great joy that will be for all the people. Today in the town of David a Savior has been born to you; he is Christ the Lord." Simeon prophesied (Luke 2:30–35) over the baby Jesus: "My eyes have seen your salvation, which you have prepared in the sight of all people, a light for revelation to the Gentiles and for glory to your people Israel . . . This child is destined to cause the falling and rising of many in Israel, and to be a sign that will be spoken against, so that the thoughts of many hearts will be revealed. And a sword will pierce your own soul too." The Wise Men declare that Jesus is "born King of the Jews" (Matthew 2:2).

It is important that we hold on to both of those key themes. If we stress the first (Jesus' birth in poverty) but ignore the second ("a Savior . . . Christ the Lord . . . light for revelation"), the story of Jesus' birth becomes merely a moving instance of human and social need; and there are those for whom

---

3. The demands of their work made it impossible for shepherds regularly to observe the ceremonial law, which branded them, in the eyes of the religious establishment, as spiritually suspect. Moreover, shepherds had a bad moral reputation, whether deserved or not, as those who would use their wanderings from place to place around the country as the cover for theft; there is some evidence that shepherds as a class were not allowed to give testimony in a law court, as they were considered too unreliable.

Jesus is primarily or solely a social reformer or political freedom fighter, causes that were close to his heart because of the circumstances of his early childhood. If on the other hand we always preach the doctrines that are encapsulated in the prophetic words spoken over the baby Jesus, but forget or ignore the human story which provided the context for those words, the birth of Jesus becomes a theological statement about salvation, but without its roots in ordinary day-to-day life with which people can identify. In the birth story, Jesus is indeed "the Word" (Savior, Lord, King) "made flesh" (a baby, a refugee, one who "stood in my shoes").

In the famous service of Nine Lessons and Carols, traditionally held in and broadcast from King's College, Cambridge on Christmas Eve, the introduction to the final reading, John 1:1–14, is: "St John unfolds the great mystery of the Incarnation." The previous readings from Matthew 1 and 2 and Luke 1 and 2 are the narrative of the birth of Jesus; and the implication might seem to be that Matthew and Luke simply tell the human story, but that it is only John who speaks of the fact that the one who was born in Bethlehem was the Son of God incarnate. That is not the case: there are a number of indications of the deity of Christ in the birth narratives: here are three fairly unambiguous ones.

1. The angels tell the shepherds in Luke 2:11 that the one born in Bethlehem is "Christ *the Lord.*" "The Lord" is an explicitly divine title; it was the Greek translation of the unique name of God *Yahweh* (or *Jehovah*) in the Old Testament. As we will have much more to say about this in a later chapter, we will for now merely note that this divine name is used of Jesus.

2. The angel Gabriel tells Mary that the one to be born "will be called the Son of God" (Luke 1:35). In the thinking of the Jewish people, "son of" did not mean, as we can often assume, "less than"—to call Jesus the "Son of God" does not mean that he is a kind of "junior version" of God—but rather "having the same nature as." That is why, when Jesus speaks of God as his own Father, John adds the comment, "For this reason the Jews tried all the harder to kill him . . . he was even calling God his own Father, *making himself equal with God*" (John 5:18).

3. Matthew's account of the visit of the Wise Men stresses several times that they have come to worship Jesus. It is of course true that these men were not strictly monotheistic Jews, but the fact remains that Matthew—the most traditionally "Jewish" of the four Gospel writers—has chosen to include in his book the fact that Jesus was worshiped. For Jewish people whose first religious principle was that worship could

be directed to none other than God himself, the implication for who Christ is could not be clearer.

The Historical Reality of Jesus' Birth

"In those days Caesar Augustus issued a decree that a census should be taken of the entire Roman world. This was the first census that took place while Quirinius was governor of Syria" (Luke 2:1–2). There is a lot of discussion in commentaries about when the kind of census described by Luke might have happened, whether the registration for a tax would have necessitated a journey to one's original family home, and the implications of the reference to Quirinius, who is known to have held a governorship in Syria from AD 6–9, and held a number of political and/or military offices before that time—he was, for example, a consul in Rome in 12 BC[4]—for the dating of the birth story. I do not propose to discuss these questions here, not because such discussion is of no value, but simply because it is not my purpose: I want to explore the spiritual and devotional lessons that we can learn from the text itself. But there is no doubt that the kind of social and political background Luke describes—such as crippling taxation and enforced registration in a census—is consistent with what we know of the practices in the Roman Empire in the first century, whether or not historians can identify the specific census referred to in Luke 2:1.

The important point is that Luke sets the birth in its historical and political context. This is important for a number of reasons.

The Real World

It emphasizes the historical reality of the incarnation; it takes place in a recognizable world, at a (more or less) datable time, when well-known historical characters were governing; Augustus was emperor from 27 BC to 14 AD. This is not a featureless or escapist world that exists in some spiritual fourth dimension. It is the world of political reality, of economic pressures—like poll taxes—and of authoritarian regimes. That is the world into which Jesus came. And his Gospel is preached today, not to lift people out of that human world, but to change their lives whilst they continue to live within it.

---

4. *NBD*, 993.

Human Politics

God uses the economic laws of a Roman ruler to bring about his will for his people. The Old Testament had prophesied that Jesus would be born at Bethlehem (Micah 5:2), the city of David. A decree about a Roman poll tax means that Joseph and Mary have to go to Bethlehem. God overrules in the affairs of nations in order to bring about his spiritual purposes for his people.

That does not mean, as the cynic might think, that God "made" Caesar order a poll-tax affecting thousands of people for no reason other than to engineer a way of getting Joseph and Mary to travel from Nazareth in the north to Jerusalem in the south; that would suggest an amoral desperation, not all that different from Herod's terrible (and ultimately unsuccessful) plan to kill Jesus by killing all the local baby boys. However we understand the relationship between the choices and actions of people and God's sovereign over-ruling of events in human history, it has to be in ways that are more subtle than that. Caesar chose to impose his tax, just as all people choose to pursue the courses of action that they do; and they, like Caesar, remain accountable to God for the choices they make and the actions they pursue. And yet, through all—indeed, in spite of all—the machinations of human action and worldly politics, God's sovereign will and purpose is brought about. Whatever laws are passed in Parliament that impinge on the church, the appropriate Christian response is not to bemoan them, and not even merely to campaign against them, but rather to ask the Lord how we can best live our lives in society so that more of God's Kingdom will come to more of our land. Everyone will in one way or another be part of bringing about God's purposes; but it makes an incalculable difference to them whether they serve his purposes as Mary and Joseph did or as Caesar did. And that is each person's choice.

Spiritual Life

We can see here an encouraging point about the relative importance of politics and God's Kingdom. The great issues of the empire are actually far less important in the history of the world than an obscure birth to a homeless teenage mother in a village in Judea. Many Christians may feel relatively powerless in terms of affecting the world they live in; they have no political influence, unlike Caesar or Quirinius—they are "ordinary people," much more like Joseph and Mary. But by bringing Jesus into the world, Mary and Joseph did more good for the world than all the Caesars or Quiriniuses put together. In terms of eternal significance, it is the believing people of God who can have the most profound effect on those around them, not the political leaders of nations. Many politicians will say that the reason they chose to enter parliament was the desire "to make a difference." That can of course be a perfectly honorable ambition, and we are instructed in the Scriptures to pray for those who govern us. But it is important for Christians to realize that they do not need to stand for political office or become prominent in order to make a difference. The believer who shares the love and the truth of Christ with others can make a more lasting difference than Prime Ministers and Presidents ever will.

Ordinary People

Following on from that, it is interesting that, whilst the birth itself happened in obscurity, its reality and significance were revealed by God to unusual people: the shepherds (Luke 2:8–20), who were as we have said a despised class in Jewish society; Simeon and Anna (Luke 2:25–38), simple believing people who prayed for God's Kingdom to come; the Wise Men (Matthew 2), who were foreigners from the east, probably in or around Persia. Simeon and Anna saw the significance of what was happening, whilst Caesar and Quirinius were quite unaware of it, and Herod (Matthew 2) was grimly determined to oppose it. But they saw it because God revealed it to them: he spoke to Simeon through the Holy Spirit (Luke 2:26–27), to the shepherds through angels, to the Wise Men initially by means of a light in the sky. Historical investigation into the person and life of Jesus can have its value; but the true meaning of Jesus' coming will never be learned from historical archives or from specialist research, and certainly not from typing "Jesus" into a Google search; it will be seen when God's Spirit reveals it to the hearts of those who are hungry for spiritual life, rather than simply interested in exploring religious speculations.

Continuing in Luke 2, two other things stand out. Luke stresses that Jesus as a baby was taken to fulfill all the Old Testament requirements following childbirth. On the eighth day after his birth, he was circumcised (2:21, Leviticus 12:3); Mary fulfilled the required period of purification after childbirth[5] (2:22, Leviticus 12:4), after which she offered the prescribed sacrifice (2:24, Leviticus 12:8). Furthermore, Mary and Joseph went to the temple in Jerusalem in order to dedicate their baby to God (2:22), and Luke points

---

5. The fact that Mary was regarded as having been made, by Jewish standards, ceremonially unclean by the birth is further evidence of the reality of the incarnation.

out that this fulfills the law which said that every first-born male must be consecrated to the Lord (Exodus 13:2); in fact, such a consecration did not require a journey to the temple, so it is likely that Joseph and Mary, knowing that their child has a special purpose in the bringing of God's Kingdom, are also presenting him before God in order to consecrate him to God's service. Luke summarizes all that happened following the birth in the words, "When Joseph and Mary had done everything required by the law of the Lord . . ." (2:39).

So all the religious requirements of the law following a birth were fulfilled. But the way in which this happened went far beyond what was normal. The Holy Spirit leads Simeon to the temple, and he prophesies over Jesus. Jesus is born as part of the Jewish people, "born under the law," as Galatians 4:4 says; but right from his birth, he is seen to go way beyond conventional religious norms. The coming of Jesus injects new life into familiar "religious" practices. He doesn't ignore them and set them aside—but he does transcend them. The Christian church should always expect him to do the same in every part of our life and ministry. All our worship, whether officially liturgical or "free," will take certain familiar forms, either actually prescribed or simply by tradition. That is in itself entirely acceptable, if not actually inevitable. But just as the presentation of Jesus in the temple went far beyond what was normal, and became the occasion when God spoke prophetically through his Spirit, so it should be the constant prayer of all believers that God will visit us in our worship and, without necessarily setting aside our "forms" of service—Jesus *was* formally circumcised and consecrated,—will breathe life into what can so easily become the dry bones of church. And this can be as necessary in what would be called "lively" or charismatic churches as in formal and liturgical ones. Charismatics can sometimes be snootily dismissive of liturgical worship and regard it as mere formality, without apparently noticing that the worship in their own fellowships can be just as set in its ways as any "prayer book" service: it always starts with two or three bouncy songs, each repeated two or three times, followed by everyone speaking or shouting in tongues for about three minutes, followed by three or four testimonies, and so on, as the meeting runs along well established lines. I am not for one moment saying that the worship offered in such contexts cannot be real, from the heart and pleasing to God, and I would like to think that it often is. But all of us, whatever our style, need to be ready to let the Holy Spirit breathe new life into our worship, and speak in ways that may not be what we expect. Mere decibels are not the evidence that he is already doing that.

What happened at the temple caused Joseph and Mary to "marvel" (2:33); is the modern western church sufficiently open to God, so that he comes and reveals himself in holiness and power in our meetings in ways that cause people to marvel?

And finally, a very frequent theme in Luke 1 and 2 is *joy*. The coming of Jesus brings great joy to people. The birth of John the Baptist "will be a joy and delight to" Zechariah (1:14), when Mary visited Elizabeth, the baby in Elizabeth's womb "leaped for joy" (1:44), Mary said that her spirit "rejoices in God my Savior" (1:47), Zechariah and Elizabeth's neighbors "shared her joy" when John was born (1:58), the angels announced "good news of great joy" (2:10). In addition, there are many other references to people "giving thanks," "praising God," or similar phrases: Elizabeth exclaims with a loud voice and blesses Mary (1:42); Zechariah is filled with the Holy Spirit and declares "Praise be to the Lord . . . !" (1:68); the angels sing "Glory to God in the highest" (2:14); having found the baby, the shepherds return "glorifying and praising God" (2:20); Simeon gladly blesses God when he sees the infant Jesus (2:28-32); and Anna gives thanks to God for Jesus (2:38). I commented above about the danger of lively charismatic churches assuming that, unlike those in a more formal tradition, they are immune to the danger of becoming set in their ways. But there is of course the opposite danger. There are those who will refer to lively churches as "happy-clappy," and the term always implies superficial and undignified. Sometimes, it can be. But the fact is, the coming of Jesus *does* fill people with joy; being happy is not unbiblical, nor is deep solemnity an invariable sign of holiness and devotion. The fruit of the Spirit is joy, and the joy of the Lord, far from being mere froth, is our strength. If the angels themselves announced good news of great joy, it is legitimate to ask (sensitively!) of those who disapprove of lively and joyful expressions of church whether their own absence of joy might perhaps be because they have not truly grasped or entered into the reality of that good news.

The Wise Men

We said earlier that the biblical story of the birth and its significance have been so overlaid with additional elements that even Christians who are fairly well grounded in the Bible are not always clear about which parts of the traditional nativity story are actually biblical history and which are extra-biblical or legendary accretions. No part of the story has suffered more in this regard than the account in Matthew 2 of the visit of the Wise Men.

So let us start by separating fact from fiction, or at least from popular and traditional folk-lore. The Bible does not say how many Wise Men there were. The tradition that there were three is based on the three gifts, on the assumption that three individuals brought one each, which is obviously not necessarily the case. Matthew gives us no reason at all to call them "kings," although they were obviously wealthy and socially prominent men. The tradition that they were kings arises from the prophecy of Psalm 72:10–11 ("The kings of Tarshish and of distant shores will bring tribute to him; the kings of Sheba and Seba will present him gifts. All kings will bow down to him . . ."), which is a psalm about the coming of the Messiah, and the fact that foreign powers and rulers will recognize him and submit to him. This came to be seen as foretelling the visit of the Wise Men. It is certainly true that Matthew 2 fulfills this prophecy; but that does not mean that the Wise Men's visit is all that Psalm 72 can ever refer to. There will be a further and greater fulfillment at the end of history, when all the rulers of the earth will bring tribute to Christ. So there is no reason to assume that the visitors to the infant Jesus were kings, and it is most unlikely that they were. Moreover the conventional names of the visitors, Melchior, Balthasar and Caspar, which are first mentioned in a Greek document from around 500 AD, have become part of traditional Yuletide folk-religion, but are no part of the biblical story. In the line of the Christmas carol "We three kings of Orient are . . . ," the only word that touches base with what the Bible says is "Orient"—the Wise Men certainly came from the east![6]

We do not know much about the Magi; we cannot be completely certain who they were, or in what their "wisdom" consisted. But it is too simplistic to say, as many do, that they were astrologers. (The *Good News Bible* does not help by calling them "some men who studied the stars"!) It is true that a lot of the religion of the ancient world included astrological elements, which the Old Testament prophets repeatedly condemn (e.g. Isaiah 47:13–14); and the story in Matthew 2 must never be regarded as in any way endorsing or condoning astrology. But in ancient cultures, the distinction between astronomy as a science and astrology as a mystical art was far from clear; and ancient Babylonian astronomy, despite its astrological elements, has been credited with laying the foundation for our present understanding of the planetary solar system.[7] It is therefore unfair to dismiss the Magi merely

---

6. The phrase in Matthew 2:2 translated in some Bibles as "in the east" is not the same as the phrase in verse 1, "Magi from the east." In verse 1, it is the normal phrase in the plural meaning "the east"; in verse 2, it is the singular word, which in the Bible is used to mean "rising": it is used twice in Revelation to refer to the rising of the sun. So the NIV footnote to verse 2 is probably right to prefer the sense of "in its [= the star's] rising" or "when it arose"; but verse 1 says explicitly that the Magi came "from the east."

7. Isaac Asimov, in an essay debunking the modern practice of astrology, says that astrology in Sumeria (that is, Babylonia) began as an enquiry into the patterns found in the natural order, because it was believed that if "the gods" wanted to communicate with people, they would do so through the regular phenomena of nature, and adds the

as superstitious and ignorant pagans. The word translated "Wise Men" or "Magi" was originally an Iranian word for a tribe of Zoroastrian priests, and came to be used more generally for (pagan) priests or religious counselors; such "Magi" generally believed in one God, in the need to practice virtue and avoid evil, and in prayer. And however much superstition their religion may have included alongside these more wholesome elements, the Wise Men in Matthew 2 certainly seem far closer to the heart and mind of God than Herod, the king reigning in Jerusalem.

We should also remember that since the exile in Babylon in the eighth century BC, Jewish people had been scattered all around the Persian (later, Greek; later still, Roman) empires. There were communities of people all over the known world, including in Persia, who were at least familiar with Old Testament teaching, and with that strand of Jewish teaching known as "wisdom," of which Proverbs is the greatest example in the Bible. When these "Wise Men" saw a special star in the sky, they were at least sufficiently familiar with Old Testament teaching to associate it with the promised King who would be born to the Jews, and whose coming is described in Numbers 24:17 as being like a brilliant star arising in Judah. Hence their journey to Jerusalem. And though they may well be "pagan" in terms of their religious and cultural background, they have come to worship the King of the Jews (Matthew 2:2).

This touches on a point with which many evangelicals, for entirely laudable reasons, are not very comfortable, and which must certainly never be pushed beyond acceptable biblical limits. But this story shows us that God is prepared to speak to people standing outside the tradition of biblical revelation from within aspects of their own culture with which they are familiar. It is entirely right that Christians reject astrology as a form of false religion which is completely incompatible with faith in Jesus. The embarrassing fact remains that God used an aspect of the religious culture of these Magi, which is at least tinged with astrological thinking, in order to get their attention. Having done that, he leads them on a spiritual journey of discovery which is as real and perhaps as challenging as their physical journey over "field and fountain, moor and mountain": having arrived in Jerusalem, they are pointed in the direction of Bethlehem not by the star but by the Scriptures (Matthew 2:4–6); and when God needs to warn the Magi not to return to Pharaoh, he does it, not through stars or any other of

---

comment that "if the early astrologers argued in this fashion, and very possibly they did, they were imbued with the spirit of science, and I honor them. No scholar can be maligned for being wrong in the light of the knowledge of a later period. If he strives for knowledge in the terms of his own time he is a member of the brotherhood of science." (Asimov, *Stars in their Courses*, 6.)

the mystical aspects of the religion with which they had grown up, but by speaking to them directly in a dream (Matthew 2:12), in the same way that he regularly speaks to his own prophets. It is not going too far to say that these Magi, through their seeking and finding Christ, have discovered a relationship with the living God that brings them to something like biblically normative faith. But God first spoke to them through a star.

It is easy to see why many people find this difficult. There is a school of vague thinking today which assumes that all forms of "religion" are equally valid and are simply different journeys to the same destination. In this supermarket of world faiths, a "pick'n'mix" approach to religion is not only permissible, but, some would insist, the only one that is compatible with the expected norms of tolerance and mutual respect; even to suggest that some aspects of anybody's religion might actually be right or wrong marks one out as a bigot and a fanatic. In the face of this religious syncretism, where the only acceptable song in which all can join is Gilbert and Sullivan's "And I am right, and you are right, and everything is quite correct," evangelicals feel it is all the more urgent to affirm, however politically incorrect it may seem, that Jesus alone is the Way, the Truth and the Life, that no one comes to the Father except by him (John 14:6), and that there is no other name given under heaven by which we must be saved (Acts 4:12).

They are right, and I unashamedly stand with all who insist that Jesus is not *a* way amongst others, but *the* Way. But the fact remains that God sometimes speaks to those who are coming from a background of pagan religion from within the terms of reference of that religion, as he did to these Magi. God is not proud; just as he was prepared to empty himself and take the form of human flesh, with all its frailties, so he is prepared, out of love for people, to come to them in the midst of their idolatry, their religious blindness, and call them to come and meet him at the cross of Christ. That God speaks to the Magi in terms with which they were familiar—through a star which seemed to be some kind of religious portent—does not endorse astrology or eastern religion; but he leads the Wise Men on a spiritual journey which enables them, not to be better at seeing religious meaning in the stars, but to kneel before Jesus and worship him. They have left the stars behind, because they have discovered the Sun of Righteousness. As Jesus was later to say, "All that the Father gives me will come to me . . . no one can come to me unless the Father who sent me draws him" (John 6:37,44); and sometimes God will make use of aspects of the religious culture from which people are coming in order to begin the process of drawing them to Christ. There are numerous stories of Hindus having come to faith in Christ when, as Hindus, but having heard of "another god" called Jesus whom some worship, they had prayed a prayer to Jesus, and it was answered; that started them on a journey of discovery which led them to Christ as Savior and Lord. In that spirit Paul, preaching in Athens, started to speak from the religious pluralism of the Greeks, and rather than railing against it and denouncing it as folly, used it as the starting-point from which to speak to them of the "unknown God" who is the Lord of heaven and earth (Acts 17:22–31).[8]

For that reason, in our prayer for and ministry to those who come from a background in other world religions, the best approach is not likely to be to start by telling them that everything they have grown up with is wrong and needs to be jettisoned. It is not only more tactful but also more biblical to start by praying that God in his sovereignty will find ways to speak to them from within the norms of their present understanding (or misunderstanding) of religious practice, and to lead them positively on a spiritual journey to Christ. There are those who believe in the spiritual value of dreams; we can pray that Jesus will reveal himself to them in their dreams. There are those who set great store by religious symbols and ritual; we can pray that God will challenge their minds, so that they start pondering what spiritual realities might actually lie behind the familiar symbols. And there are those, whether in any meaningful sense "Wise Men" or not, who look to the stars for guidance; but then, the psalmist tells us that the heavens reveal the glory of God (Psalm 19:1), and we can quite properly pray that God will so speak to the mind of the religious star-gazer that he will start to see the greatness of the Creator reflected in his creation. Everybody has to start from somewhere; it's where they finish that matters. For the Magi, it was in bowing down to Jesus and worshiping him.[9] God knew what he was doing when he caused that star to appear; and it was *not* to vindicate astrology.

Regarding the star, it is worth pointing out that it was not, strictly speaking, the star that led the Magi to find Jesus. The star is not said to

---

8. It might be objected that the Old Testament prophets frequently condemn pagan religion and idolatry. They do indeed, and often in terms that are not exactly diplomatic. But such denunciations are invariably directed at the Jewish people themselves who were in danger of being, or had actually been, drawn into idolatrous practices. When those who have known God and have lived by God's Word depart from the truth and relapse into false religion, they incur the wrath of God, being seen as far more blameworthy than those who have never known anything different. In a similar way, Jesus is gracious and forbearing with prostitutes despite their sins, but very severe in his condemnation of Pharisees for their religious hypocrisy; those educated in, and claiming to live by, the law of God could and should know better.

9. It is significant, in the light of the veneration that is directed in the Catholic tradition to Mary, that, even though Jesus is here mentioned immediately after his mother—"on coming to the house, they saw the child with his mother Mary . . . " (verse 11)—this worship is said specifically to be offered to Jesus. The Magi were indeed "Wise Men": when they saw the infant Jesus with his mother, "they bowed down and worshiped *him*."

"lead" them anywhere. Matthew says that they saw a star of some kind in the sky when they were back in their homeland, and understood this to be a sign that the King of the Jews had been born. So they traveled to Judea to find him, but it does not say that the star "led" them. In Judea, they went first to Jerusalem, as the obvious place to start looking for a king. It was the Word of God in the Bible that pointed them to Bethlehem (Matthew 2:3-8). Verse 9 has sometimes been taken to mean that the star really did "lead them"; it reads in the NIV "and the star they had seen [in the east?—more correctly, 'when it rose' or 'in its rising'] went ahead of them until it stopped over the place where the child was." Literally, this reads: "and behold, the star, which they saw in its rising, went before them until standing over where the child was." That probably means that the "star" which had originally been seen, and which had first prompted their journey, reappeared, but this time in a different part of the sky; it now appeared to be over the area of Judea. "Where the child was" does not have to mean the very house where he was, but in the area over Bethlehem—the star appeared to be overhead over the Judea region. This was a kind of confirmation to the men that they were on the right track. But the Wise Men were not "guided by the star." When they needed specific guidance, God spoke to them through his Word (Matthew 2:4-6) and by his Spirit in a dream (2:12). The star was a sign to them to get them started on their journey.

Understandably, many people have tried to "explain" or identify the star which the Wise Men saw. Was it a special conjunction of planets?, was it Halley's comet?, was it some completely supernatural phenomenon that God caused to appear in the sky? However fascinating it may be to speculate on such questions, they really do not add anything to the truths that God wants us to learn from this story in his Word. God caused an unusual light to appear in the sky for his own purposes. Whether it can be identified in astronomical terms is beside the point. I understand the desire to be able to demonstrate that the Bible is historically and scientifically credible; and I believe that it is. But those who are skeptical about the Bible are not likely to be convinced by being told that the star seen by the Magi might have been a conjunction of Jupiter and Saturn, which occurred in 7 BC or (less likely) Halley's comet, which was visible around 10-12 BC. However fascinating such guesses may be, they are not likely to be much help to the scientific skeptic, who is much more likely to conclude that religious people (including Christians) are simply those who insist on seeing a supernatural significance in everything, though "we know" how to account for it perfectly well in scientific terms. If we are going to engage in apologetics—and sometimes we must—then we need to do it on better grounds that that. I recommend C. S. Lewis' *Mere Christianity*, or, if you want something more recent, Timothy Keller's *The Reason for God*, or one of Lee Strobel's *The Case for . . .* books: *The Case for a Creator*, *The Case for Christ*, *The Case for Faith*, etc., though they are far more technical and less easy to read than Lewis.

To return once more to the familiar "nativity play" presentation of the Wise Men, we need to treat the idea that the Wise Men visited the "stable" at more or less the same time as the shepherds with at best a pinch of salt. We cannot be completely sure when their visit took place, but it could have been anything up to two years later (Matthew 2:16); on being asked by Herod when the star first appeared, and presumably using that as a guide to how old the child in question might now be, Herod ordered the death of all baby boys up to two years old. Herod may of course have been as wrong in his calculations as he was in his morals; but certainly by the time the Magi found Mary and Joseph, the family was living in a "house" (verse 11). It is quite likely that, following the birth, Joseph stayed for some time in Bethlehem (probably preferring not to undertake a long journey home to Nazareth with a very little new-born baby), and found more suitable longer-term accommodation.

The Wise Men's gifts, as is often pointed out, reflect symbolically who Jesus is and what he does. Gold is associated above all with kings and royalty—Jesus is King. Incense was burned as an offering to God—Christ is God, whom we worship. Myrrh was used for a number of purposes, but, whereas almost all the uses of incense in the Bible are in the worship of God, almost all the uses of myrrh are quite human and "this-worldly": to perfume a bed (Proverbs 7:17) or a garment (Psalm 45:8), as perfume for young ladies (Esther 2:12); in bridal processions (Song of songs 3:6). It was also used to prepare bodies for burial (John 19:39–40). Jesus is King, God, and also man—and in particular, the man who will die for us. Despite my earlier reservations about the accuracy of the words of the traditional carol "We three kings of Orient are," there is a couplet in that hymn that summarizes very well the significance of the gifts: "Glorious now behold him arise: God, and King, and sacrifice." The Wise Men's gifts are a model to us, not of Christmas presents (!), but of worship: our praise can and should always celebrate Jesus as King, as Lord and God, and as the crucified Savior.

Herod was not a Jew; his family were Edomites, from the largely desert area between the Dead Sea and the Gulf of Aqaba. He had started his career as a military governor of Galilee. Through various victories, he gained more power and promotion, and the Roman senate, under Mark Antony, granted him the right to use the courtesy title "king of the Jews," so long as he always ruled in the interests of the Roman Empire. He was therefore a "puppet-governor" of Judea. He had a terrible reputation as a brutal man, who killed many people whom he saw as a threat to his own position—he executed more than half of the Sanhedrin; he once killed three hundred court officers at one go; he executed his own wife Mariamne; he had three of his sons, Antipater, Aristobolus and Alexander, put to death, because he saw them as rivals for his power; and as he lay dying, he arranged for all the notable men of Jerusalem to be assembled in the hippodrome and killed the moment his own death was announced, so that he could be sure that there would be great grief and mourning at the news of his death—so the picture of Herod in Matthew 2 is typical of what we know of him from other sources.

His killing of all the baby boys reminds us of what had happened in Egypt at the time Moses was born (Exodus 1). Pharaoh had ordered all Hebrew boys to be killed, but Moses escaped that mass-slaughter. In the same way, Jesus escapes the slaughter[10] of infants in his own day. Matthew wants to tell his Jewish readers that Jesus is the new Moses, the new leader of God's people.

In the light of that, it is very ironic that Jesus' family should flee to Egypt to find safety from Herod. Back in the days of the exodus, Egypt was the place where the Israelites were cruelly treated, and God enabled them to escape *from* Egypt and become his own people in their own land. But in Jesus' day, it is in his own land that he is threatened; and he goes *to* Egypt to find safety. We see again in this story something that we will see later in the ministry of Jesus as an adult: the fact that he is often rejected by his own people—and also that the black-and-white differentiation between the Jews (good!) and the Gentiles (bad!) is no longer valid. Now that Jesus is here, the distinction between those who are God's people and those who are not is no longer defined on the basis of race, but rather of personal spiritual and moral disposition.

The Childhood

Again, we have only Luke's account for the story of the journey to Jerusalem for Jesus' first Passover at the age of twelve (2:41-50) and the following summary statement of how he grows up in Nazareth (2:51-52).

The visit to Jerusalem is the only incident in the Bible between the birth story and the adult ministry of Jesus. We need to steer round the

---

10. Though it in no way detracts from the unspeakable evil of what Herod did, we should not think of the so-called "slaughter of the innocents" as being of genocidal proportions. Bethlehem was a very small town; and even including the surrounding area, it is unlikely that we are talking about more than fifteen or twenty children under two. But it was still an abominable sin, and is another reminder that the Bible takes place in the real world, where horrible people do horrible things; the world we live in, in fact.

possible red herrings—how could Joseph and Mary have traveled a whole day without realizing Jesus was not with them?; was Jesus in any sense doing something wrong (being naughty?) by staying behind without his parents' knowledge or consent?—and focus on the main reason why Luke includes the story. That is not to say that the "red herrings" are unanswerable. For example, we live in a culture where the nuclear family is the primary unit; so when we hear of parents going on a journey and leaving their child behind, we think either of *Home Alone* or of calling the social services. First-century Jewish society was not like that; it would be normal to travel in larger groups or caravans, and Joseph and Mary were not being negligent in taking it for granted that Jesus was with the traveling party. But such questions are not the point of the story. And to read into Jesus' response to Mary's astonished rebuke (verses 48–49) any suggestion that Jesus was "out of order" is to forget that the whole story demonstrates that Jesus is not just any ordinary twelve-year-old. This would not be the last time that his own family found Jesus' calling to be devoted to the service of his heavenly Father strange. Children and young teenagers should not see in this story any biblical precedent for doing their own thing independently of their parents; verse 51—"then [Jesus] went down to Nazareth with [Joseph and Mary] and was obedient to them"—is much more to the point! But parents also need to learn, as Joseph and Mary, despite their initial lack of understanding (verse 50), seem to have done, that God can have a special calling for believing people, however young, and should seek to encourage their children in appropriate ways to pursue that calling, rather than standing against it with a peremptory "Mum and dad know best: do as you're told!" Even in a society which granted parents far more authority over their children, Mary and Joseph were wiser than that.

What we have in verse 49 are the first recorded words of Jesus; and, as Howard Marshall says, they "set the tone for what follows in the Gospel,"[11] and give us three foundational principles that should shape our understanding, not only of the unique Person and ministry of Jesus, but also of our own calling to be God's people.

1. The key lesson of this story centers on the fact that, even at the age of twelve, Jesus is clearly aware that he is the Son of God. He refers to God as his "Father" (verse 49) in a completely natural and spontaneous way. Jews never referred to God as "my Father"; but the twelve-year-old Jesus does. Jesus' awareness that he is God's Son is not something that developed later in his thinking as an adult: here, at the age of twelve, he knows exactly who he is and where he has to be. In a similar way, the

---

11. Marshall, *Luke*, 128.

effectiveness of our own lives and service depends first and foremost on our knowing who we are in Christ: that we are adopted as God's beloved children.

2. Moreover, Jesus already knows that his heavenly Father's will has to be the over-riding principle that will shape his life—even more than his human family. Mary refers in verse 48 to Joseph as "your father"—which does not in any way fly in the face of the virgin birth; how else would she refer to Joseph, who was the father in the family into which Jesus, by a miracle, was born?—yet in verse 49 Jesus speaks of being in his Father's house; is there not perhaps in the transfer of the title "father" from Joseph to God a gentle but unmistakable expression of the fact that, for Jesus, the one who had to govern his life was not his human father, but his heavenly Father?

The words of Jesus that are translated as "in my Father's house" can also mean, as the NIV footnote points out, "about my Father's business."[12] Most commentators assume that the intended sense is "in my Father's house," since the immediate question in the story is *where* Jesus is; but the important thing is in fact not merely where Jesus is but *why* he believes he needs to be there. In theory, anyone might pay an extra visit to the temple out of a fascination with its architectural splendor or historical associations, in the same way that cathedrals are a major tourist attraction today; but Jesus' interest is focused, not in the building in itself, but in the fact that he knows he needs to grow in understand of his relationship with God and of how he will pursue God's purpose for his life. It is quite possible for Christians today to be "in church," but that does not necessarily mean that the focus of all their attention is on God and how they can live for the glory of God. Jesus later had to rebuke Peter because, as he said, "you do not have in mind the things of God, but the things of men" (Matthew 16:23), and the phrase translated "the things of [God]" is the same as the one Luke uses in 2:49, "the things of [my Father]." From the age of twelve, Jesus had in mind the things of God.

3. "I had to be . . . "; this is the first occurrence in Luke of the little Greek word *dei*, which means "it is necessary [for me to . . .]," or "[I] have

---

12. The only Bible translation known to me that reads "about my Father's business" is the *King James (Authorized) Version*. Eugene Peterson's popular paraphrase *The Message* manages to include both senses: "I had to be here [that is, here in the temple], dealing with the things of my Father"; and whilst "dealing with" may have more "business-like" connotations than the preposition Luke uses (Greek: *en*), which at its simplest means "in," the phrase "the things of my Father" is in fact the literal translation of what Luke wrote.

to," which, in addition to here in 2:49, occurs nine times in connection with the ministry of Jesus;[13] most of these references are to either the fulfillment of prophecy in the life and work of Jesus, or to his own obedience to the will of his Father.

"I had to . . . " carries no sense of fatalism or determinism; the biblical doctrine of God's sovereign will being done in and through all things does not abolish our human responsibility to make choices. God has a purpose for each person's life; but each person can choose to embrace or to reject that purpose. Here, at the age of twelve, Jesus chose to embrace it; for him, God's sovereign will (*deî* = "it is necessary") is not an impersonal destiny that he can do nothing to escape, but a heavenly calling to which he can devote the whole of his life. And so, here at the temple, sitting with the teachers of the law, he starts to explore the implications for his life of the fact that he knows that he is the Son of God.

And yet on the other hand verse 52 stresses Jesus' full humanity. Jesus grew up in a normal way, and we are told that he was "obedient" to his parents (verse 51); Luke does not want us to get the impression from the incident at the age of twelve that Jesus was a "naturally rebellious" child, who made a habit of running away from his parents. Jesus grew and developed in his all-round humanity: "in stature," that is, physically; "in wisdom," that is, in understanding and insight into the right way to live; "in favor with men," that is, in his ability to live in proper social relations with others; and—remarkably!—"in favor with God," in other words, spiritually. As the children's carol puts it, "day by day like us he grew."[14] We can speculate at great length as to what it can possibly have meant for him who is God the eternal and beloved Son to grow "in favor with God"; whilst Luke does not speculate on such mysteries, and does not invite us to, there are at least a few ideas that we can rule out. To say that Jesus grew "in favor with God" does *not* mean that there was ever a time when he was "out of favor" with God; and it is not speaking of his essentially divine nature, as though that was something that simply developed over time. In all probability, Jesus' growing "in favor with God" has to do with his growing in his devotional life, and learning what it meant for him to serve the will of his heavenly Father. Beyond that, we dare not speculate on how the One who *is* spiritual life incarnate could grow spiritually; but that is simply because we cannot hope properly to understand what it meant for Jesus to be at once the eternal Son of God *and* a human being who had, just as much as any other child,

13. Luke 4:43, 9:22, 13:33, 17:25, 19:5, 22:37, 24:7, 24:26, 24:44.
14. From "Once in royal David's city" by Cecil Frances Alexander (1818–95).

to grow up. But in this simple childhood story, Luke states and emphasizes both the humanity and the deity of Christ. Those two sides of Jesus' nature are seen in the fact that he is sitting talking with teachers of the Law. On the one hand, Jesus (as a human being) needs to grow in understanding, as we all do. So he talks with senior religious teachers; he explores spiritual truth and develops his understanding of it. On the other hand, these teachers of the Law are amazed at Jesus' "understanding and his answers" (verse 47). This twelve-year-old boy seems to have an instinctive awareness of spiritual truth, which these men have spent a lifetime trying to study and discover.

"For he is our childhood's pattern"; and not just our childhood's. The four-fold growth of Jesus in verse 52 is an excellent model of how God wants to help us, as his adopted children, to grow as disciples. Just as Jesus grew in size and strength, so the Spirit enables us to grow in moral strength, to develop "spiritual backbone." Jesus grew in wisdom; and we too are called to grow in wisdom and understanding of God, his Word and his ways. Jesus grew in favor with God; and we too are called to "love him more dearly, follow him more nearly." Jesus grew in favor with men; and part of our discipleship has to mean growing in fellowship relationships with our brothers and sisters in the church. Unless we are growing in all four ways, we are not growing in Jesus' way.

4

The King and Judge

"Hosanna to the Son of David!" (Matthew 21:9)

We now jump forward some twenty-one years or so. As was said in the introduction, my intention in this book is not to comment on the public ministry of Jesus, but to reflect on Jesus' birth, and on the grand finale of his time on earth: his death and resurrection.

And so, as we move, so to speak, from Christmas to Easter, we come to the final week leading up to the cross, which in the liturgical tradition of the church is referred to as "Holy Week," starting with Palm Sunday, as we usually call it. In all four Gospels, the details about this week, and the cross itself, take up a large proportion of the whole book—nearly 36 percent of Matthew, over 37 percent of Mark, 33 percent of Luke, and over 34 percent of John; and through the events of this week we see Jesus fulfilling his various roles as God's Messiah. The last week shows Jesus as the "all-round Christ."

Jesus as King

We start on Palm Sunday with the triumphal entry into Jerusalem, which is recounted in all four Gospels (Matthew 21:1–11//Mark 11:1–11//Luke 19:28–44//John 12:12–19). In fulfillment of Zechariah 9:9 Jesus rides into Jerusalem, and is hailed with enthusiasm as King. Despite the opposition of the religious establishment and the disillusionment of some who had previously followed Jesus (John 6:66), many people were clearly still hoping that Jesus might turn out to be the promised Messiah-King (Matthew 21:9-11//Mark 11:9-10//John 12:13), although they almost certainly did not understand the precise nature of his Kingship. The shouts and actions of the crowd show that they are greeting a king: spreading their cloaks on the ground in front of Jesus recalls the coronation of King Jehu (2 Kings 9:13), and the exclamations of "Hosanna!"[1] are taken from Psalm 118:25-26, the latter part of which is a psalm of victory, welcoming back a conquering and triumphant king—maybe the crowd borrowed the words of the psalm, not in celebration of a victory already won, but in anticipation of one which they were hoping their king was about to win; and the palm branches which the people waved are themselves a reflection of verse 27 in that psalm, "with boughs in hand, join in the festal procession."

That Jesus is King is an important theme in John's Gospel in particular. Although the phrase "the Kingdom of God" with which we are familiar from the other three Gospels is hardly ever used in John—only in 3:3,5 and 18:36—he uses the title "King" for Jesus far more than any other of the Gospels: fourteen times, as opposed to eight in Matthew, six in Mark and five in Luke. Moreover, John says a great deal about the "glory" of Jesus, but invariably in the context of speaking of his death on the cross; and in the same way the overwhelming majority of John's references to Jesus as King come in the account of his suffering, trial and crucifixion: Jesus is the King who suffers for his own people. There are already hints of that in the account of the triumphal entry: even on this day of celebration, there are two indications that Jesus' Kingship might not be of the kind that the crowds were hoping for. One is the fact that Jesus rode on a donkey. This was of course a fulfillment of Zechariah's prophecy of one who would come, "righteous and having salvation" (9:9); but might those who were still hoping for a military Messiah to stand against the occupying forces of the Roman Empire have wondered whether a king who rides on a donkey was really what they were looking for? Jesus is indeed the King, but he is also the humble servant (riding on a donkey), who brings his Kingdom not by conquest but by self-sacrifice.

The other hint is in the context of the cries of "Hosanna!" in Psalm 118. For just three verses earlier in that psalm we find the words, which Jesus was soon to quote of himself (Matthew 21:42//Mark 12:10), "The stone

---

1. The Hebrew word "Hosanna" is formed from the verb *hôsâ* ("save") plus the suffix *nā*, which expresses a plea or entreaty; it was traditionally translated by phrases like "we beseech you," and is a rather more urgent form of our modern "please"; so "hosanna" means literally "please save [us]!" As an exclamation of praise it is a joyful declaration that the Lord is our Savior.

the builders rejected has become the capstone," or, more correctly, as the NIV footnote says, the "cornerstone": the phrase is literally "the head of the corner," though "head" means, not "at the top of the building," but "the most important." The "head of the corner" means the first foundation stone to be laid; as Hendriksen says, "the cornerstone of a building, in addition to being part of the foundation and therefore supporting the superstructure, finalizes its shape, for, being placed at the corner formed by the junction of two primary walls, it determines the lay of the walls and crosswalls throughout. All the other stones must adjust themselves to this cornerstone. Such is the relation of Christ to his church."[2] The King would certainly fulfill his calling, and become the cornerstone; but only after he had first been rejected by the very people to whom he had come. Just as a builder might decide that a particular stone did not fit the criteria he was looking for to be used in his building, and cast it aside, so the people would decide that Jesus was after all not the kind of king they wanted; he would be rejected as, to use the modern phrase, "not fit for purpose." Yet paradoxically, it is only because Jesus is the kind of "stone" he is that he can become, not just "a" stone in the building, but the chief cornerstone.

Luke's version of the story of the triumphal entry contains one remarkable (and perhaps ironic?) reflection of the fact that Jesus is coming to fulfill his mission to save the world, but that the way in which he will do it will not be accepted by most of the crowd who are at present celebrating him as King. The shouts of acclamation which greet Jesus include the words "Peace in heaven and glory in the highest" (Luke 19:38), and "peace" and "glory in the highest" are phrases that had been used by the angels when they sang praises to God at the birth of Jesus (Luke 2:11). The angels' song of praise is being repeated, no doubt unwittingly, by human beings: Jesus is about to accomplish the purpose for which he had come into the world in the first place, and the Kingdom which the angels proclaimed at his birth is about to be realized through the suffering that awaits the King in Jerusalem. The crowds who now shout enthusiastically about the arrival of their King will in less than a week be amongst those who by their shouts of "Crucify him!" will be instrumental in inflicting that suffering.

That rejection of Jesus will be seen very soon. But before we come to it, there are some lessons we can learn from the fact that Jesus is King. Our problem is of course that our conception of kingship is inevitably colored by the fact that we live in the UK in a constitutional monarchy, in which the Queen is the head of state but not the head of government: she has no political or executive power. But Jesus is not merely a ceremonial King, and

---

2. Hendriksen, *Matthew*, 787.

he is certainly not a nominal King. He is the King of kings and the Lord of lords, and he reigns in absolute—and absolutely righteous—power. For us to affirm that Jesus is King necessarily means that we recognize that he has the authority to govern our lives. If the fact that Jesus is Lord means that we bow before him in reverence and worship him, then the fact that he is King means that we stand humbly before him as servants, ready to receive our instructions. In the film *Mrs Brown* the Scottish servant John Brown (Billy Connolly), who has been summoned to try and persuade the grieving Queen Victoria (Judi Dench) to take occasional horse-back rides as a first step towards ending her withdrawal from public life, stands for a whole day alongside his horse, motionless, outside the windows of the Queen's residence at Osborne House on the Isle of Wight. When he is asked what he is doing, he replies that he is awaiting his orders from Her Majesty. Despite the later liberties that he will take with court etiquette, that is a good example of the attitude that the Christian for whom Jesus is King is called to adopt: we are to be available to the King, and we await his orders.

But with that goes a second consideration. The people in the crowd on Palm Sunday had a concept of kingship which was not that of Jesus; and when that fact became apparent, and they were faced with the choice of either changing their ideas about what kind of King they wanted, or rejecting Jesus as King, they chose the latter course. They thought that they knew better than the King how he should be King. But before we rush to rebuke such arrogance and silliness, it is worth asking ourselves the sobering question how often we have done the same. Jesus is King; but we sometimes have our own ideas about the life and conduct of his Kingdom, which may or may not have much in common with his own sovereign will. Here is the challenge for the servants of the King: are we ready to let Jesus be King in his own way, on his own terms?; or do we still harbor the hope that the King will let us pursue our own agenda and give it his "royal assent"? Are we sometimes, like the Palm Sunday crowds, very keen to enjoy the *celebration* of the King—we will shout "Hosanna!" to our heart's content—but rather less ready to serve the *will* of the King, if he should bring his Kingdom in ways that we had not expected?

But the joyful celebration of Jesus' Kingship is in itself right and valid. When the Pharisees, perhaps in the spirit of King David's wife Michal rather than in that of David himself (2 Samuel 6:14–16), complained that the crowds were behaving in ways that they found unseemly, Jesus dismissed their objections (Luke 19:39–40): "I tell you . . . if they [= the disciples] keep quiet, the stones will cry out." In other words, when the King is present, praise and celebration are entirely right, and should not, indeed cannot, be stopped. It is wonderfully encouraging that praise and celebration have found vibrant new expression in the life of the church in recent decades. There will sadly always be those who disapprove, who prefer a church atmosphere of quiet, even of solemnity. And it is true that what is termed "a lively time of worship" can sometimes seem to be regarded as an opportunity for young people to let their hair down. But the fact remains that Jesus' Kingship is to be celebrated; and the question whether those who tut-tut in disapproval at "modern," lively and joyful praise have in fact ever known in their own experience the glorious and liberating life of God's Kingdom is not illegitimate. It must always be asked with a concern for the spiritual welfare of, rather than a contempt for the spiritual "stuffiness" of, the objectors. But it should be a cause for genuine concern—"concern," not complaint or criticism—when people object to joyful praise and celebration in a spirit that seems to have more in common with the Pharisees, who saw in the Palm Sunday celebrations nothing except a rowdy street party, than it has with Jesus' disciples, who, whatever the shortcomings in their understanding, did at least see Jesus as a King worth celebrating.

"Rejoice, the Lord is King!" But whilst we shout our hosannas to the King, let us always remember that to enjoy celebrating Jesus' Kingship without at the same time submitting every part of our lives to his kingly authority is at best shallow, and at worst a form of spiritual treason. The true measure of our awareness of Jesus' Kingship is not merely the decibel-count of our praise, but the devotion of our lives.

One aspect of the biblical understanding of kingship which is perhaps less obviously present to our modern western minds is that of conquest and victory. In the ancient world kings were military rather than political leaders. When Israel first asked for a king to govern them, it was primarily so that they would, like the nations around them, have "a king to lead us and to go out before us and fight our battles" (1 Samuel 8:20). What people in biblical days expected their king to do was not to implement policy but to defeat their enemies.

This presents us with a remarkable paradox, when we speak of Jesus as King. There can have been few characters in history who have shown less inclination towards, or whose whole ethos was more manifestly poles apart from, military aggression. But not only were there many people in Jesus' day who hoped that his ability to draw a crowd could be enlisted in the cause of an uprising against the Romans—in John 6, following the feeding of the five thousand, we are told that Jesus knew that the crowd intended to "come and make him king by force" (verse 15), which could only have been with the intention that he should lead or at least inspire a coup against the occupying power—but throughout history there have been repeated military actions supposedly in the name and the cause of Jesus, most famously the crusades. "Onward, Christian soldiers, marching as to war" has not always been understood metaphorically; and although the New Testament insists that our struggle is not against flesh and blood (Ephesians 6:12) and that the weapons with which we fight are not those of the world (2 Corinthians 10:4), the church has all too frequently seemed only too willing to make use of worldly weapons, and not necessarily as a last resort.

Jesus was about to make it clear that he was not a worldly or military king; "my Kingdom is not of this world," he would tell Pilate (John 18:36), and by "not of" he meant, as always, that it neither derives from nor shares the character of the human world. Jesus' Kingship is from heaven, and it has the character of heaven: he is the Prince of Peace. But a significant aspect of the achievement of the cross is that by his death Jesus conquered evil and won the decisive victory over all the principalities and powers of evil. Although making Christianity a military cause is a terrible distortion of Scripture,[3] the New Testament does frequently use military metaphors to describe Jesus' work at the cross: "Having disarmed the powers and authorities, he made a public spectacle of them, triumphing over them by the cross" (Colossians 2:15).

Spiritual warfare is always a popular subject in evangelical-charismatic circles, though not always for entirely wholesome reasons. It can sometimes seem that zealous Christians, aware that they are not really supposed to be aggressive towards people, can quite enjoy working out their aggression by spending a lot of time shouting at demons and justifying it by saying that they are engaged in spiritual warfare. Moreover ranting about the devil, who is, we assume, to blame for everything that is wrong in our lives and churches, is far easier (and, dare I say, far more fun) than actually seeking to make better, godlier and more disciplined choices about how we live. I would not be misunderstood: I believe that spiritual warfare is real, that the devil and demons are real, and that they are out to oppose Christians who engage seriously in Kingdom mission; I know not only from Scripture but also from experience that there is still a real place in our ministry for casting out demons from those whom the enemy has taken captive. But I am equally convinced that a great deal that is done in the name of spiritual

---

3. There are many reasons why the medieval church developed into a political institution which in its structure and ethos was poles apart from the church of the New Testament. But once the church has come to be seen as a branch of the state, it will often resort to the powers of the state to advance its cause: hence the crusades, as well as the enforcement of church rules by law. That is emphatically *not* the church founded by Jesus, but a corrupt and secular distortion of it; but a dream not all that different may have been in the minds of some who hailed Jesus as King on Palm Sunday.

warfare has more to do with pandering to a fascination with the weirdly paranormal than with faithfully exercising ministry in a biblical spirit. In particular the language of Ephesians 6:10–18—invariably cited as the classic New Testament passage about spiritual warfare—has often been grotesquely misapplied; I am quite convinced that when Paul talks about the full armor of God—the belt of truth, the breastplate of righteousness, the boots of peace, etc.—he is not referring primarily to anything mystical but to the moral qualities of Christian discipleship: the way to ensure that we are fully defended against the attacks of the enemy, that we leave no chink in our moral and spiritual armor, is to ensure that we speak the truth, live lives that are righteous, share with others in a spirit of peace, and so on. That is how we avoid giving the devil a foothold (Ephesians 4:27); we will be able to stand against all his attacks, because he can find no point of weakness in us to exploit in order to undermine our service and mission.

That no doubt sounds less glamorous and less exciting than what is often portrayed as "taking spiritual warfare seriously"; but if it is what Ephesians 6 is about—and I am sure it is—then we need to spend less time rebuking the devil for everything and more time asking the Spirit of God to help us to grow in spiritual grace and practical godliness. But it remains gloriously true that Jesus our King has conquered the devil and won the victory over all the works of darkness. We most truly celebrate that victory, however, not by continually going on about the devil, or even about the fact that the devil is defeated, but by exalting Jesus as King. We inflict the most damage on our enemy when we do not refer to him, but celebrate the fact that the Lord reigns. It has been said that dramatists and actors don't mind being criticized, so long as they are not being ignored; in his novel *The Picture of Dorian Gray*, Oscar Wilde said, "There is only one thing in the world worse than being talked about, and that is not being talked about." I suspect the devil feels the same way. The less we talk about him, and the more we celebrate Christ as King, the better we will know what it means to live as "more than conquerors."

Jesus as Judge

Jesus has been acclaimed as King. But his next actions soon make people turn against him. The Jews were looking for a King who would come and judge the Romans, and cast them out of Jerusalem. So when Jesus arrived in Jerusalem, they probably expected him to turn to the west side of the city, where the Roman authorities had their headquarters, and bring God's judgment on the Romans. Instead, he stayed in the east of the city, where the Jewish temple stood, and brought God's judgment on his own people.

Jesus demonstrates that he is Judge in two ways. First, he curses a fig tree that, despite its abundant foliage, had no fruit (Matthew 21:18–22//Mark 11:12–14,20–25); then he goes to the temple, and drives out the money-changers and "all who were buying and selling there" (Matthew 21:12), to the indignation of the religious leaders (Matthew 21:12–15//Mark 11:15–18//Luke 19:45–48).

Jesus is bringing the judgment of God on two things in particular. One is *corrupt religion*. The priests and the leaders of the Jewish religious establishment were using the temple as the base for what was, not to mince words, a commercial racket. The practice in Jesus' day was for people who wished to come to the temple and offer sacrifices in worship to buy the animals for those sacrifices at the temple; that was not quite how God had first intended the sacrificial system to operate—originally people brought offerings from their own livestock—but the real corruption lay in the fact that the temple animals were sold at an inflated price that guaranteed a generous profit to both the merchants who supplied the animals and to the priests. In addition to the stalls selling livestock for sacrifice, there were also the tables of the "money-changers": foreign money—that is, Roman or Greek currency—was deemed unacceptable in a holy building like the temple; so those wishing to buy animals for sacrifice within the temple precincts, or those who had come from Jewish communities throughout the Roman Empire to pay the temple tax, who would often have with them only Roman or Greek money, would exchange it for Jewish shekels at a kind of first-century *bureau de change*. Needless to say, the exchange rate was fixed so that the profit went to the "money-changers" rather than to the worshipers. In other words, the temple authorities had devised a clever way of turning to their own pecuniary advantage the desire of pious Jews from various parts of the Middle East to be able to come and worship at the temple.

But there is another side to this corrupt commercialization of the life of the temple. The tables for the sale of animals and those of the money-changers were in the outer court of the temple, known as the court of the Gentiles. Whilst only Jewish men could go into the inner court, the outer court was open for anyone—people of all nations—to come, and it was supposed to be a place where Gentiles, even though they could not go through into the inner court, could at least be in the presence of the God of Israel, and could spend time there in prayer. But the temple authorities had turned this court of the Gentiles into a trading market. They themselves could, if they wished, go into the inner court, and there be able to pray undisturbed; but the Gentiles had to be content with finding whatever devotional atmosphere they could in a bustling cattle market, where the aim was to relieve Jewish people of as much of their cash as possible; so far as the priests were concerned, the fact that this also deprived the Gentiles of a place of peace where they could approach God as much as they were allowed under Jewish law was of no great consequence. That is why Jesus quotes from Isaiah 56, where God says that his house should be a "house of prayer *for all nations*"—"all nations" meaning, of course, Gentile nations—and condemns the fact that the temple has instead become the means by which already wealthy priests could further line their own pockets at the expense of poor but devout Jewish worshipers, whilst denying Gentiles even the limited access to the presence of God that they should have been able to enjoy.

It would not be difficult, though it would be depressing and it is hardly necessary, to compile a catalog of abuses as least as bad as that in the history of what is, at least in name, the church of Jesus Christ, through the centuries and on into our own day. The story of this dramatic sequel to the triumphal entry demonstrates unambiguously that Jesus the King is also Jesus the Judge; that judgment begins in the household of God; and that one of the things that most seriously incurs Jesus' judgment, and the specific thing that aroused his anger in the temple, is when religion is used, and devout worshipers exploited, by mercenary religious leaders as a cover for personal gain, or where a religious "inner circle" organizes the life of the church so that it suits their personal needs, whilst excluding those whom they regard as outsiders from being able to approach God.

It makes sense. If Jesus is King, if he is the Head of the church—and he is—then he alone has the absolute authority to decide what is right and wrong in the life and conduct of his church, and to take action against whatever is wrong. Unfortunately, the church has frequently been guilty of two errors in this respect. The first is to remember, and to remind other people, that Jesus is coming to judge the world, and to warn people, in the words of John the Baptist, to "flee from the coming wrath" (Matthew 3:7). That in itself can be quite right and biblical: the error is to forget that Jesus is also—indeed, first of all—the Judge of the church. The letters in Revelation 2 and 3 show that Jesus, as well as commending and blessing all that is good in the seven churches of Asia Minor, can and will intervene to bring judgment on churches that persistently refuse to submit to his will. The phrase in the letter to the church in Ephesus, that unless they repent "I will come to you and remove your lampstand from its place" (Revelation 2:5) means, bearing in mind that the lampstands represent the churches (1:20), that Jesus will close the church down, or will at least so remove his presence and his blessing from the church that, even if it still continues to exist, it will be as a human organization that is no longer part of the Body of Christ, and is no longer a light to the world.

That that has been the fate of a number of "churches" throughout history is scarcely in doubt. But that brings us to the second error, which is to assume that the branches of the church that Jesus has judged and will judge are "the others." The classic expression of this is the frequent assertion from evangelical Protestants that the Church of Rome is a false church, and that Jesus will judge it. Here I will nail my colors to the mast and risk incurring the wrath of the ecumenical movement: they are right. Where they are not right, however, is if they assume that Jesus sees nothing to judge in the Protestant church, or that, if he does, he will let us off because we are doctrinally sounder than the Catholics.[4]

"If you think you are standing firm, be careful that you don't fall" (1 Corinthians 10:12). Jesus will act in judgment against any church, or any part of any church, that consistently offends his name, ignores his Word, betrays his Kingdom or abuses his people. When we read the story of Jesus purging the temple, do we automatically identify ourselves with Jesus, the purifier of the church, or with the money-changers, the "church" that desperately needs to be purified?

Jesus will judge religious corruption. Sometimes his judgment can be seen to fall within human history; what is quite certain is that his judgment will fall at the end of history, when the Lord returns to "weed out of his Kingdom everything that causes sin and all who do evil" (Matthew 13:41).

But before the purging of the temple and the judgment of corrupt religion, we have the story of Jesus cursing the fig-tree: the other thing that he is seen to judge is *fruitless religion*. The cursing of the fig-tree, which is the only miracle of Jesus that illustrates the condemnation of sin rather than salvation from sin, is an enacted parable of judgment. Just as he judges the tree for having all the outward signs of life, but actually lacking any real fruit (Mark 11:13), so he will judge his people if, despite the outward signs of religion, they lack any real spiritual fruit in their lives.[5] The fig-tree is of

---

4. I am emphatically *not* saying that all Catholics are under the judgment of God simply because they are Catholics. I believe that the institution of the Catholic Church is a false, i.e., unbiblical, form of church; but each individual in a Catholic Church—or for that matter in any other—will be saved if he or she believes in Jesus as Savior, or rejected if he or she rejects Jesus. The principle that "God does not show favoritism" (Romans 2:11) applies to denominational affiliation just as much as to nationality or ethnicity.

5. Some people find Mark 11:13—" . . . because it was not the season for figs"—rather embarrassing; since it was not the right season to expect to find fruit, Jesus' reaction when he found, predictably, that there was none might seem somewhat petulant and unreasonable. But that is to make too much of a passing comment. Jesus saw in the

course a symbol of the situation that Jesus will find at the temple: a great deal of impressive foliage—lots of religious hustle and bustle, not least from the sellers of livestock and the money-changers—but no real spiritual life, worship or devotion. The same might be said of the life of some churches: activities galore, meetings, clubs and programs every day—enough foliage to make a really impressive tree, a church where there is obviously a lot going on. But Jesus is not looking for busy churches, but for fruitful ones. Where is the real fruit of Jesus' Kingdom?

In this judgment against the fig-tree Jesus acts out exactly what he teaches in parabolic or metaphorical form in John 15, where he compares his people to the branches in a vine.

> "My Father is the gardener. He cuts off every branch in me that bears no fruit, while every branch that does bear fruit he prunes so that it will be even more fruitful[6] . . . No branch can bear fruit by itself; it must remain in the vine. Neither can you bear fruit unless you remain in me. I am the vine; you are the branches. If a man remains in me and I in him, he will bear much fruit; apart from me you can do nothing. If anyone does not remain in me, he is like a branch that is thrown away and withers; such branches are picked up, thrown into the fire and burned . . . This is to my Father's glory, that you bear much fruit, showing yourselves to be my disciples."

Foliage—religious decoration, the church equivalent of Christmas tree tinsel—does not show us to be Jesus' disciples. Fruit does.

So the question needs to be asked, what does Jesus mean by "fruit"? What kind of fruit is he looking for, the absence of which will incur his judgment? The answer must be that he is looking for the life of his Kingdom. There are a number of places in the New Testament which use the metaphor of bearing fruit to suggest various qualities of that life, starting with the fruit of *character*, as described in Paul's list of the fruit of the Spirit in Galatians 5:22–23—love, joy, peace, patience, kindness, goodness, faithfulness,

---

fruitless tree an opportunity to teach his disciples an important lesson about spiritual fruitfulness; and even if we cannot literally "blame" a tree for not bearing fruit out of season, people undoubtedly *are* blameworthy for not bearing spiritual fruit: and that is the object of the lesson.

6. It is worth stressing that Jesus says, "*My Father* is the gardener . . . *he* cuts off . . ." To decide which members of the church are to be finally "cut off" is the prerogative of the Lord alone; branches do not decide which other branches need pruning or lopping off. There is a proper place for pastoral discipline in the life of the church, but that discipline has always to have as its goal the restoration of the wayward or lapsed believer. It is not given to the church, or to anyone in the church, to pronounce definitively on who is to be consigned to "the outer darkness"; God alone can decide that.

gentleness and self-control—or passages like James 3:17, which says that "the wisdom that comes from heaven is first of all pure; then peace-loving, considerate, submissive, full of mercy and good fruit, impartial and sincere." Colossians 1:10 speaks of the fruit of *good works*, works done in the service of God's Kingdom and which display to others the love, the grace, the justice, the compassion, the mercy of Jesus. Jesus' words in John 15:16—"I chose you and appointed you to go and bear fruit"—can perhaps be understood to embrace the all-round fruit of Christian *lifestyle*, as Jesus' followers live out their discipleship and their devotion in the ways he taught, for example in the Sermon on the Mount; but there is perhaps also a more specific reference to the fruit of *Gospel mission*: Jesus had originally appointed his disciples to go out and proclaim his Kingdom, and his use of the phrase " . . . to *go* and bear fruit . . . " anticipates his later commission to the apostles to go and make disciples of all nations, to reach out to the unbelieving world with the Gospel and seek to win others to Christ. Hebrews 13:15 speaks of the fruit of *praise and worship*—" . . . a sacrifice of praise, the fruit of lips that confess his name"—in the light of which we need always to remember Jesus' words in John 4:23 about true worship being that which is offered "in spirit and truth"; the phrase "in spirit and truth" is almost certainly primarily a reference to worship which comes from the heart, which is sincere,[7] as opposed to mechanical or formulaic ritual which is really little more than "going through the motions," or an approach to worship which focuses on merely physical criteria like the right place (Jerusalem or Samaria?, John 4:21), the appointed times, prescribed words, correct postures, etc. And Philippians 1:11 and Ephesians 5:9 both use the metaphor of fruit to describe *holiness and purity of life*, a life that is lived in righteousness which mirrors the righteousness of God himself.

Where many or all of these are lacking—where a church is pursuing a quite secular or social agenda, or where the only character-qualities in evidence are what Paul describes as the works of the sinful nature, or where

---

7. The Greek contains no definite articles: it says "in spirit and truth" rather than "in *the* Spirit and *the* Truth," which would be much more obviously a reference to the Holy Spirit and to absolute theological truth. It is likely that "in spirit and in truth" is an instance of the rhetorical device known as hendiadys (pronounced "hen-dire-diss"), when a single idea is expressed using two terms linked by "and": an example in English might be the phrase "nice and warm," which does not mean that something is [a] nice, and also [b] warm, but that it is "nicely warm." In the same way, "in spirit and truth" almost certainly means "in a truthful spirit," that is, with a sincere attitude. Having said that, it is tempting to see in the phrase "will worship the Father in spirit and in truth" at least a reflection of the Trinity: the Father, the Spirit, and the Son who is "the Truth." And whilst the phrase "in spirit" is rightly to be taken as referring to the human spirit, and to characterize a genuinely devotional as opposed to a mechanical attitude, it is also true that the Holy Spirit himself inspires and enables us so to worship.

people are living lives that in their values and priorities are indistinguishable from the world, except that they go to church on Sundays—there Jesus, as Head of the church, may well, in the language of John 15, start to prune his church; and if the church still refuses, even after pruning, to abide in him, to cut them out of the vine.

Underlying all the biblical language about fruit is a vital principle; in Galatians 5 Paul explicitly contrasts the "works" of the sinful nature with the "fruit" of the Spirit. The point about fruit is that it is *grown*; it is the result of a seed being sown and putting down roots. Human "works," whether good or bad, are things that we have to *do*; but fruit is what God grows in us from the seed of his Word sown into our lives by the Holy Spirit. Jesus' words in John 15:5—"If a man remains[8] in me and I in him, he will bear much fruit"—give us the vital key to fruitfulness. Jesus does not command us to bear fruit: the *command* is that we abide in him; if we do that, the *promise* is that we will bear much fruit. We do not become fruitful by trying harder to bear fruit; we become fruitful by abiding in Christ, by putting down deeper roots into his Word, by remaining in prayer to him, by seeking to live in as close a relationship with him as possible. Remaining in Christ is, in a sense, our responsibility; growing fruit is God's.

The crowds on Palm Sunday were only too happy to celebrate Jesus as their King; they were extremely offended when he demonstrated that he was also their Judge. Jesus the Messiah is the Lord of and Head over the church, and those branches in the vine that refuse to respond to his disciplinary pruning have no grounds for being similarly offended when they face his judgment. In the New Testament, the judgment of God is less part of the message we proclaim to the world—because you will be judged, repent!—and is much more a warning to the church to prevent us from becoming complacent or corrupt. If the modern western church often seems not to be overly concerned to heed the warning, is that perhaps because we do not take sufficiently seriously the fact that Jesus is our Judge?; and because, when we read of Jesus purging the temple, we assume that the story is saying something about "them" rather than about "us"?

But we cannot end this section on Jesus as Judge without a caution. There are people who are only too willing to judge the church, or at least

---

8. John uses the word "remain"—traditionally "abide"—many times in this passage about the vine and the branches; and it is significant that Jesus, having spoken of his disciples "abiding" in him nine times in verses 1–10, then uses the same word for the fruit that his disciples are to bear: "I appointed you to go and bear fruit—fruit that abides" (verse 16). If we want our fruit to abide—if we want the things we do for Jesus to continue to be of lasting value and significance—then we ourselves need to abide in him.

to insist that the church deserves judgment. But we cannot see these acts of Jesus' judgment without setting them alongside some other passages which speak of his words as he approached and entered Jerusalem. As he drew near to the city he said, "O Jerusalem, Jerusalem, you who kill the prophets and stone those sent to you, how often I have longed to gather your children together, as a hen gathers her chicks under her wings, but you were not willing" (Luke 13:34); and Luke also tells us that, between entering Jerusalem on the donkey and going to the temple to clear out the money-changers, he wept over the city, and said, "If you, even you, had only known on this day what would bring you peace—but now it is hidden from your eyes" (Luke 19:42). The people he is referring to—those whom he would love to gather under his wings, those over whom he wept and for whom he longed for peace—are, or at least include, the very Pharisees and priests whom he would later have to judge for their corruption. Jesus is Judge—but he judges, as it were, with tears in his eyes; he would much rather be able to gather these wayward people under his wings. That they are not willing to be gathered under his wings arouses his deep sorrow and compassion. We must never assume that Jesus' words and acts of judgment against the Jewish religious leaders are simply a harsh rejection of those who practice corrupt religion; they are an expression of the deepest possible regret that people whom Jesus would love to save and comfort will not allow themselves to be saved and comforted. If that is true of the Lord Jesus, who alone is the righteous Judge of the church, how much more must it always be true of us, his people. Those who condemn other Christians or branches of the church for their moral or doctrinal deviance should rather be asking God for a heart that would love to gather them together with us, as fellow chicks under Jesus' wings.

That lesson is reinforced in the words that Jesus speaks in Mark's Gospel immediately after cursing the fig-tree. When his disciples express astonishment that the tree has withered, Jesus urges them to have faith that God can and will answer their prayers; then he immediately adds, "And when you stand praying, if you hold anything against anyone, forgive him, so that your Father in heaven may forgive you your sins" (Mark 11:26). Far from being out of context, these words could not be more apposite. The disciples have seen Jesus perform an act symbolic of judgment against moral and spiritual wrong; but they should not infer from that that they too have the right to curse whatever "fig-trees" in the spiritual world they think are not all they should be. It is Jesus' prerogative to judge where he sees judgment is needed; but, as forgiven sinners, our place is not to judge others' sins, but to forgive them.

5

The Teacher, Lord, and Prophet

"Every day he was teaching at the temple" (Luke 19:47)

If Palm Sunday shows Jesus to be King and Judge, the next couple of days show him as Teacher; he spends time in the temple courts, teaching the people (Matthew 21:23//Mark 11:27//Luke 20:1).

Jesus as Teacher

Most of what is recorded in the Gospels are Jesus' answers to questions raised by various people; and he also tells some more parables, those of the two sons (Matthew 21:28–32), the tenants (Matthew 21:33–44//Mark 12:1–12//Luke 20:9–19) and the wedding banquet (Matthew 22:1–14).

People ask Jesus questions, broadly speaking, for one of four reasons. Some asked *genuine questions*, because they were eager to learn about the Kingdom of God. A teacher of the law asked which was the greatest commandment (Matthew 22:34–40//Mark 12:28–34), and in response Jesus gave what we might call a straight answer, the wisdom of which the teacher recognized. Others asked *hostile questions*. The Pharisees challenged Jesus' authority (Matthew 21:23–27//Mark 11:27–33//Luke 20:1–8), not because they genuinely wanted to inquire into its nature and origin, but as an accusation that he in fact had none. Jesus' response did not answer their question, but demonstrated the hypocrisy that lay behind their having asked it, and the fact that their only interest in authority was as a tool to be used to their own advantage. Third, there were *trick questions*. The Pharisees, looking to trap Jesus into giving an unwise answer on the basis of which they could accuse him, raised the issue of whether or not it was right to pay taxes to Caesar (Matthew 22:15-22//Mark 12:13-17//Luke 20:20-26), thinking that, if Jesus said "yes," they could accuse him to the Jewish people by showing him to be siding with their oppressors, whereas if he said "no," they could accuse him to the Romans of advocating breaking the law. Jesus' reply turns the tables on them by pointing out that the coins used to pay taxes bear the name and the impression of Caesar; so they should "give to Caesar what is Caesar's, and to God what is God's." Coins bear the image of Caesar, but people themselves are made in the image of God; so if it is right, according to the law, to give your coins to Caesar, how much more right must it be to give your lives to God. Finally, the Sadducees, the sect amongst the Jews who did not believe in the supernatural, asked a *theoretical question*. Their query about marriage at the resurrection, and their somewhat artificial story of the woman who became, as a famous Broadway musical very nearly put it, "one bride for seven brothers" (Matthew 22:23-33//Mark 12:18-27//Luke 20:27-40), was not prompted by any serious interest in the nature of the resurrection—on that subject, the Sadducees had already made up their minds—but was simply an attempt to trip Jesus up by asking the difficult question that, they assumed, he would not be able to answer.

A number of useful lessons can be learned from Jesus' teaching here.

Religious Questions

There is an important place in the ministry of the Gospel for letting the world ask its questions. A great deal of traditional evangelism has reduced the audience to being passive listeners whilst Christian preachers talk to them, whether or not they want to hear. Whilst there must always be at the heart of any Gospel ministry the straightforward preaching of the Good News, the western church is at last starting to learn again the importance of doing what Jesus did, and also being open to questions. Part of the reason for the great success of the *Alpha* course as an evangelistic tool is that it gives people the space to raise and think through their questions about and objections to Christian faith, rather than, as has sometimes seemed to be the case, feeling chastised for having questions and objections at all. It is understandable that many Christians, including experienced speakers, can feel somewhat nervous about being exposed to the spiritual equivalent of *Question Time*; there is a vulnerability in not being in a position to control what we may be required to speak about, as well as the ever-present concern, "suppose they ask me a question that I don't know how to answer?" But maybe that highlights precisely the problem with our understanding of evangelism: it is *not* in our hands to control. When Jesus told his disciples that the Spirit would lead them into all truth (John 16:13), he certainly did not mean that they would be given pre-packaged words of truth which they could simply repeat, and which their audiences would absorb like so many spiritually thirsty sponges. Jesus was prepared to take questions; and, as we rely on guidance and wisdom from his Spirit, we can and should do likewise.

Spiritual Discernment

Another lesson is that we need, like Jesus, to seek to discern what lies behind the questions that people might ask. Jesus could tell whether a questioner was genuinely seeking the truth, or was trying to catch him out, or just wanted to spark off a debate. That is why he answered the question from the teacher of the law who asked which was the greatest commandment in a very different way from the Pharisees' question about paying taxes to Caesar. Unlike many a politician being interviewed on the radio or TV, Jesus never simply ducked a question. But he did always seek to address the spiritual attitude that lay behind the question rather than merely the question itself. It is having the spiritual discernment to do that that can prevent what we had hoped would be an evangelistic conversation from degenerating into a sterile argument, in which every time we have more or less succeeded in answering, or at least fending off, one question designed to catch us out, the questioner comes up with another, and then another, and then another. This kind of witness can never be a merely intellectual exercise; whilst there is a real place for apologetics in Christian witness, what is in fact needed is not the ability to come up with the answers to people's questions, but the spiritual gift of discernment so that we can respond appropriately to why they asked them in the first place.[1]

1. For those unfamiliar with the term, "apologetics" means giving a reasoned argument to demonstrate that Christian faith makes sense and is not irrational. It is interesting that one of the greatest Christian apologists of the twentieth century, C. S. Lewis, whilst recognizing that it has a place, accepted that it was a limited place; he wrote in his 1945 essay *Christian Apologetics*, "If I speak only of the intellectual kind [of witness], that is not because I undervalue the other, but because, not having been given the gifts necessary for carrying it out, I cannot give advice about it. But I wish to say that where a speaker has that gift, the direct evangelistic appeal of the 'Come to Jesus' type can be as overwhelming today as it was a hundred years ago . . . I cannot do it, but those who can ought to do it with all their might. I am not sure that the ideal missionary team ought not to consist of one who argues and one who, in the fullest sense of the word, *preaches*."

Responding to Questions

Following on from that, Jesus frequently uses the approach of answering a question with a question. He did it with the Pharisees who asked from where he derived his authority: "I will also ask you one question . . . John's baptism—where did it come from? Was it from heaven, or from men?" (Matthew 21:24–25//Mark 11:29–30//Luke 20:3–4). He did it with their question about paying taxes: "Whose portrait is this? And whose inscription?" (Matthew 22:20//Mark12:16//Luke 20:24). He would do it when he asked his hearers what they understood Psalm 110:1 to be saying about who the Messiah is (Matthew 22:41–45//Mark 12:35–37//Luke 20:41–44). As well as requiring his questioners to think through for themselves the implications of what they were asking, to answer a question with a question can often be a helpful way of discerning what lies behind the question. It was Jesus' so responding to the Pharisees' query about the source of his authority that made clear that they were not particularly interested in where his authority was from: their "question" was in fact a hostile denunciation of Jesus disguised as a question, which is why Jesus declined to answer it; it left the Pharisees with the challenge of thinking seriously about whether they were actually interested in who Jesus might be. As it turned out, they were not. And Jesus usually leaves people with questions in order to get them to think about things for themselves. Again, in speaking about the fact that he is Lord, he points them to the wording of Psalm 110:1 in Scriptures and asks them what they think it must mean (Matthew 22:41–45//Mark 12:35–37//Luke 20:41–44). He does not always tell them directly; sometimes, he leaves people to see the truth for themselves from the Scriptures.

One of the reasons why it can help to answer a question with a question is that, behind many questions and objections, there can often lie a misunderstanding of what Christians actually believe; many people can use Christian terminology, but mean by it something that is quite different from its meaning in the Bible. It can be useful to ask questions that seek to expose what people actually mean by the words they use. So if we respond to the person who says, maybe sarcastically, that believing in "going to heaven" is childish and naïve, not by rushing to defend ourselves but by asking what he thinks "heaven" actually means, it is likely that we will then find ourselves able to point out that what Jesus means by "heaven" is very different, and probably to go on to describe what it really means, namely a different kind of life that we start to live now in relationship with God and which will not end at death but will become even more real and more substantial.

(Lewis, *Timeless at Heart*, 25.)

The hackneyed question, "Why do you have to go to church?—can't people believe in God and pray on their own?," is more likely to lead to a fruitful conversation if, rather than launching into a list of reasons why church matters, which is humanly speaking very unlikely to convince the person who does not already share our basic understanding of what the life of faith really is, we start by asking something like, "Why do you think Christians do meet together in church? What do you think they see as the value of it?"

Submission to Christ

Finally, the parables that Jesus teaches in the temple all make the point that it is no use merely paying "lip-service" to Jesus; if he really is our Teacher, then we need to do what he says, not merely approve of it, admire it, or even agree with it. Those asking Jesus questions are treating him as a teacher, but are they actually submitting to his teaching? Are they like the son in the parable who said to his father that he would work for him, but then did not (Matthew 21:30)?, or like the people who were supposedly tenants, but who abused their landlord (Matthew 21:33–40)?, or like the people whose names were on the invited guests list for the wedding, but who did not bother to come (Matthew 22:1–5)? It has been said that you are only a leader if someone is following you; and Jesus is only our Teacher if we are actually following his teaching. It is quite normal in modern education for pupils to debate with, even argue with, their teachers; and in a sense a good teacher should want his pupils to develop to the point when they can challenge him. But Jesus is not that kind of teacher. When Jesus began to teach the crowds during his Galilean ministry, what struck his hearers as most unusually distinctive about him was that he taught *with authority* (Matthew 7:28–29); and that should be remembered when we read about his teaching in the last week in Jerusalem. Jesus does not merely discuss ideas about truths, and leave it up to us to agree or disagree with him; he *is* the Truth. There is of course a real place for serious discussion of the best ways in which to apply Jesus' teaching in today's world; but for the Christian the challenge of Jesus the Teacher can never be whether we agree with him, but whether we will obey him.

Jesus as Lord

Up to now, Jesus has been teaching in the typical style of a Jewish Rabbi, which was by giving answers to questions put to him by others. But now his approach changes. From answering questions, he suddenly departs from the rabbinical norm and takes the initiative himself: he raises the question about his own identity—who is the Christ? (Matthew 22:41–46//Mark 12:35–37//Luke 20:41–44). Referring to Psalm 110:1, he makes the point that he is not just "Son of David," since David himself addresses him as "Lord"; and he invites his hearers to reflect on the implications of that.

Jesus' teaching is important; but the Gospel writers want to remind us again, by turning to the question of Jesus' Lordship, that the really central thing is not simply the content of his teaching, but the person of Jesus himself. There are many teachers, but there is only one Lord. The most fundamental Christian confession of faith is that "Jesus is Lord" (Romans 10:9). When the risen Christ met with the skeptical Thomas, the former doubter did not merely say that he had revised his opinion about the rumors of Jesus' resurrection: he addressed Jesus directly as "My Lord and my God!" (John 20:28).

That is ultimately the challenge of Christian faith. People can discuss Jesus' teaching, admire it, even seek to try and live by it; but Christian life begins when we say to Jesus "my Lord and my God."

One of the implications of Jesus' Lordship is stressed by Mark and Luke immediately after Jesus has challenged the crowds about his own Lordship; he warns them, "Watch out for the teachers of the law. They like to walk around in flowing robes and be greeted in the market-places, and have the most important seats in the synagogues and the places of honor at banquets" (Mark 12:38–39//Luke 20:46). The Lordship of Christ necessarily has connotations of splendor and magnificence; and although those qualities were laid aside when the Son of God became man, they will be seen in all their fullness when he returns in glory. But his followers, unlike the Jewish teachers of the law, must never aspire to such signs of glory and honor. If Jesus is Lord, then we are not to presume to wear the insignia of Lordship for ourselves; since he is Lord, we are his servants. The high church or Catholic tradition, with all the pomp and paraphernalia of the higher echelons of their ecclesiastical hierarchies, has not always been noticeably different from the teachers of the law in their "flowing robes."

Matthew includes even more than Mark or Luke: he recounts Jesus pronouncing a series of woes against the Pharisees (Matthew 23:1–39). "Woe" should not be taken lightly: it can be a serious word expressing the judgment of God against those who have the outward signs of religion, but who are not living rightly. The Greek word translated "woe" is *ouai*: it was in classical Greek an onomatopoeic exclamation of anguish or anger. There are two sides to its New Testament use, both as an exclamation, as here in Matthew 23, or as a noun, as in Revelation 9:12 and 11:14. It can express the serious judgment of God against evil (e.g. Jude 11); but, as Norman

Hillyer says,[2] "In the New Testament *ouaí*, more often than not, expresses sympathetic sorrow rather than condemnation." That is another indication of the truth of which we spoke previously: that Jesus' judgment is invariably shot through with grief at the sins of people whom he would much prefer to be able to bless than to have to condemn. But his righteous judgment is nonetheless real, as Jesus speaks his "woes" over the Pharisees, with their impressive show of religion but total lack of spiritual character. If Jesus is Lord of our lives, we must have more than the outward show of religion; and certainly more than the finery of religious rank. Like the great medieval cathedrals, many of the splendid articles of established ecclesiastical apparel and ceremony may well have been created out of a quite proper desire to worship God in ways that were a worthy reflection of his own Lordship and majesty. But the great danger is that the connotations of Lordship come to be applied to the leaders of the church rather than to Christ alone, a danger that is hardly lessened by the fact that the formal mode of address for an English bishop is "my lord" and his installation is referred to as his "enthronement." In George Orwell's *Animal Farm* the picture of an ideal community in which "all animals are equal" degenerates into a form of dictatorship in which the pigs start to walk on two legs and their original slogan is changed, in one of Orwell's most brilliant phrases, to "all animals are equal, but some animals are more equal than others." Orwell's satire was aimed at political dictatorship, but it is also a disturbingly apposite indictment of forms of hierarchical church, in which it may be claimed that all Christians are equal, but in which the splendor and finery that are the traditional insignia of the senior clergy leave the distinct impression that some Christians are more equal than others.[3]

However it is all too easy for those of us in the Free Church tradition to denounce the established churches for their priestly pomp. Two cautions are in order. First, in the light of Jesus' denunciation of the Pharisees, it is clearly not just the formal priesthood and its ceremonial accoutrements that are at fault: Pharisees were not normally priests. It is anything that suggests

---

2. In his article on the term "woe" in *NIDNTT*, vol. 3, 1052.

3. Anthony Trollope's 1855 novel *The Warden* contains a delightfully ironic passage, which contrasts the awe-inspiring dignity of the senior clergy with how they are seen by their wives when dressed for bed: "He has all the dignity of an ancient saint with the sleekness of a modern bishop . . . 'Tis only when he has exchanged that ever-new shovel hat for a tasselled night-cap, and those shining black habiliments for his accustomed *robe de nuit*, that Dr Grantly talks, and looks, and thinks like an ordinary man . . . A dean or archbishop, in the garb of his order, is sure of our reverence, and a well-got-up bishop fills our very souls with awe. But how can this feeling be perpetuated in the bosoms of those who see their bishops without their aprons, and the archdeacons even in a lower state of dishabille?"

that religious leaders are in any sense more dignified, worthy or elevated than the mere mortals who sit in the pews. The contemporary evangelical church can hardly pour scorn on the papal motorcade when a number of high-profile evangelical speakers travel around the world in private jets and stay in five-star hotels. But even more importantly, what really matters is not primarily appearance but attitude. If Jesus alone is Lord, then the concomitant attitude has to be that all his people, from the most experienced bishop to the newest and rawest convert, can only ever be servants. Servanthood is a *mind-set*, not a dress-code. So whilst it may be true that splendid priestly apparel can hardly avoid implying that those privileged to wear it are worthy of veneration, it behooves every church leader, even if he or she always wears jeans and T-shirts, to practice the discipline of thinking of themselves as servants of others. If Tennyson was right when he wrote,[4] "'Tis only noble to be good; kind hearts are more than coronets," then it is equally true that a servant spirit must mean more than simply the absence of cassocks and stoles.

The title "Lord" can all too easily come to be seen as a kind of courtesy or conventional title for Jesus; it is part of the traditional religious language of western liturgy, it is what we call Jesus. We cannot however use the title Lord and avoid its clear doctrinal implications: it is the name of God himself. "The Lord" was how the Greek translators of the Old Testament in the second and third centuries BC chose to render the sacred name of God that is variously transliterated into English as Jehovah or Yahweh. Most traditional English Bible translations adopt the convention of printing the title of God in capitals as "the LORD" wherever it is translating the unique name of Yahweh, by which God identified himself to Moses at the burning bush (Exodus 3:14–15).

So when we say, with the New Testament, that "Jesus is Lord" we are unambiguously saying that he is God. The fact that many people feel far less comfortable with the phrase "Jesus is God" than they do with "Jesus is Lord" is partly because of a dual use of the word "God": it can sometimes be used as a title for the whole Trinity ("God exists eternally as Father, Son and Spirit") and sometimes specifically as a title for the Father ("Jesus prayed to God"). So to say that Jesus is God can grate slightly on our theological nerves: it appears to be encroaching on the province of the Father. In fact, of course, this is just one example of a number of ways in which divine titles can sometimes be used to refer to one of the Persons in the Godhead, and sometimes for the whole Godhead; just as "God" is often used to mean

---

4. In his poem *Lady Clara Vere de Vere*.

specifically the Father, so "Lord" is often used specifically to mean the Son, but to call Jesus "Lord" does not in any way detract from the Lordship of the Father, any more than to call the Father "God" implies that the Son is less than or other than God.

It is the witness of the New Testament that Jesus is fully divine. Nothing less than that is involved in the confession that he is Lord. And therefore he is the object of our worship. We cannot sit at Jesus' feet as our Teacher if we are not also kneeling at his feet as our Lord. Those who have truly grasped who Jesus is are not those who can explain him, or can write learned dissertations on the co-existence of his humanity and deity; they are those who worship and adore him. The verb "to worship" is used a number of times in the New Testament with Jesus as its object: Matthew 2:2, 2:11, 14:33, 28:9, 28:17, John 9:38, Hebrews 1:6; and there are also a number of doxologies ascribed equally to the Father and the Son, such as Revelation 5:13. In their desire to water down the biblical witness to Jesus' deity, the Jehovah's Witnesses' *New World Translation* avoids the word "worship" of Jesus, and says instead "[do] obeisance to." Quite apart from being a somewhat stilted expression, that is simply wrong:[5] the verb used in all the passages listed is the Greek verb *proskuneō*, which means explicitly "to worship," and is the same word that is used in all the references to worshiping God, such as Matthew 4:10 ("Worship the Lord your God") and Revelation 19:4 ("the four living creatures fell down and worshiped God").

But the title "Lord" has political as well as theological implications; it was one of the titles that the Roman emperors claimed for themselves. To say "Jesus is Lord" was to say in effect that Caesar was not; that Jesus is a higher authority than Caesar. The fact that he is does not make such a statement any less controversial or politically offensive. The tyrannical Roman emperor Domitian (81–96 AD) was the first to accord himself the title *dominus et deus noster* ("our lord and god"), which is interestingly the very wording of Thomas' confession of faith to the risen Christ (John 20:28) and of the affirmation of the worshiping elders in heaven (Revelation 4:11); since there is a possibility that John's writings date from the era of Domitian, he seems to be making not merely a theological point about Jesus but also a very explicit political one, which could have been part of the reason for his ending his days in the Roman penal colony of Patmos (Revelation 1:9). The

---

5. The English word "obeisance" is derived from the verb "to obey," and originally meant simply obedience; it is normally used to refer to bowing to a human monarch or other dignitary as a sign of respect. *SOED*, following the first sense of "obedience," adds the later definitions "a respectful salutation; a bow or curtsy; respectfulness of manner or bearing, deference; homage, submission," but adds the comment, "in modern use, regarded as figurative." There is nothing "figurative" about worshiping the Lord!

challenge is no less radical for Christians today; relatively few political leaders, it is true, claim for themselves titles like "lord" and "god,"[6] but if we say that Jesus is Lord we are affirming that he alone receives not only our worship but also our submission and surrender; he is the highest authority for the Christian believer. It is valid to ask whether the tradition in the higher catholic streams of the church of treating leaders, especially the Pope, with all the veneration that is normally accorded to monarchs—and for that matter in the modern evangelical church of putting celebrity preachers on a pedestal—is not at best a distraction from Jesus' unique Lordship, and at worst a denial of it.

Jesus as Prophet

Jesus continues to teach, but now moves into a more prophetic style: he talks about the coming downfall of Jerusalem and the end of the world (Matthew 24:1–51//Mark 13:1–37//Luke 21:5–38). In this address, Jesus combines two things. He is describing what was to happen in the year 70 AD, when the Roman armies besieged Jerusalem, invaded it and destroyed the temple. He is also speaking of what will happen at the end of the world, just before he comes again. In the disciples' question in Matthew 24:3//Mark 13:4//Luke 21:7 these two things are both mentioned: "When will [1] this [= the destruction of the temple, as Jesus predicted in Matthew 24:2//Mark 13:2//Luke 21:6] happen, and [2] what will be the sign of your coming and of the end of the age?" The disciples may well have assumed that the two would happen together; that when the temple was destroyed, Jesus would return. But Jesus does not say that. Like many Old Testament prophets, he uses events *within* history, like the destruction of the temple, as illustrations and foreshadowings of what will happen *at the end of* history.

That is what can make the interpretation of prophecy in the Bible quite complicated. The things Jesus speaks of in this discourse can be divided into three categories.

- There are, first, statements which can only really refer to the fall of Jerusalem in 70 AD. One such is the comment that people should pray that their flight from Jerusalem will not be on the Sabbath (Matthew

---

6. Even though they would not use divine titles for themselves, the ways in which many dictators in the world demand and receive total submission and obedience from their subjects certainly suggests that their status is more that of "secular gods" to be venerated than political leaders exercising an office. The New Testament insists that Christians pay proper respect to government leaders (Romans 13:1–7), and it is worth remembering that this was written under what we would today call a totalitarian regime; but our *absolute* allegiance is to Jesus alone.

24:20); that clearly applies to the Jewish citizens of Jerusalem forced to flee from the city when the Roman armies marched in; another (probably) is Luke's phrase, "When you see Jerusalem being surrounded by armies" (Luke 21:20), that is, the Roman armies under the newly appointed emperor Vespasian.

- The second, rather larger, category is those statements that can only be referring to events at the end of history and the second coming of Jesus, such as the shaking of the sun, moon and stars just before the Son of Man appears in the sky (Matthew 24:29–30//Mark 13:24–26//Luke 21:25–27).

- The third category, which is probably the largest, is those statements which are initially a prediction of the events of 70 AD, but which also at a deeper level apply to the end of the world: these include the puzzling words about the appearance of the "abomination that causes desolation" (Matthew 24:15//Mark 13:14), of which we shall speak shortly.

Those three strands—statements which are only, or at least primarily, a prediction of events in history, those which only or primarily refer to the end of the world, and those which apply at two levels, to the events of imminent history and also to a deeper fulfillment in the coming of God's Kingdom—are not kept separate: they are all interwoven. That can make it quite difficult to analyze a prophetic passage like this; it would be so much easier, and would appeal to our western delight in logical analysis, if Jesus had spoken first of what would happen in 70 AD, and then said explicitly that he would go on to speak separately of what will happen at the end of human history. But he didn't. In speaking as he does, Jesus is standing in the tradition of the great Old Testament prophets, whose prophecies can often be seen as being fulfilled both at a human level in the events of the history of God's people, and also at a spiritual level, in the coming of God's Kingdom in Christ. A classic example is Isaiah's famous words about the one who will be a voice in the desert calling "Prepare the way for the Lord" (Isaiah 40:3). The immediate historical reference is to the return of the Jewish people from exile in Babylon in the sixth century BC; their return to Jerusalem would take them through the Syrian desert, and the prophet pictures the Lord himself going ahead of them, leading his people through the desert back to their homeland. But in the New Testament, that prophecy is also seen as applying spiritually to the work of John the Baptist, the one who, by his ministry of calling the people to repentance in preparation for the appearance of Christ, prepared the way for the Lord Jesus to come and bring God's Kingdom (Mark 1:3–4).

We may not know whether or to what degree the Old Testament prophets understood that their words had this double level of application. Maybe they assumed that the words God had given them were simply about what would shortly happen in Jewish history; but Peter's language about the prophets who "searched intently and with the greatest care" as they tried to fathom the spiritual significance of the words they were inspired to speak (1 Peter 1:10) suggests that they sensed that their prophecies had a deeper spiritual significance, but that they couldn't quite see what it was. Be that as it may, we need have no doubt that Jesus knew that he was speaking of both the historical fall of Jerusalem, and of his own return at the end of history. Holding on to that double level of fulfillment of his words—even though we cannot easily analyze it—safeguards us from a number of errors, such as thinking that Jesus was speaking only of the fall of Jerusalem, and that the more overtly supernatural language about the end of the world is mere poetic hyperbole, or that he mistakenly thought that the fall of Jerusalem would itself herald the end of the world. It does not take a particularly robust faith to believe that Jesus knew better than that what he was talking about, whether or not we can always understand it perfectly.

Concerning his own return and the end of the world, Jesus ends his discourse by saying that no one will know the exact time or date when it will happen (Matthew 24:36//Mark 13:32). The whole of the preceding address speaks of various things that will happen in the world before he comes. Some, but not all, of these "signs" would start happening in the years before the fall of Jerusalem in 70 AD; all would continue until Jesus' final return. These things do not give us a time-table for the "last of the last days," but they do give us a picture of the whole era between the first and second comings of Jesus, building to a climax in the days immediately preceding his return. Jesus speaks first of wars, rumors of wars (that means, news of wars in other parts of the world),[7] famines and earthquakes (Matthew 24:4-8//Mark 13:7-8//Luke 21:9-11). These things are described as "the *beginning* of birth pains" (Matthew 24:8//Mark 13:8), and Matthew 24:6 and Mark 13:7 say explicitly that, even though these things happen, "the end is still to come" (literally, "is not yet"): Jesus seems to be warning his disciples here not to have the kind of extreme apocalyptic mind-set that sees every

---

7. The reference to "wars" must refer to later history between the first and second comings of Jesus rather than to the time leading up to the fall of Jerusalem; the first two centuries AD were a period of almost complete peace within the Roman Empire, the famous *pax romana*. That social stability was, in the providence of God, one of the reasons for the early spread of the Gospel, as apostles and other evangelists could travel freely and safely over most of the known world.

catastrophe in world history as a sign that "the end is nigh." Things like this have been happening consistently through the last two thousand years.

From the life of the world, Jesus turns to the life of the church. Three things are mentioned: persecution (Matthew 24:9//Mark 13:9,11,13//Luke 21:12,17); a growth in the numbers of people who fall away from their faith (Matthew 24:10–12); and the Gospel being preached in every nation[8] (Matthew 24:14//Mark 13:10). By 70 AD persecution had started to happen in the church, and the Gospel had spread to three continents. The letter to the Hebrews was probably written during or shortly after the first major period of persecution of the church under emperor Nero in 64 AD, and its purpose is to encourage Jewish Christians in danger of doing what Jesus speaks of here, namely falling away from their faith in Christ, to keep going despite the pressure. But of course, both the spread of the Gospel and the persecution of the church have continued and increased greatly in more recent times. In fact, without wishing to encourage the wrong kind of "last days" mentality, we can be rather more specific about recent developments: in the last century, and specifically in the last thirty to fifty years, there has been an unprecedented increase in the amount of persecution in the world—it is estimated that there are now over two hundred million people in the world who are being denied their basic human rights solely because they are Christians;[9] and of all those who have since the time of Jesus been put to death for their Christian faith, over 65 percent are from the last hundred years.[10] And in the same period there has been a similar increase in the number of countries where the Gospel has been preached, and in the numbers of Christians in the world. According to the 2010 edition of *Operation World*, the handbook of statistical information about the countries of the world and the growth of Christian faith, in 1900, 16.7 percent of the world's population was Christian; in 1960 it was 35.3 percent; in 2010 it was 63.2 percent.[11]

---

8. "Nations" (in Matthew 24:14//Mark 13:10) does not just mean political states; it means that the Gospel will be preached in all *people-groups* in the world.

9. Those who assume that such things could never happen in the UK might like to ask Mrs Caroline Petrie, a professional nurse suspended without pay in December 2008 and threatened with the sack and being struck off, because she offered to pray with a sick patient; the patient in question incidentally made no complaint and said she was not offended by the offer. For those who are wondering, that strange sound you can hear is probably Florence Nightingale turning in her grave.

10. I am writing this chapter around the anniversary of the 9/11 bombings. Whilst I would never wish to minimize the sheer horror and evil of what was done on that day at the Twin Towers, it is perhaps sobering to reflect that the number of people who died in that attack is approximately the same as the number of Christians in the world who are put to death for their faith every two or three weeks.

11. Mandryk, *Operation World*, 5.

In Africa as a whole, well over 503 million people (over 48 percent of the total population) are Christians,[12] and in many individual African countries the figures are far higher: Kenya is over 82 percent Christian, Angola over 94 percent, the Democratic Republic of Congo over 92 percent, Zambia 87 percent.[13] No Christian was allowed to live in Nepal until 1970; there are now over 850 thousand Nepalese Christians.[14] In 1900 South Korea had no Protestant church; today the country is over 30 percent Christian.[15] Asia as a whole has over 368 million Christians;[16] China has over 105 million.[17]

Having said that, these figures of growth in the things Jesus mentions do not give us the right to claim that the return of Jesus must necessarily be imminent. He turns next, however, to the signs that will accompany the more immediate prelude to his coming. And he starts with the most notoriously puzzling phrase in the whole discourse, namely the appearance of "the abomination that causes desolation" (Matthew 24:15//Mark 11:14). These words describe someone or something that is so terrible and loathsome ("abominable") that he (or it) will cause people to flee from Jerusalem and the temple in horror (that is, will cause the temple to be "desolated"). It was first used by Daniel (Daniel 9:27) to prophesy the blasphemous desecration of the temple by the Syrian king Antiochus Epiphanes, who between about 171 and 164 BC dedicated the temple in Jerusalem to Zeus, filled it with pagan images, and made offerings of pig's flesh on its altar. Jesus uses the same phrase to refer to the coming desecration of the temple by the Roman armies under Titus Vespasian, who brought the flags and standards of the Roman Empire into the temple itself; this "abomination" did indeed cause many Jews to flee from Jerusalem and from the temple.

But we come again to the "double application" of prophecy; as well as speaking of the Romans' desecration of the temple in 70 AD, these words have always been understood, rightly in my view, as looking ahead to the appearance of the one who elsewhere in the New Testament is called the "Antichrist" (e.g. 1 John 2:18) or the "man of lawlessness" (2 Thessalonians 2:3), the major figure who will lead the last great movement of opposition to God and God's people. He will make arrogant and blasphemous claims for himself; he will bring to a climax the spiritual opposition to God and to God's Kingdom; he will appear to be gaining ground, but the Lord Jesus will

---

12. Ibid, 32.
13. Ibid, 29.
14. Ibid, 619.
15. Ibid, 509.
16. Ibid, 59.
17. Ibid, 215.

return when he is at the height of his power, and will destroy him "with the breath of his mouth" (2 Thessalonians 2:8).

There has inevitably been a great deal of speculation about the Antichrist, and I have no desire to fuel any more. The most we can say is that the New Testament appears to be referring to an actual individual who will appear at the end of history, though John does recognize that there are many "antichrists" who have already appeared (1 John 2:18), people who have opposed Jesus and his Kingdom; just as many figures in the Old Testament can be seen as foreshadowings or "types" of Christ, so *the* Antichrist will come at the end, although he has been preceded by many people and movements throughout history who have opposed Christ. Moreover he would appear from Paul's phrase "the man of lawlessness" to be a human figure, though he is obviously an instrument of Satan.

Following the appearance of the Antichrist, Jesus says that people will flee from Jerusalem in large numbers (Matthew 24:16-20//Mark 13:14-19//Luke 21:21-23); there will be great turmoil and distress in the area around Jerusalem (Matthew 24:21//Mark 13:19). It is of course possible that the specific "Jerusalem" references refer to the historical assaults on the temple under Vespasian in 70 AD, and that the Antichrist's activity will be more global or focused elsewhere. "Jerusalem" may imply that the Antichrist's activity will arise and be focused in the Middle East, or it may be a symbolic way of speaking of the fact that his target will be the believing people of God, rather than the city itself; after all, the New Testament uses the image of a temple to describe the church (1 Corinthians 3:16-17, 2 Corinthians 6:16). We should be wary of those who claim to be confident about all the fine detail of the Antichrist's activity. But there is no doubt that Jesus predicts a period of severe persecution of and opposition to the Christian church in the time before his return. 2 Thessalonians 2:8 says of the "man of lawlessness" that it will be during the time of his apparent power and victory that Jesus will return and destroy him. And there will be many who will falsely claim to be the Christ (Matthew 24:23-24//Mark 13:21-22). This has often happened in various places around the world; it is possible that these verses mean that there will be an increase in "false Christs" in the days of the Antichrist.

Throughout history there have been many confident claims that this or that person was clearly *the* Antichrist—the best known candidates have been the Pope, Napoleon, Hitler and Stalin—and I have no doubt that a few years ago there were many people trying desperately to work out ways of "proving" that Osama bin Laden and/or George W. Bush were definitely the Antichrist. The fact that such claims are futile will not stop them being made; but the New Testament never invites us to speculate on the identity of the Antichrist, but rather challenges us to live lives that are so devoted to Christ that, even if we should find ourselves living under his dreadful rule, we will stand firm in our faith whatever the cost.

Finally, Jesus speaks of the signs in the heavens that are the immediate prelude to his coming again in glory (Matthew 24:29//Mark 13:24–25// Luke 21:25–26); and this part of the discourse, as we have said, is most obviously a reference to the end of the world, rather than the events on AD 70. Immediately following the distress in the days of the Antichrist, there will be disturbances in the heavenly bodies, the sun, moon and stars. Then the Lord Jesus himself will appear.

What are we to make of all this? It would be good to begin by saying what it is *not* intended to mean.

1. It is not intended to give us a time-table of events at the end of the world, or to enable us to know when the coming of Jesus will occur. Jesus says very explicitly that we will never be able to pinpoint the date when he will return (Matthew 24:36//Mark 13:32); in other words, we need to be ready all the time. And in the New Testament, teaching about the end of the world and the coming again of Jesus is never the basis for drawing up plans and time-tables about events in the future, but is always the basis of an appeal for holy living *now*.

2. We need to avoid becoming drawn into a mind-set that has, unfortunately, become extremely common these days, namely getting bogged down in apocalyptic speculation. There is an endless stream of theories about the Antichrist, of people tracking events in the Middle East to try and spot anything that they can link to something Jesus says about the signs to come, of sensationalist articles, especially on the internet, of the "Are we living in the last days?!?" kind. There are many who will say that such things are largely a waste of time; on the contrary, I would suggest they are *completely* a waste of time. It is worth remembering that what prompted this whole discourse was a question from his disciples about when these things would happen. Whilst not evading the question, Jesus clearly wants to distinguish what it is profitable for his people to know—that he will indeed return with power and glory—from what they need to avoid, namely theorizing about when, how and how soon it would happen.

3. Furthermore, we need to understand why Jesus mentions the signs in the world (earthquakes, etc.) and, to some extent, the signs in the church (like growing opposition and persecution); it is *not* to say that they mean that the end is imminent, it is precisely to say that they do not. As we said above, Jesus mentions disturbances in the world to

warn us that they do not mean that the end is coming: he wants to counter the kind of paranoid speculation that sees in every natural disaster a sign that the world is about to end.

More positively, there are a number of things that can be said.

"The Last Days?"

We need to be careful how we use the phrase "the last days." It tends to be used to refer to the time immediately preceding the return of Jesus, and to imply precisely the kind of apocalyptic speculation against which Jesus wants to warn us. But the New Testament uses it rather to refer to the whole period between the two comings of Jesus: Hebrews 1:2, having mentioned how God spoke in Old Testament days through various prophets, continues, "but in these last days he has spoken to us by his Son." Jude says (verse 18) that "in the last times there will be scoffers who will follow their own ungodly desires," then immediately continues, "these are the men who divide you"—in other words, it is happening *now*, that is, in Jude's day: it is not a prophecy about the dim and distant future. If people ask "are we living in the last days?," the New Testament answer is, "yes—and we have been for two thousand years." The coming of Jesus initiated the beginning of the "last days."

It is because of this that the New Testament can speak of Jesus coming "soon" (Revelation 22:7,12,20), or of his coming being "near" (James 5:8). It has often been said, with some embarrassment by Christians and with cynicism by unbelievers, that since the Bible declared confidently that Jesus was coming back "soon" two thousand years have come and gone. It may be—though it is not as certain as some might suppose—that when the New Testament writers said "soon," they were genuinely thinking in terms of dates and times, even though Jesus had not only warned against being preoccupied with the time-table of the last days, but had also hinted on a number of occasions that some considerable time would elapse before his coming again.[18] But it is quite proper to understand "soon" to mean, not chronologically imminent, but spiritually imminent. The unfolding of God's plan of salvation is not so much like a straightforward race as like a hurdle race. In a simple race, the only question is how far there is to run—is it a hundred meter sprint, or a thousand meter run, or a marathon? But in a

---

18. For example, "the bridegroom was a long time in coming" (Matthew 25:5), "after a long time" (Matthew 25:19). Luke 19:11 says that Jesus told the parable of the ten minas—sums of money given by a ruler to ten of his subjects—in order to correct the mistaken thinking that "the Kingdom of God was going to appear at once."

hurdle race, there is also the question of how many hurdles remain to be jumped. In Old Testament days, there were many things that still needed to happen before God's Kingdom could come in its final fullness—there were still a lot of hurdles to be overcome: Christ had to be born, he had to inaugurate the Kingdom, sin had to be atoned for, the Gospel had to be preached, the Spirit had to be made available. Now that Jesus has returned to the Father, relatively little remains to be done before Jesus can consummate the Kingdom: there are far fewer hurdles remaining. It is probably that sense of "spiritual imminence," rather than the idea of chronological time-table, that lies behind the assertion that Jesus' coming is now "at hand."

"Be Prepared"

Jesus' teaching about his return is always to urge us to be ready in our lives, never to furnish us with questions to ponder in our minds. Wherever the New Testament letter-writers speak of the coming again of the Lord, they always follow it with a call to readiness, and in particular to holy living. "The day of the Lord will come like a thief . . . Since everything will be destroyed in this way, what kind of people ought you to be? You ought to live holy and godly lives . . . " (2 Peter 3:10–11). "We know that when he appears, we shall be like him, for we shall see him as he is. Everyone who has this hope in him purifies himself, just as he is pure" (1 John 3:2–3). Those who have understood Jesus' prophetic teaching are not the people who debate whether this or that event in the world is a further sign that the Antichrist will appear at any moment, but those who devote themselves to living holy and pure lives.

"Coming in Glory"

The language used in the Bible about Jesus' return—that he will appear "in the sky . . . on the clouds . . . with power and great glory" (Matthew 24:30//Mark 13:26//Luke 21:27)—has given rise to a great deal of debate about the degree to which Jesus' words are to be understood metaphorically or literally. What is beyond dispute is that he speaks of his coming again as a wholly supernatural event. When Jesus came in history, he was born as a human baby and lived as a man; most of the world was completely unaware of the fact that he had arrived in human history, let alone of the significance of his coming. His coming again will be quite different: it will be heavenly, not human; public, not hidden; glorious, not squalid; and supernatural, not natural. People can argue as much as they like about whether "on the clouds" means actual clouds as we see them in the sky and whether the "trumpet call of God" (1 Thessalonians 4:16) refers to an actual musical instrument, or whether these phrases are symbolic ways of speaking of splendor and glory. Personally, I think it is always best to take the language of Scripture at face value. That does not mean that it has to be interpreted in a boringly literal and wooden way; the Bible can and does use metaphorical language, but to say that a biblical phrase is a metaphor does not mean that it is not true: it is using a figure of speech to refer to something that is even more gloriously real than the inadequate human language we have to depend on to try and describe it. Far from being crude or simplistic, the description of Jesus coming on the clouds "with a loud command, with the voice of the archangel and with the trumpet call of God" (1 Thessalonians 4:16) is a very powerful way of conveying the sheer magnificence of his coming again; theologians who dismiss such phrases on the grounds that some of them might be metaphorical all too often end up with language that is more abstract, more boring and less understandable, and which conveys very little except that the theologians in question don't actually believe in or expect an real glorious coming of the Lord. But if we take the verbal inspiration of the Bible seriously, and believe that all Scripture is inspired by God (2 Timothy 3:16)—and I do,—then we should accept that the ways in which the Bible actually speaks are the ways in which God has chosen to convey his truth to us. I do not believe that anyone's faith or growth in grace will ever be hindered by their taking literally something in the Bible which might later turn out to have been intended as a figure of speech; but I am sure that the opposite error—failing to take biblical statements at face value—will always eat away at Christian confidence and undermine Christian life.

However much of the language used to describe Jesus' return may or may not be metaphorical, there is no doubt that the return of Christ is portrayed as utterly supernatural: the splendor and glory being spoken of are *heavenly* splendor and glory. As Jesus himself warned us, there have throughout history, and especially in recent decades, been a number of "false Christs," people who have claimed to be—or whose followers have claimed that they are—Christ returned to earth. But all of these messianic imposters are "ordinary people"; they were born, they grew up, they live as men and will one day die as men. When Christ returns, he will unmistakably be seen to be the Lord of heaven.

In our age, there is, for understandable reasons, a great deal of concern about "the end of the world," and about the two features of modern life that pose a threat to the ongoing existence of planet earth, namely atomic weapons and environmental damage. Without for a moment denying that Christians should take those issues seriously and handle them responsibly, the fact remains that the end of the world will come neither with an atomic bang nor an environmental whimper. The event that brings about the end of human history will not arise from within human history; it will be the heavenly and supernatural advent of the Lord of glory himself. Our modern world may regard such an idea with cynicism; but it is as much a part of core Christian belief as anything.

"Take Heart"

And finally, Jesus speaks as a prophet about his later return in order to give us a firm assurance about the future dimension of the Kingdom. We are not merely those who live here and now with the measure of faith and love that we have; we are those who are filled with a hope that is steadfast and sure. Jesus is coming back; the fact that we cannot know for certain precisely *when* he is coming is infinitely less important than the fact that we can be completely confident *that* he is coming. Christians are those who have something to look forward to.

We need to be reminded of this in a church culture which has become, at least in the west, increasingly "this-worldly"; where the focus of our mission is so often what Jesus can do for people today, rather than what they can become in heaven; where the offer of the Gospel is not so much eternal life as a better life. Yet ironically, the very things that Jesus mentions in this discourse—that in this world there will be troubles, conflict, opposition, and confusion—are things that this generation is perhaps more aware of than any previous one. Few people today have a real confidence that there are answers here and now to the unrest of the world; even though they would not necessarily phrase it in theological ways, most people know that "heaven and earth will pass away" (Mark 13:31). Jesus alone can assure them that his Kingdom, like his Word, will never pass away.

One final point concerning this teaching about the signs of Jesus' return needs to be remembered: all three synoptic Gospels point out that Jesus gave this teaching, not to the crowds in the temple courts, but to his own circle of disciples; and both Matthew and Mark stress that this discussion took place in private (Matthew 24:3//Mark 13:3). It is important to reinstate the fact that Jesus is coming again, and the promise of the future consummation of the Kingdom, as vital elements in the Gospel we proclaim to the world; but the same is not true of the complicated discussion about the signs of the times and whether we can know how near we are to the end. Rehearsing those arguments in public is likely to do little for the cause of the Gospel, and is much more likely to leave our listeners with the impression that Christians are—to put it far more politely than most people would—rather eccentric. I have occasionally overheard earnest Christians speaking to unbelievers, supposedly witnessing to the Gospel and challenging them to faith, and getting into intense and impassioned warnings about the Antichrist, the wars and rumors of wars in the world, and the fact that the prevalence of false cults and false Christs proves that the end is near; in such circumstances I find myself cringing with embarrassment and even hoping, if not actually praying, that God would do for these no doubt well-meaning but misguided zealots' powers of speech what he did for Zechariah when he doubted Gabriel's message that he would become the father of John the Baptist. We need Jesus' teaching about the signs of his return; but he spoke about these things in order to remind his followers to be ready, not to give us something we can share with the world in the hope that it will frighten people into faith.

In Matthew's Gospel this discourse about the end of the world is followed by a series of parables about judgment (25:1–46). The most famous of these parables, the third, about the sheep and the goats,[19] is often quoted out of context, and is assumed to imply that the only criterion for judgment is whether we have looked after poor people. But this is the third of three parables which together describe all-round Christian life. That life starts when we receive "oil in our lamps" (verses 1–13), the new life of God's Spirit. This then involves us starting a new life as active disciples; unlike the foolish servant (verses 14–30), we are not to leave the life Jesus gives us just "lying around" or "hidden in the ground" (verse 18), but to do something with it.[20] The fact that this second parable is always referred to as the parable of the "talents" has led to a widespread idea that it is about using our gifts; but a "talent" is simply a measure of weight and a unit of currency—it does not mean a "talent" in the modern English sense of ability or skill. Spiritual gifts are of course part of Christian life, but it is of that life as a whole that

---

19. Strictly speaking, this third story is not actually a "parable"; unlike the first two, it does not start with the typical introduction to a parable ("the Kingdom of heaven will be like . . . "), and it is in fact a straightforward description of the final judgment. Of course the reference to "sheep and goats" is a simile (verse 32, "*as* [= *like*] a shepherd separates the sheep from the goats"), but the rest of the story is a factual description of what will happen at the last judgment, albeit using, necessarily, very "this-worldly" language. But it is convenient to group the three stories in chapter 25 together, and to speak of them as three "parables" of judgment.

20. Commenting on the similar parable in Luke 19:11–27, A. M. Hunter sees in the wicked servant who kept his coin "laid away in a piece of cloth" (verse 20) a picture of "the pious Pharisee who hoarded the light God gave him (the Law) and kept for himself what was meant for mankind. Such a policy of selfish exclusivism yields God no interest on his capital; it is tantamount to defrauding him and must incur his judgment." (Hunter, *New Testament Theology*, 81.)

Jesus is speaking. A talent was a quite considerable amount of money: it would take an ordinary laborer many years to earn such a sum; and we have been blessed in Christ with every spiritual blessing in the heavenly realms (Ephesians 1:3)—in spiritual terms, Christians are all multi-millionaires. The fact that Jesus mentions different amounts given to different servants should not lead to speculation about whether and on what grounds people are given different "amounts" of spiritual life, blessings or gifts; the lesson is that, irrespective of "how much" faith we have—not that it can be easily quantified—what matters is that we *do* something with it, rather than compare it with others who may appear to have more or less than us. Finally, the third parable shows us that one of the things that this new life will always involve is service to the poor and needy (verses 31–46).[21]

What is often forgotten is that Jesus addressed these parables, not to the unbelieving world, as a warning that they need to "get saved," but, like the discourse about the signs of his coming, to his own disciples, as an incentive to make something positive of their Christian lives now, because there will be a day of reckoning in the future. Simply having been invited to be a Christian bridesmaid is not enough: we need oil in our lamps. Having been allocated the talent of Christian faith is not enough: we need to make something of it. Saying we are ready to serve Jesus is not enough: if we cannot see opportunities to serve him in the needs around us ("Lord, when did we see you hungry or thirsty . . . ?"), we cannot see at all. Matthew 25 poses the challenging question: why is the church so much better at preaching judgment to unbelievers than at living in a way that prepares *us* for it?

The New Testament speaks about the future judgment of Christians in two different ways, which need to be, but in the history of the church have not always been, kept in proper balance. On the one hand, there are numerous assurances that those who believe in Jesus will never face judgment: "I tell you the truth, whoever hears my word and believes him who sent me has eternal life and will not be condemned; he has crossed over from death to life" (John 5:24—the phrase translated "will not be condemned" is literally

---

21. The fact that Jesus says that he will gather "all the nations" to judgment (verse 32) has led some to suggest that this story is about the criteria by which Jesus will judge those who have never had the opportunity to become his people by a response to the Gospel; "the nations" would mean to most Jews "the Gentiles," that is, outsiders to the people of God. Whilst this is not impossible, it is far more likely that "all the nations" simply means the entire human race; and the frequently forgotten fact that this parable is the third in a series of three means that what comes under scrutiny in the judgment is the whole of the life of faith leading to discipleship and service. Maybe the "goats" in the parable, those who did not serve the cause of Christ in the world, include the people Jesus referred to in the Sermon on the Mount, who regularly say "Lord! Lord!," but never do the will of the Father.

simply "does not come to judgment"); "since we have now been justified by [Christ's] blood, how much more shall we be saved from God's wrath through him" (Romans 5:9); "there is now no condemnation for those who are in Christ Jesus" (Romans 8:1). On the other hand, there are also reminders, addressed to Christians, that "we must all appear before the judgment seat of Christ, that each one may receive what is due to him for the things done while in the body, whether good or bad" (2 Corinthians 5:10).

As with all biblical doctrines that are multi-faceted, to focus solely on one side of the truth and ignore the other inevitably leads to serious problems, not only theologically but also pastorally. There are those churches—for example, the medieval Catholic Church, and also perhaps some of those that belong to what is often called the "holiness" tradition—who have repeatedly warned believers about the judgment of God, but have not taught them about the basis of our assurance that in Christ we are free from judgment; that can lead to Christians living their lives in the paranoid fear that, despite their faith and devotion, if they slip up even once—if at any point they put a foot wrong morally or spiritually—they might lose their salvation and be condemned to hell. Other denominations, especially those in the Calvinist tradition,[22] have repeatedly reassured people that there is absolutely no judgment to come for them since they are in Christ, which has sometimes led to the kind of casual attitude that assumes that we can do or not do whatever we like here and now because we will never be called to account for it—we'll be saved anyway. Healthy Christian life requires that we hold on to both of two equally important truths: that so long as we continue to believe in Jesus as Savior,[23] we will never face judgment in the sense of condemnation for our sins and exclusion from heaven; *and* that we are called to live our lives in the light of the fact that we will be judged by God, not in terms of a "heaven or hell" judgment—that is no longer an issue, since God has brought forward into human history the judgment that was due to be passed on us for our sins, and has passed it on Jesus on the cross, which is why "whoever believes does not come to judgment" (John 5:24)—

---

22. And also, unfortunately, those on the extreme liberal wing of the church who simply don't believe in judgment at all. Jesus did; so whilst we must not distort or misapply his teaching about judgment, those who take him seriously do not have the option of simply disregarding it.

23. That is the vital basis of Christian assurance; I can be assured of heaven, not merely because I once made a decision to believe in Jesus, but because I "abide in him." That does not mean that assurance is any less assured; but it is an important safeguard against complacency. It is important to note that the verbs in verses like the famous John 3:16—"that whoever believes in him . . . [should] have eternal life"—are in the present (continuous) tense: the sense is that "all who continue believing in him will continue having eternal life."

but rather an assessment of the quality of our discipleship and service. In 1 Corinthians 3:11–16, Paul says,

> "No one can lay any foundation other than the one already laid, which is Jesus Christ. If any man builds on this foundation using gold, silver, costly stones, wood, hay or straw, his work will be shown for what it is, because the Day will bring it to light. It will be revealed with fire, and the fire will test the quality of each man's work. If what he has built survives, he will receive his reward. If it is burned up, he will suffer loss; he himself will be saved, but only as one escaping through the flames."

Faith in Jesus as Savior is the "foundation," and it is having that foundation that secures our salvation and acceptance into heaven; but what each person has built on that foundation—the quality of life and service that he or she achieved as a Christian—will be tested, and those who really made something of their Christian lives, who, in Paul's language, built with silver and gold, will receive special rewards, whilst those who frankly did not—who, though they remained Christian believers, never really did anything of Christian quality with their lives—will "suffer loss": they will lose out on the rewards that could have been theirs. Paul adds of such a believer that "he himself will be saved": even those Christians who never do anything of value with their Christian lives will be accepted into heaven; but they will be saved, as it were, by the skin of their teeth, with nothing much to show for their lives. University students, at the end of their course, usually take final exams, and on the basis of those exams (and, these days, increasingly of their course work during the whole of their time as students) will be graded, in UK universities, as "first class," "second class," etc. No matter how they do in their finals, they are still students (provided they do not behave so badly that they get sent down before their finals!); so the Cambridge student who just about scrapes a third-class degree can still legitimately call himself a Cambridge graduate: it's just that some of his fellow students got firsts or seconds. In an analogous way, all Christians will "graduate" to heaven, so long as they remain in the faith of Christ; but the Bible assures us that there are special "honors" for those whose quality of Christian service is deemed to be "first class": though I should of course add that, unlike in my university analogy, the quality of life that we lead is in no way at all related to our ability, and certainly not to academic ability, but only to the degree to which we devote ourselves to holy living and Gospel service. I would not be at all surprised if some people who, in their earthly lives, were barely literate and had no human skills worth speaking of, might find themselves being honored with the heavenly equivalent of a first-class degree, whilst some professional theologians, with more letters after their names than would fit on any business card, might have to be content with a modest "third": but, so longer as they genuinely believed in Jesus, they will be saved. Of course we have no idea what kind of special "rewards" are in store for those who with God's help build a Christian life that is of gold or silver quality; but Paul was clear that he did not want to miss out on them, and he urged his readers to have the same spiritual ambition. For the Christian believer, the fact that we will appear before the judgment seat of Christ is not to do with the fear that we might be rejected: as it says in 1 John 4:17–18, "Love is made complete among us so that we will have confidence on the day of judgment, because in this world we are like him. There is no fear in love. But perfect love drives out fear, because fear has to do with punishment. The one who fears is not made perfect in love"—in other words, our coming "judgment" is nothing to do with punishment, and if we fear that it might be, we have not grasped what it true of us because of the love of God which has atoned for all our sins. Rather, the judgment to come is, for the believer, an incentive to devote ourselves to holy living and Kingdom service. There are many students who, realizing that their final exams start next week, suddenly wake up to the fact that it might not be a bad idea to start doing some revision. The New Testament would encourage those who by free grace are students in Jesus' school of discipleship: don't leave it that long to allow God to help you to make something positive of your Christian life, because we don't know when we will find ourselves turning up for our graduation ceremony.

6

The Passover Lamb

"I have eagerly desired to eat this Passover with you" (Luke 22:15)

In the second half of the last week, we start to see those aspects of Jesus' all-round ministry that focus on the approaching cross; and we begin with one thing that was not part of the normal expectations of the Messiah, but which becomes a central theme in the New Testament: the fact that Jesus is the Lamb of God who takes away the sins of the world.

The Last Supper

In the account of the Last Supper, we find the preparation for the Passover (Matthew 26:17-19//Mark 14:12-16//Luke 22:7-13) and the Passover itself, which includes the account of Jesus washing his disciples' feet (John 13:3-17), the argument amongst the disciples (Luke 22:24), the Last Supper (Matthew 26:20-30//Mark 14:17-26//Luke 22:14-23), and the prediction of Peter's denial (Matthew 26:31-35//Mark 14:27-31//Luke 22:34//John 13:38).

I shall follow the conventional assumption that the Last Supper took place on the Thursday of Holy Week. Admittedly, the exact date of the meal is not as clear as we might wish: the first three Gospels all say that it was the Passover meal itself, whereas John says that the meal took place "just before the Passover" (John 13:1). "*Just* before" is perhaps an overstatement:

the Greek simply says "before." I do not propose to discuss the question of the day on which the meal took place; Howard Marshall is obviously right when he agrees "that in *character* the meal was a Passover supper, and that paschal [that is, Passover] features are present both in Mark and in John,"[1] even though the words in the different Gospels which speak of *when* the meal took place are slightly ambiguous. But the lessons we can learn from the Last Supper all arise from its character; none is dependent on our being able to pin-point the calendar date on which it happened.[2]

The Passover is one of the main annual festivals of the Jews. It commemorates the time when God rescued his people from slavery in Egypt (Exodus 12). The Israelites were told to kill a lamb and to smear its blood on the outside of their doors (12:7). When God passed through Egypt, he killed the first-born son in every household (12:12); but where he saw the blood on the doors (that is, in the homes of the Israelites) he "passed over" that house and did not bring judgment (12:13).[3] Exodus 12:30 reads, literally, "there was not a house without a death." That is quite true: in the homes of the Egyptians the firstborn sons were dead; in the homes of the Israelites a lamb was dead. We see here another instance of the frequent biblical theme of substitution; where the lamb's blood had been shed, the people's lives were saved.

This is of course a striking picture of what God has done for us through Jesus. We are all by nature in slavery to sin. Jesus is the "Lamb of God" (John 1:29), our "Passover Lamb" (1 Corinthians 5:7), who died to atone for our sins, so that we might not suffer the punishment that they deserve, since he has already suffered in our place. When we trust in Jesus, his blood covers

---

1. Marshall, *Luke*, 790.

2. As a point of interest, the conventional English name for the day on which we traditionally commemorate the Last Supper, "Maundy" Thursday, refers to the ceremony of washing the feet of the poor. The word "maundy" is derived from the Latin *mandatum* ("commandment": our English word "mandate" is from the same Latin root) and refers to John 13:34, where Jesus says, having washed his disciples' feet, "A new command I give you: Love one another"; hence the practice of distributing "maundy money," that is, charitable gifts for the poor.

3. The Hebrew word for the feast of Passover, *pesah*, is connected with the verb *pāsah*; the exact meaning of this word is not easy to determine, as it is used only four times in the Old Testament, but it has usually been thought to mean something like "to go over" or "move over." Apart from the three places where it is used specifically of the original Passover in Egypt (Exodus 12:13,23,27), its only other occurrence is in Isaiah 31:5, "Like birds hovering overhead, the Lord Almighty will shield Jerusalem; he will shield it and deliver it, he will *pass over* it and will rescue it"; this seems to reflect the sense that, when God went through Egypt on the night before the exodus, whilst he brought judgment on the Egyptians, his presence hovered over the homes of the Israelites to protect them.

us, just as the blood was put on the outside of the doors in Egypt. Where God sees the blood—when he sees that we are trusting in the death of Jesus—he "passes over us" on the day of judgment. Jesus used the Passover meal as a time to teach his disciples about the meaning of his death, and that his blood is being shed as a sacrifice to take away sins (Matthew 26:28). He is the one through whom God's New Testament people are rescued, not from physical slavery like that which the Israelites were suffering in Egypt, but from the far greater spiritual slavery to sin; and in him, everything that the Jewish Passover symbolized and represented is consummated.

Throughout the history of the church there has been much theological debate about the nature and significance of the Lord's Supper. The Catholic tradition has developed a view of the Supper that sees it as a solemn and mystical ritual, in which grace is supernaturally conveyed to those who receive the bread and the wine; at the other end of the ecclesiastical spectrum, apart from those groups that practice no sacraments at all, like the Salvation Army, there are many who understand the Lord's Supper primarily as a fellowship meal and a memorial of Christ. Apart from affirming that, on the one hand, the high catholic view goes way beyond anything that the Bible itself would sanction, and, on the other, that the decision of some churches to practice no sacraments at all is hard to justify in the light of Jesus' explicit command to "Do this"—that is, break bread—"in remembrance of me" (Luke 22:19), I do not intend to enter here into a debate between a purely memorial and a more "sacramental" understanding of the Supper; on this, I am quite prepared to say, with Paul, that "each one should be fully convinced in his own mind" (Romans 14:5). What we can however say with confidence is that Jesus clearly sees the Last Supper, not as an end in itself, but as a pointer to the nature and meaning of his own death on the cross. It is Jesus' atoning death that secures our salvation, not our taking bread and wine. The bread and the wine are given to us as "signs" of his death, which is why Paul says that each time we break bread together, we "proclaim the Lord's death" (1 Corinthians 11:26); we do not proclaim simply that we are taking communion. Whether we see the Lord's Supper as a sacrament or as a memorial, unless it and the whole of our faith are focused in the fact that Christ died for our sins, it is meaningless.

The most controversial debate about the Lord's Supper concerns the meaning of Jesus' words "This is my body" and "This is my blood." The medieval Roman Catholic Church developed the doctrine of "transubstantiation," the idea that the substance of the bread and wine are actually transformed into the substance of the body and blood of the Lord. The official statement of this doctrine as a dogma to be believed was made by the Synod of Rome in 1079, which spoke of the bread and the wine being "converted" into the actual body and blood of Christ; the term "transubstantiation" was first formally used in the Fourth Council of the Lateran, convened by Pope Innocent III, which began in November 1215.[4] Earlier Christian writers certainly spoke of the body and blood of the Lord in the context of the Lord's Supper, but whether they understood this terminology to be figurative or "literal" and mystical is not certain. The comment of Michael Smith on the early church practice of the Supper is very wise: "It is tempting to try and read back later practice into the early days of the church, but it must be resisted. Although Justin [that is, Justin Martyr, who died in 165] might seem in some ways very 'Catholic,' in other points the worship he describes would have greater similarity to that of the Brethren today."[5]

It is impossible to derive the Catholic understanding of the bread and the wine that are served at our communion services from the Bible; there are a number of reasons for saying that Jesus' words "This is my body" are intended figuratively.

1. The Bible frequently uses the verb "to be" in the sense of "to represent" or "to symbolize": examples are Genesis 41:26 ("The seven good cows *are* seven years, and the seven good heads of grain *are* seven years"), Daniel 7:17 ("The four great beasts *are* four kingdoms that will rise from the earth"), Luke 8:11 ("The seed *is* the word of God"), Galatians 4:24 ("These things may be taken figuratively, for the women [= Hagar and Sarah] *are* [NIV: 'represent'] two covenants"), and Revelation 1:20 ("The seven stars *are* the angels of the seven churches, and the seven lampstands *are* the seven churches"). So when Jesus says "this *is* my body" it is unnecessary to insist that this can refer to nothing other than the mystical nature of the bread; it can quite properly be taken, in the same way as in the passages just listed, to mean, as Galatians 4:24 explicitly says, this bread "may be taken figuratively" as representing my body.

2. There are many instances in the ministry of Jesus when he spoke figuratively, and people mistakenly thought his words were meant in their immediate physical sense, and so missed the point that he was making. Examples are:

    "Jesus said to them, 'Be on your guard against the yeast of the Pharisees and the Sadducees.' They discussed this among themselves and said, 'It is because we didn't bring any bread' ... Then they understood that he was not telling them to guard against the yeast used in bread, but against the teaching of the Pharisees

---

4. Briggs, *Theological Symbolics*, 131–133.
5. Smith, *From Christ to Constantine*, 72.

and Sadducees" (Matthew 16:6–7,12); "Jesus answered them, 'Destroy this temple, and I will raise it again in three days.' The Jews replied, 'It has taken forty-six years to build this temple, and you are going to raise it in three days?' But the temple he had spoken of was his body" (John 2:19–21); "'No one can see the Kingdom of God unless he is born again.' 'How can a man be born when he is old?' Nicodemus asked. 'Surely he cannot enter a second time into his mother's womb to be born?'" (John 3:3–4); "The water I give him will become in him a spring of water welling up to eternal life.' The woman said to him, 'Sir, give me this water so that I won't get thirsty and have to keep coming here to draw water'" (John 4:14–15); "He said to them, 'I have food to eat that you know nothing about.' 'Then his disciples said to each other, 'Could someone have brought him food?' 'My food,' said Jesus, 'is to do the will of him who sent me...'" (John 4:32–34); "'Our friend Lazarus has fallen asleep; but I am going there to wake him up.' His disciples replied, 'Lord, if he sleeps, he will get better.' Jesus had been speaking of his death, but his disciples thought he meant natural sleep" (John 11:11–13).

Hendriksen's comment on this repeated tendency to misinterpret Jesus is apposite: "In all of [these passages] the symbolical or figurative character of our Lord's language was disregarded by those who first heard it. In each case also, the context made clear that those who interpreted Christ's words literally were mistaken.[6] Is it not high time that the implied lesson be taken to heart?"[7]

3. It is impossible to see how the words "This is my body" could have meant what the Roman doctrine of transubstantiation implies at the time they were first uttered: Jesus was standing before his disciples in his own human body, and he handed them pieces of broken bread which were clearly distinct from his own physical body.

4. In the Last Supper, Jesus bases all he says and does on the Jewish Passover. The various elements of the Passover meal were understood to be representative of aspects of the story of the original exodus—the

---

6. Evangelicals, like myself, are usually defined as those who take the Bible literally. That does not however mean that we do not recognize figures of speech (metaphors, poetic images, etc.) for what they are and interpret them accordingly. To take the Bible "literally" should always mean that the sense we take from the text is whatever it is to be understood as meaning, by all the normal criteria of literary judgment. So where for example a metaphor is used, the correct interpretation of the words is to accept the truth of which they are a figurative illustration rather than to insist that they cannot be metaphorical.

7. Hendriksen, *Matthew*, 909.

bitter herbs represented the bitterness of the condition of the Hebrew slaves, the roast lamb represented the lambs that were slaughtered in the Jewish homes in Egypt—and by sharing in the meal, Jews understood themselves to be spiritually identified with the first generation of their people who came out of Egypt in the exodus. The person who presided at the Passover meal would, for example, take the unleavened bread and say over it, "This is the bread of affliction, which our fathers ate in the wilderness"; as Michael Green says, "It wasn't, of course, but it represented it, and brought it vividly to mind."[8] There was never any hint that anything supernatural or mystical happened which changed the nature of the elements of the Passover meal; but by sharing in the meal generations later, Jews were invited to see themselves as spiritually one with their forefathers in the deliverance which God had accomplished for them, making them the people they were. When Jesus adapts the Passover words, presenting himself as the Passover lamb who accomplishes the far greater deliverance from sin, it makes sense to assume that he intended his words in the same way.

For those reasons, the Catholic theory of transubstantiation has to be seen as a later doctrine which is quite alien in spirit to anything in the Bible. The historical controversies about the nature of the elements in the communion have, tragically, distracted many people from the fundamental truth that its meaning is found, not in the physical nature of the bread and the wine, but in the fact that Christ died on the cross. When in October 1529 a somewhat heated debate took place in Marburg between the leading reformers about the nature of the Eucharist or Lord's Supper, Martin Luther, who maintained a more strongly "sacramental" view of the Eucharist, is said to have written in chalk on the table *hoc est corpus meum* ("this is my body") as a sign to Huldrych Zwingli that he was not prepared to change his stance on the mystical nature of the elements in the sacrament; he was in effect saying, "If Jesus said 'This *is* . . . ,' that's an end of the matter." With all due respect to the great reformer, it is far from being as simple as that: if Jesus was using a metaphor (as all agree he was) when he said "I am the bread of life," why is it impossible to suggest that he was speaking in a similarly metaphorical way of a piece of bread he held in his hands and over which he said, "This is my body"? That is not to say that an understanding of the breaking of bread as a sacrament in which God works to impart grace and blessing is ruled out; as stated above, I am prepared to let each person make up his or her own mind on that. But what it does mean is that, however we understand the nature of the relationship between the historical crucifixion of Jesus and the

---

8. Green, *Matthew for Today*, 253.

bread served in the communion—whether like Zwingli we see the latter as simply a representative token or symbol of the former, or whether with Luther we believe that the benefits of the cross are in some real sense conveyed to the participant in the sacrament—the fact is that what the communion is "about" is the death of Jesus on the cross. The sacrament can never be an end in itself, separate from the historical work of the atonement, and any benefits that the believer can receive from sharing in the bread and the wine were made possible only because Jesus died as the Lamb of God, to take away the sins of the world.

Even whilst the disciples were sitting with Jesus at the meal, a quarrel broke out among them about which of them was the most important (Luke 22:24). And at the meal, Jesus predicted that all his disciples would desert him (Matthew 26:31//Mark 14:27), and that Peter would deny him (Matthew 26:34//Mark 14:30//Luke 22:34). Those two facts show us two things about Jesus at the Last Supper. First, they show us how badly we all need the forgiveness and salvation that Jesus was going to achieve. Even whilst they were sharing in a solemn and sacred meal, the disciples' sinful human nature kept coming to the surface. They squabbled, they all wanted to be seen as the most important, they all made arrogant and unrealistic claims about how loyal they were. That is why all people need Jesus to forgive and save them. Entering into a "religious" setting does not stop people from being sinners. Paul tells the Romans that "the Kingdom of God is not a matter of eating and drinking"—and, we might add, not even, as ends in themselves, of eating the bread and drinking the cup—"but of righteousness, peace and joy in the Holy Spirit" (Romans 14:17). Without that, as he tells the Corinthians (1 Corinthians 11:20), "it is not the Lord's Supper you eat."

Second, they show us the amazing grace of Jesus, who shares this meal with people who he knows will desert him and deny him. If we need a reminder that simply "taking communion" is not in itself a guarantee that our lives are pleasing and acceptable to God, it is found in the disturbing fact that Judas shared in the Last Supper with the Lord; it was only after the meal that he left to betray Jesus. Any idea that participation in the sacrament automatically ensures that we are justified before God is a form of superstition, not faith. But Jesus in his mercy wants to share fellowship with those who are unworthy of him. Salvation (and the Lord's Supper) are not for those who are good enough to deserve to sit with Jesus—they are for sinners who need his grace.

The Lord's Supper

The two great sacraments which Jesus left for his church as signs of the salvation we can share in him—baptism and the Lord's Supper—have over the centuries of church history become the grounds of some division and confusion. That is true of baptism; but differences over the understanding and practice of water baptism are as nothing compared to the controversy that has surrounded the breaking of bread, Lord's Supper, Eucharist or Holy Communion. Much, though not all, of this confusion and controversy arose from the way in which the medieval Catholic Church turned the Lord's Supper into a ritual full of symbolic mystery, in which those who receive the sacrament, though they are not expected to understand it, can somehow receive or forfeit grace according to whether they take or fail to take mass in the way properly prescribed by the church.

I have already said that this understanding of the mass, with its attendant doctrines like transubstantiation and its view of the sacrament as a sacrificial offering[9] goes way beyond anything that is found in the Bible, and represents an understanding of the nature not only of the communion service but of Christian faith as a whole which is quite different from that of the New Testament. Beyond that, I am prepared to recognize a range of understandings of the communion service—as a fellowship meal, a memorial of Christ or a sacrament in which God bestows spiritual grace on the communicants—as biblically possible.

From what is said of the communion in the rest of the New Testament, especially 1 Corinthians 10:14–22 and 11:17–34, a number of things can however be said with some confidence about the place of the breaking of bread in Christian life. But it is worth saying first that in these passages Paul is not attempting to offer a theological overview of the significance of the breaking of bread. He writes to rebuke and challenge the ways in which the Corinthian Christians were behaving when they came together to break bread; and that intention affects both what he says and how he says it. That should always be borne in mind as we read these chapters; although different churches have their cherished and traditional ways of administering the Lord's Supper, the New Testament would strongly suggest that what matters most is the moral and devotional attitude of those who share in the service: it was the fact that such an attitude was lacking in Corinth that caused Paul to write to the church as he did, rather than the need to establish a correct understanding of the theology and practice of the Lord's Supper.

---

9. Hence the practice of calling the table from which the elements in the mass are served the "altar": free churches invariably speak of the "table," which is the word used in the account of the Last Supper (Matthew 26:20//Mark 14:18//Luke 22:14).

"Do This"

The simplest thing to say about the Lord's Supper is the fact that believers are told to do it: as was said above, Jesus' words "Do this in remembrance of me" (Luke 22:19) are just as much a straightforward command as "Love one another" or "Follow me." I can understand and sympathize with the reasons why some groups within the Christian church like the Salvation Army chose from the beginning not to practice any form of sacrament—William Booth had seen how easily ritual could become a mechanical substitute for real spiritual life, and he was determined to avoid that danger—and the superstition that came to surround the Catholic mass has led to many evangelical believers wanting to have as little to do with anything sacramental as possible; and in many Protestant denominations, the importance of the breaking of bread has at various times been similarly played down: Horton Davies says, of the life and worship of the early seventeenth-century Baptist Churches in England, "The Sacrament is already becoming a materialistic superfluity, an extra that can be dispensed with, as long as the experience it channels is obtainable elsewhere."[10] But the fact remains that Jesus said "Do this." There is a Latin proverb, *abusus non tollit usum*: "abuse should not take away [right] use." If we believe that the way in which some churches practice the Lord's Supper is wrong, for those of us who want to follow Jesus according to the Scriptures the appropriate response is to get it right rather than to avoid doing it at all.

"Break Bread"

In the New Testament the phrase "to break bread" was used at its simplest to refer to having an "ordinary" meal. It is used of Jesus' feeding the five thousand (Matthew 14:19//Mark 6:41//Luke 9:16) and the four thousand (Matthew 15:36//Mark 8:6),[11] of the meal Jesus shared with Cleopas and his friend at Emmaus (Luke 24:30), and of the meal Paul encouraged those with

---

10. Davies, *Worship and Theology*, 503.

11. There has long been a tradition of seeing the feeding of the crowds as a kind of picture of the communion meal, largely because of the similarity of language—Jesus took the bread, broke it, etc.—to that used in the account of the Last Supper. Without going into too much detail about what is a much debated subject, it is at least as likely that the reverse is the case: that the language used of an ordinary occasion of people eating together, like the feedings of the crowds, is also used of the occasion when Jesus shared the Last Supper with his disciples. That does not mean that the communion meal cannot in addition have an extra layer of significance, but it is the more likely explanation of the terms used in the New Testament.

him in the storm on the Mediterranean Sea to share in order to keep their strength up (Acts 27:35). It was the phrase used in Jewish society for what would be done by the head of the family or the host at the formal start of any social meal, including those with more sacred significance like the Passover: we might say that for the head of a Jewish family to begin a meal by taking bread, giving thanks and breaking it was in their culture the equivalent of the traditional practice of "saying grace" at the start of a meal; though like the western "grace" the degree to which this was a conventional formality or a genuine act of thanksgiving to God would vary, depending on the spiritual character of the people concerned.

There are those who, because of this, would claim that all the New Testament means by "breaking bread" is having a meal together, without any spiritual connotations, and that that is what is referred to in passages like Acts 2:42, "They devoted themselves to the apostles' teaching and to the fellowship, to the breaking of bread and to prayer." It is true that the interpretation of such verses has long been swayed by the tendency to read back into the New Testament church practices that developed centuries later, and so to assume that when it says that the early church "broke bread" it must be referring to the symbolic sacrament as practiced in our churches today. But it is also true that the language of 1 Corinthians 11:20–22 suggests that the context in which the more formally "sacramental" breaking of bread took place was a social or fellowship meal, since Paul has to rebuke some members of the church for rushing ahead and eating before others, who probably had to work longer hours, arrived, with the result that when those workers got there, there was no food left.[12] However the fact that the early church had meals together does not have to mean that, as part of those meals, there was not also the practice of breaking bread with a distinctly spiritual purpose as an act of worship and a commemoration of Christ; the fact that the model for our Lord's Supper is the Jewish Passover, which was a shared meal with a specific spiritual purpose as a commemoration of God's great act of deliverance in the exodus, suggests that there probably was.

---

12. The only direct reference in the New Testament to the church practicing the *agápē* or "love feast," the fellowship meal, is in Jude 12. From that two things follow: first, the fellowship meal was clearly a feature of early church life; but second, the fact that in both 1 Corinthians 11 and Jude the writers have to address abuses of the practice should be a warning to those groups who believe that simply holding "love feasts" is in itself more pleasing to God and more immune to the danger of abuse than the traditional sacrament.

"A Participation in the Body"

Paul's language in 1 Corinthians 10:16, that to share in the breaking of bread is a "participation" in the body of Christ, suggests that, just as baptism includes the spiritual principle that the baptized believer is incorporated into and becomes one with Christ in his death and resurrection, so in the breaking of bread the Christian's incorporation into and unity with Christ is affirmed and renewed. The word translated "participation" is the frequent New Testament word *koinōnía*, often translated as "fellowship" or, in its older sense, "communion," from which that name for the Lord's Supper is derived; it means "sharing together in" something, or "being partners in" something. That in which the members of the church are "sharers" is of course the new life of God's Kingdom, made available through the death of Jesus; to break bread together declares, consolidates and strengthens our sharing together in the eternal life of Christ as fellow-members of the new covenant community of faith.

From that follows the truth affirmed in the next verse (10:17), that "because there is one loaf, we, who are many, are one body, for we all partake of the one loaf." Again, without addressing the question of the degree to which the sacrament is a metaphorical picture or a mystical channel of unity, it is beyond dispute that sharing together in the Lord's Supper is about unity, being one with our brothers and sisters in Christ, which is why Paul has such harsh words for those in Corinth who were denying that unity by their selfish behavior towards others in the church. To break bread with anyone else is to affirm that we are one with them in Christ; and that means that a genuine desire to grow in positive unity with our fellow-believers has to be one of the attitudes that we bring to the communion service.

"In Remembrance of Me"

Paul quotes in 1 Corinthians 11:24-25 the words recorded by Luke, that Jesus said, "Do this *in remembrance of me*." The breaking of bread is about remembering Jesus. The word translated "remembrance" is used only four times in the New Testament; apart from the three occasions referring to the Last Supper, it is also used in Hebrews 10:3-4, where we read, "Those sacrifices [that is, Old Testament sacrifices that had to be repeated annually] are an annual *reminder* of sins, because it is impossible for the blood of bulls and goats to take away sins." That gives us a clue to the meaning of "in remembrance of me"; the fact that again and again God's Old Testament people had to bring sacrifices for sin was a regular reminder to them of their spiritual state—they were not free from sin and its consequences once and for all, because they had to keep offering sacrifices of (symbolic) atonement. In the same way, but to the opposite end, the breaking of bread reminds the Christian again and again of his or her spiritual state before God: that we *are* free from sin and forgiven once and for all, because of the blood of Jesus. If the Old Testament sacrifices are a regular reminder of the fact of sin, the breaking of bread is a regular reminder of the forgiveness of sin. The sacrament is sometimes seen as a means of conveying forgiveness to the believer; it is perhaps more in keeping with Scripture, though without of course denying the need to confess any sins that have spoiled our relationship with God, to say that it re-affirms to the believer his or her forgiven-ness, and in particular how our salvation was achieved by Jesus' atoning death.

There may be a metaphorical reminder of that in the account that John, who does not narrate the Last Supper itself, gives us of the other significant action of Jesus with his disciples in the upper room, namely his washing of their feet. When Peter urges Jesus to wash not only his feet but also his hands and head, Jesus replies, "A person who has had a bath needs only to wash his feet; his whole body is clean. And you are clean . . . " (John 13:9–10). That John wants us to understand Jesus' language as referring to spiritual cleanliness is not in doubt; and one indication of that fact which does not come across in the English translation is that the verb "[who] *has bathed*" is in fact in the passive form: it is literally "the one who *has been* bathed." We do not wash ourselves clean from sin; Jesus washes us, and when he has done so he can say to us, as he did to his disciples, "You *are* clean." We do from time to time need to have our feet washed; as we walk through the world as Jesus' disciples, we can pick up some of the dirt of the world—we can commit sins which need to be confessed to God—but just as the person who has been bathed does not need a new bath just because his feet are dirty, so the believer may well commit sins which need to be confessed, but having been washed in the blood of Christ his essential status is that of forgiven-ness. Sharing in the Supper "in remembrance" of Christ crucified reaffirms to us that living in the status of forgiven children of God is our spiritual birth-right, made available to us by Jesus' death.

"Until He Comes"

Paul's phrase in 1 Corinthians 11:26, that we are to practice the Lord's Supper "until he comes," reminds us that in the breaking of bread we look both back (to the cross) and forward (to Jesus' return). Jesus himself referred to the future fulfillment of the Supper when he said to his disciples that he would not drink the fruit of the vine with his disciples until he drank it in a new way in the Kingdom (Matthew 26:29//Mark 14:25//Luke 22:16); and that saying, though it may of course have an initial partial fulfillment in the meals that the risen Christ shared with his disciples before his ascension and in the practice of the communion service, is certainly to be understood as above all a promise of the heavenly banquet in the new Jerusalem. In breaking bread together, Christians are reminded of the fact that we stand between the finished work of Jesus on the cross on the one hand, and the promised consummation of our salvation when Jesus returns on the other.

"Recognizing the Body"

In 1 Corinthians 11:29 we find another phrase that has been the grounds of much theological debate over the centuries: that "anyone who eats and drinks *without recognizing the body of the Lord*[13] eats and drinks judgment on himself." What does Paul mean by "recognizing the body of the Lord"? There are those on the Catholic wing of the church who cannot see these words other than against the background of the doctrine of transubstantiation, the idea that the bread eaten in the communion service becomes transformed, in some sense, into the actual flesh of Christ; and those who so understand the Lord's Supper would assume Paul to mean by "recognizing the body" the need to have a proper understanding of the doctrine of transubstantiation. But since that doctrine is quite alien to and incompatible with the Bible, we need to seek an understanding of Paul's words that is consistent with what the Bible itself teaches.

There are two main ways in which "recognizing the body [of the Lord]" can be interpreted. The first is to understand "the body" in the sense that Paul regularly uses it, not least in 1 Corinthians 12, as a way of referring to the church; he is shortly to say to the Corinthians, "Now you are the body of Christ" (12:27). So the sense of Paul's warning is that believers who participate in the Lord's Supper, but who think only of themselves and ignore the fact that they are fellow-members of the fellowship of the church, are in fact abusing the Supper. It is interesting, in the light of the centuries of debate about the theological significance of the communion, that what Paul

---

13. Strictly speaking, the phrase "of the Lord" is almost certainly not part of what Paul wrote; the best manuscripts read simply "without recognizing the body." But that makes little difference to the sense of the term: the meaning of "the body" is surely the same as in verse 27, which speaks of "the body and blood of the Lord" in a way that can only mean the historical body of Christ nailed to the cross and his blood that was shed there.

says has incurred the judgment of God[14] is not that they have got their theology of the sacrament wrong, but that they are behaving in ways that offend against the unity of the fellowship. And since that is indeed the behavior for which Paul has had to reprimand them (verses 20–22), it is very likely that this is part of what Paul means by "recognizing the body"; do we understand that, by saving us, Jesus has made us part of his body, the church, and that in the church we are all members of one another? If not—if when we break bread we ignore the fact that we are together fellow-members of the body of God's redeemed people, or, worse, if we behave as the Corinthians did in ways that despise, belittle or offend others in the church—then, although we may eat and drink in church, "it is not the Lord's Supper that you eat" (verse 20), because the Lord is the Head of the body.

The other way of understanding "recognizing the body" is that Paul means, do you understand that the breaking of bread is related to Jesus' death on the cross? Although the bread is still bread, it is a reminder of the body of Christ crucified for our sins. That is why to participate in the Lord's Supper "in an unworthy manner" (verse 27)—which in the case of the Corinthians specifically meant in ways that despise and disregard their fellow-Christians—should be a moral contradiction in terms. Christ's death on the cross has set us free from sin—so how can we commemorate it in a sinful way?! If people see the breaking of bread as simply a meal for them to enjoy, but do not see it as a way of focusing on the fact that Jesus died on the cross, and giving thanks for all that his cross achieved, then, again, "it is not the Lord's Supper that you eat."

"Look"

Finally, we said that the breaking of bread, as described in 1 Corinthians 11, looks back at the cross, and also forward to Jesus' coming again. In fact, we

---

14. By "judgment" Paul means that God has acted to discipline the members of the church who are out of order; we must not take the word in the sense of "the last judgment," and the question of whether people are admitted to or excluded from heaven. It is completely incompatible with both the letter and the spirit of the New Testament to suggest that the kind of wrong behavior that Paul is here rebuking can in itself be the grounds of anyone forfeiting their eternal salvation, as the words of verse 32 show—"when we are judged by the Lord, we are being disciplined so that we will not be condemned with the world." The kind of behavior Paul is challenging is certainly serious—hence the serious way in which God has had to intervene to discipline some in the church—but it is serious because it damages and undermines the very life of the church now, not because of any rule that the wrong approach to the Lord's Supper incurs damnation.

can go further: in verses 20–32 we see five ways in which those who share in the Supper are to "look."

- *We look back.* Verse 23 takes us back to what the Lord Jesus did "on the night he was betrayed." Just as the Jewish Passover looked back to the historical event of the exodus, so the Christian communion looks back to the historical event of the cross, and the fact that Christ died once for all for our sins. It is Jesus' sacrifice on cross that is the root of the whole of our life and faith.

- *We look forward.* As we said, verse 26 reminds us that we break bread "until he comes." Jesus himself, in the upper room, had spoken of the fact that his death on the cross contains an anticipation of the final glorious triumph of God's Kingdom: "I tell you, I will not drink of this fruit of the vine from now on until that day when I drink it anew with you in my Father's Kingdom" (Matthew 26:29). At the Last Supper, Jesus is pointing his disciples to the future feast in heavenly glory. Eating and drinking, feasting, is of course a frequent picture of the heavenly Kingdom; Jesus taught about heaven by telling a number of parables about a wedding banquet. The Lord's Supper is a foretaste of that heavenly banquet; we who share in the Supper are the community of those who are looking forward to the Lord's return.

- *We look around.* That is, we look around at one another. The problem in Corinth, as we have seen, is that in fact they weren't: the motto for their communion services was not "we are the body of Christ," but rather, "every man for himself!" The Lord's Supper is not an individual experience, but a fellowship meal. "Because there is one loaf, we, who are many, are one body, for we all partake of the same loaf" (1 Corinthians 10:17). The one loaf reminds us of, and is a sign of, the one body, and of the fact that we belong to each other.[15] So in the breaking of bread we declare our fellowship with one another, and recommit ourselves to each other as those who share together in the salvation of Christ.

---

15. Without wishing to make more of this than is appropriate, this is one reason why I find the common practice of serving individual communion wafers less than helpful. Where in that form of communion do we see any reflection of the vital truth that because there is one loaf we are one body? I am not suggesting that people who take communion in churches where wafers are used are necessarily "missing out" spiritually; but the models of practice that God has given us in his word, including the practice of breaking "one loaf," are there for a purpose, because they have something to teach us; where we change the practice, we are always in danger of missing some of the significance of what is happening.

- *We look inward*. Paul says in verse 28 that "a man ought to examine himself before he eats of the bread and drinks of the cup." This is of course because of the terrible abuses of fellowship that were going on in Corinth; Paul urges people to look into their own hearts, and ask themselves the question, am I one of those who have been guilty of such sins? Am I living as someone who is part of the Body? Am I in good relationship with my fellow church members? There have been many branches of the church that have advocated a practice of intense self-scrutiny in preparation for the breaking of bread; Christians have been urged to "examine themselves" to see whether they have been guilty of any sins that need to be confessed before they can come to the communion table. That can of course be a very healthy and profitable practice, and it is certainly to be preferred to the casual approach that assumes people can simply turn up and take communion, no matter whether or not their lives in recent days and weeks have in any sense been in step with God. But the danger against which such a practice needs always to be on its guard is that of becoming petty and "navel-gazing," and even worse, of leading people to feel that they cannot share in the breaking of bread because they have somehow fallen below the acceptable standard required of communicants. That is poles apart from the biblical spirit of grace: we come to Christ as sinners who have been cleansed from sin by his blood shed on the cross, not as those who have proved that we are good enough to come. And again, the specific context of the issue at Corinth should be borne in mind: Paul urges people to "examine themselves," not in a perfectionist or self-flagellating spirit, but to encourage them to ask, do I discern the body? Do I understand that this is all about Jesus and his death on the cross, and have I come in a spirit of wanting to reaffirm my commitment to Christ crucified as the grounds of my hope of salvation? Do I recognize the body that is the church, and am I living in good fellowship relationships with the rest of the church? Jesus, after all, had himself encouraged the same self-examination: "Therefore, if you are offering your gift at the altar and there remember that your brother has something against you, leave your gift there in front of the altar. First go and be reconciled to your brother; then come and offer your gift" (Matthew 5:23–24). The language of "offering your gift at the altar" is of course a reflection of Jewish sacrifices and temple worship; a Christian equivalent would be, "if you are about to break bread, and you remember . . . " It is first and foremost the need to put right any differences with a fellow church member before breaking bread together that lies behind Paul's call that we "examine ourselves."

- Finally, *we look outward*. In verse 26 Paul says that, every time we break bread, "we proclaim the Lord's death." We do not only "remember" the Lord's death—we "proclaim" it. That has been taken by some to mean that the Gospel should be preached at every communion service. Maybe; it would certainly do no harm. But "we proclaim" may have two senses. The main one, which is probably what Paul intends above all, is that, as we have said a number of times, what the communion service is "about" is the death of Jesus on the cross. When Christians break bread, they are affirming that Christ crucified is the focus of their faith and their hope. What Paul was declaring in words when he wrote that "[this] is of first importance, that Christ died for our sins" (1 Corinthians 15:3), every Christian "proclaims" in the very act of breaking bread. But there may be another sense in which we "proclaim the Lord's death": the Supper reminds us of what is at heart of Gospel that we have to proclaim, that "we preach Christ crucified." The church is never to be an inward-looking clique; and in the Lord's Supper, we are refreshed in our faith, and reminded of what is at the heart of our faith, so that we can go out and share the saving news of Christ and his cross with those who as yet do not know him. It was so in early church; Acts 2:46–47 remind us that the breaking of bread in the fellowship and fruitful evangelism in the world went side-by-side.

It is possible for the administration of communion to be somewhat private and introspective. Whilst not denying that there can be a place for the personal and quietly devotional celebration of the Lord's Supper, Paul's words in 1 Corinthians 11 remind us of the bigger context in which we break bread. As we come together as the people of God to share in the Supper, we are urged to look in those five directions: we look back to the death of Christ, forward to the coming again of Christ in glory, around at our fellow Christians with whom we are one in the body of Christ, inward to ensure that we are living in proper fellowship relationships, and outward at the world for which Jesus died. Wherever our theology of the communion may come on the scale from Luther's high view of the sacrament to Zwingli's memorial fellowship-meal, it is having those five different perspectives in proper balance that is most likely to enable us to benefit from the Supper in the ways that Jesus intended when he instituted it.

7

The Leader and High Priest

"My children, I will be with you only a little longer" (John 13:33)

Jesus, the Leader

One aspect of the office of the Messiah was as the leader and head of a renewed people of God. In John's Gospel, the Last Supper is followed by a long discourse containing Jesus' last words to his disciples (John 14–16). Jesus speaks in this address about his being the way to the Father; about the Holy Spirit who will come; about the importance of remaining in him; and about the opposition that the disciples will face in the future. Jesus is preparing his disciples for the time when he will no longer be with them in person, and they will be guided instead by his Spirit. Like the Sermon on the Mount in Matthew 5–7, these chapters are another "manual of Christian discipleship," and they are especially important for what they teach about the work of the Holy Spirit in our lives. Jesus is giving his people the guidance and resources they need to be the people of God under his leadership, even after he is no longer (physically) with them.

John 13–16 introduces us to the second major half of John's Gospel. In the prologue, John gave us the summary of what would become the two main sections of his Gospel: "He came to his own,[1] but his own did not

---

1. The NIV translates this as "he came to that which was his own"; that probably gets

receive him. Yet to all who received him, to those who believed in his name, he gave the right to become children of God . . . " (1:11–12). Chapters 5–12 show how his own people, the Jews, by and large, and with some notable exceptions, did not receive Jesus; with chapter 13, we come to the second major section of the Gospel, as Jesus spends time with those who *did* receive him, and to whom he has given the right to become God's children. It is significant that 13:1 begins by speaking of how Jesus had loved "his own," meaning his disciples: it is as though Jesus has a new people who are constituted as "his own": not the national people of Israel, but the believing fellowship of those who will receive him.

The key thread that runs through this whole discourse is that what has been true of Jesus will be true of his followers after he has returned to the Father. What Jesus leads us into is a continuation of the life that he has lived and the ministry that he has exercised. That theme occurs in a number of ways.

Knowing Jesus' Father

The disciples will have the same kind of *knowledge of the Father* as Jesus has always had (14:7,9); they will know the Father in much the same way as they have known Jesus—that is, the Father will be as personally real to them through the Spirit as Jesus has been to them in his incarnation. There was often amongst God's people in the ancient world, and there can often be today, the idea that God is a remote mystery; the disciples had over the last three years got to know Jesus really well, but God himself is essentially, as Isaiah said, the "God who hides himself" (Isaiah 45:15). There is a vital truth in the mystery and the hiddenness of God, as a balancing corrective to an over-familiar and over-domesticated view of God; but Jesus promises that there will be a direct correlation between the way in which the disciples had known him, and the way in which he would enable them to know the Father. The departure of Jesus will not mean the end of that sense of the immediate presence of God: it will continue, and will be just as real, only in a different way.

The verb "know," as is often rightly pointed out, does not in the Bible refer primarily to "head-knowledge"—knowing that certain things

---

the sense of the words John uses, which is the neuter phrase *ta ídia* = literally "his own things" or "his own possessions." Actually, this phrase could mean a person's "home"; exactly the same expression is used in 19:27 of how John took Mary "into his home"—when Jesus came into the world, he did not come as an alien; rather, he "came home." But in the second phrase, "his own did not receive him," the words are the masculine *hoi ídioi* = "his own *people*," meaning the Jewish people.

are true—but above all to "relationship-knowledge." We English speakers have to make use of the same verb "to know" to express different kinds of "knowledge" for which a number of European languages have quite separate words. In French the verb *savoir*, and in German *wissen*, both mean "to know facts," "to be informed" ("I know that Nairobi is the capital of Kenya"). The French *connaître* and the German *kennen*, on the other hand, mean the personal knowledge of acquaintance, experience or relationship ("I know Nairobi well: I spent the first thirty years of my life there"); and the two words are completely distinct, which is why a Frenchman or German will be puzzled or amused if English speakers use the wrong one. When Jesus says to his disciples, and us, that "If you really knew me, you would know my Father as well. From now on, you do know him . . . ," he means it in the sense of *connaître/kennen*. He is not saying that we can understand in our heads everything that can be known about God; he means that we can live with the same assurance of being in a secure relationship with God as Father as the disciples had known for three years with Jesus as their Master. There is of course a sense in which God's being is a mystery beyond our understanding: as Paul says in Romans 11:33, "Oh, the depth of the riches of the wisdom and knowledge of God! How unsearchable his judgments, and his paths beyond tracing out!" Yet earlier in that same letter (8:15–16) Paul had spoken of the personal assurance of a relationship with God that the Holy Spirit makes real in our hearts: "You received the Spirit of sonship. And by him we cry, '*Abba*, Father.' The Spirit himself testifies with our spirit that we are God's children." To know God means to have an inner assurance that we stand in relationship with God as children with a loving Father. Jesus always had that assurance: his disciples will know it too.

Doing Jesus' Works

The disciples will *do the works* the Son has been doing (14:12), indeed, even greater works. The question is often raised, in what sense can Christians perform "greater" works than Jesus? What could possibly be greater than raising the dead? But this is a misunderstanding, based on our tendency to rate miracles according to their apparent difficulty, and to give them, so to speak, marks out of ten for impressiveness. That is *not* what Jesus is talking about, and not what he is remotely interested in. The frequent answer, that the disciples' works will be "greater" in the sense that they will do more works over a larger area than Jesus accomplished in a few years in one small country, is probably only partly the answer. It is helpful to understand this saying about "greater works" in the light of Jesus' parable of the growing seed in Mark 4:26–29. Jesus, in his own ministry, sowed the seed of the Kingdom. Seed, by definition, is small, but then grows. The Kingdom was inaugurated by Jesus; it is now growing all over the world, and as time goes on, the presence and influence of the Kingdom can and should become more and more evident, leading to the full and final harvest when Jesus returns.

But the key to making sense of Jesus' words about "even greater works" is that the disciples' ministry, including their works, will be Jesus' ministry continued and developed in and through them. Jesus says that the reason the disciples will do "greater works" is "because I am going to the Father." The ascended Jesus will be able to do even more in his heavenly glory than he could in his human incarnation. When musicians, artists or writers die young, it is often said with regret how much more they might have achieved if they had lived longer, but now we will never know: they were cut off in their prime. The disciples might well have thought that the same would be true of Jesus, who was, after all, only thirty-three years old: they had already seen him do remarkable things, but how much more might he have gone on to do if he were able to continue living in the world! Instead of which, he is speaking of the fact that he will leave this world and go to the Father. But Jesus reassures them: far from cutting short his ability to perform great works of the Kingdom, his ascension to the throne of heaven will actually increase it. And the remarkable promise is that the ascended and exalted Christ will do these ongoing and greater works through his disciples.

Sharing Jesus' Life

The disciples will *share in the resurrection life* of Jesus (14:19); because Jesus lives, they too will live. "You also will live" is not simply a prediction of the future resurrection of believers at the end of the age; more immediately, it is a promise that the risen Christ will return to his disciples and will impart to them a share in his own spiritual life. They will not remain as they are; they will be made new, with a different kind of life. The resurrection of Jesus will mean, not only that Jesus will not remain dead, but that his disciples will not remain "ordinary."

Receiving Jesus' Peace

The disciples will live in *the same peace* that Jesus knew (14:27). When Jesus says "Peace I leave with you," the word translated "leave" is the word for a bequest; Jesus is here giving his last will and testament. He will bequeath his own inner quality of peace—the peace of God that passes all understanding—to his disciples. And he stresses that he does not give as the world gives. "Peace" (or *shālôm*) was of course a formal greeting in the Middle East, but those who used it could at best be expressing a hope—we hope that peace may be with you—in much the same way as our English "good-bye" is derived from the pious wish "[May] God [be] 'by' [= with] you"; but when Jesus pronounces his peace over us, he actually deposits it into our lives: we "have" peace with God through our Lord Jesus Christ.

Understanding Jesus' Will

The disciples will also start to have the same *understanding of the Father's will* that Jesus, who said that he never did anything except what the Father told him to do, had all his life (15:15). Jesus says, "I no longer call you servants... instead, I have called you friends." That does not overturn his earlier teaching about the importance of being humble servants, and the New Testament writers invariably stress that they are servants of God; but Jesus is drawing a distinction between one who is merely a slave and is therefore not privy to his master's thinking—he just has to do as he is told, very much in the spirit of Tennyson's "Theirs not to reason why, theirs but to do or die"[2]—and his disciples, to whom God will reveal his heart and, to some degree, his will and purposes. To say we are God's servants does not mean we are mere tools or instruments; what we are called to is not blind obedience, without any awareness of or share in the meaning and purpose of what we are doing, but rather responsible and purposeful partnership with God in the ongoing work of his Kingdom.

Facing Jesus' Enemies

Jesus also challenges his disciples to be prepared for the fact that they will be *treated by the hostile world* in the same was as he was treated (15:18–20). Jesus says that the reason his disciples will face opposition is that "you do not belong to the world... that is why the world hates you." Jesus' disciples belong to a different reality and jurisdiction from that of the secular world: they are citizens of the Kingdom of heaven. And there is an inherent tension between those two realities, which Paul expresses in terms of the opposition between "flesh" (that is, ordinary human nature) and "Spirit" (that is, the new life of God's Kingdom which the Holy Spirit makes it possible for us

---

2. From his poem, *The Charge of the Light Brigade*: often misquoted as "Ours is not to reason why..."

to receive and live); he says in Galatians 5:17 that "the sinful nature [= the flesh] desires what is contrary to the Spirit, and the Spirit what is contrary to the sinful nature. They are in conflict with each other . . . " That we face opposition should not surprise us; there is a fundamental incompatibility between darkness and light, between the world and God's Kingdom. We are told that we must never invite, cause or provoke a hostile reaction—"If it is possible, as far as it depends on you, live at peace with everyone" (Romans 12:18)—but the Christian who can always fit in perfectly comfortably in the world, without any sense of being on different sides, should ask himself how seriously he is living the life of Jesus' Kingdom.

In his earlier Sermon on the Mount Jesus had said that "love your neighbor" did *not* mean " . . . and hate your enemy," and there is a similar contrast here: following on from his instruction that his disciples are to remain in his love (15:10), he points out that the world will hate them. That does not mean that they are to hate the world; after all, God so loved the world that he gave his one and only Son. Disciples are to love those who hate and are hostile to them.

In fact, "love the world" is a potentially ambiguous phrase. God loved the world and sent his Son to save it; and in that spirit Christians are to go to the world with the grace of Jesus, and serve the world with his love. But 1 John 2:15 says, "Do not love the world . . . if anyone loves the world, the love of the Father is not in him." Here "love" means "be devoted to": Christians are not to be committed to the values or lifestyle of the world; they are not to make the things of this world what they most cherish. When a couple gets married, part of their vows often includes the phrase "forsaking all other": that does not mean that no one else in the world will ever mean anything to them again; it means that no one else can ever hold the place in their lives that their new husband or wife holds. In the same way, to love God and not love the world never means that we are to be negative, hostile or indifferent towards the world; it means that nothing in the world can ever hold the place in our lives that belongs to God alone.

Following Jesus' Spirit

The way in which they will be *taught by the Spirit* will be a continuation and a completion of the way in which they have hitherto been taught by Jesus. In 16:13 Jesus says that the Holy Spirit "will tell you what is yet to come." Many commentators assume this is a reference to "last things," to the end of the world. It probably includes that. But I am personally quite sure that the primary reference is to what is about to happen to Jesus, his death on the cross. At this stage, the disciples clearly cannot get hold of what that is all about (13:36, 14:5, 16:17), hence Jesus' words in 16:12, "I have much more to say to you, more than you can now bear." Whilst the Spirit can and does from time to time inspire predictive prophecy in the church, and whilst he will reveal much about the final consummation of God's Kingdom, his primary task will be, in words that I heard the late Lesslie Newbigin use in a talk to probationary pastors in 1989, "to interpret to the church the coming passion of Christ." The Spirit will make clear the true significance of what is about to "come," the death and resurrection of Christ, and will teach the church how to live in the light of them.

The other famous and much quoted phrase in verse 13 is that the Spirit will guide the disciples "into all truth." What Jesus says is literally "into all *the* truth," and the distinction is of some significance. Jesus clearly does not mean that the disciples will know everything that there is to know—they will not become omniscient—but that they will grasp the full truth of Jesus himself, who is (14:6) "*the* truth." At this stage, they may well understand something of who Jesus is—though, as Jesus' response to Philip in 14:9 indicates, not perhaps as much as they could and should—but it is largely theoretical knowledge, doctrinal knowledge. When Jesus has been crucified and raised, and when the Spirit has come, he will make those truths real to the disciples in a new way; they will be enabled to *live in* the truth. That is an important distinction: Christian truth is not just to be believed as doctrine but lived as reality, as the Holy Spirit guides us into what it means to live with Jesus as the Way, the Truth and the Life. Leon Morris is surely right to say that, by "he will lead you into all truth," Jesus means "the whole Christian system . . . the whole Christian way."[3]

One important fulfillment of this promise that the Spirit would lead the disciples into all truth—though I would not claim that this is what Jesus was explicitly or exclusively referring to—is found in the way in which the canon of New Testament Scripture came so quickly and with such remarkable unanimity to be recognized as authoritative. The church as a whole, without any rulings imposed by its leaders, was led to recognize the New Testament writings as God's inspired Word. Once the canon of Scripture was established, it laid down the unchanging parameters of objective truth for the Christian church; and the Spirit was actively instrumental in laying that foundation.[4]

---

3. Morris, *John*, 701.

4. For a simple but very helpful summary of the process by which the canon was formally recognized, I recommend Don Carson's essay *Approaching the Bible*, in his *Collected Writings on Scripture*, 19–37.

Sharing Jesus' Victory

The disciples, finally, will *share in Jesus' victory* over the world (16:33). Although they will "have trouble" in the world, they will not face defeat. Because Jesus has overcome, they will overcome, or, as Paul was later to write, they will be "more than conquerors" (Romans 8:37). The fact that Jesus has overcome the world does not mean that his followers will not face persecution, or that they will always remain unscathed by the world; but the world cannot rob them of their spiritual inheritance, and need never succeed in undermining their faith or their assurance of salvation. The church may lose the occasional battle; but Jesus has already won the war.

Jesus, the Master

In the midst of this teaching about how the life and service of the disciples will through the Holy Spirit continue to be that of Jesus in his years with them, there are in chapters 14–16 of John some specific commands. Until we come to the upper room, none of the teaching in John is about what disciples ought to do; it is all about who Jesus is. But in these three chapters, Jesus tells them to do seven things.

"Do Not Let Your Hearts be Troubled"

The first of these commands may seem puzzling. There are three reasons why it might seem strange that Jesus says "Do not let your hearts be troubled" (14:1,27). First, the disciples have every reason to be troubled: Jesus has spoken about leaving them, about being betrayed by one of them, and about the fact that Peter will deny him. So his words, "Do not let your hearts be troubled," are not a bland and naïvely optimistic denial that there are any grounds for concern, in the way that we might say to someone from whom we feel the need to hide the fact that they are in grave danger, "It's alright, there's nothing to worry about!" Humanly speaking, the disciples *did* have a lot to worry about, and Jesus does not conceal the fact. Yet he says, "Do not let your hearts be troubled." Second, the same word that is used here has in the last few chapters been used three times of Jesus himself being "troubled" in his heart (11:33, 12:27, 13:21): how can Jesus tell his disciples not to do something that he himself has done? But there is a third, more general question that might arise, especially in our age, with our awareness of the psychological and emotional aspects of life: is Jesus telling his disciples not to "feel" troubled? And if so, to what extent can people control what they feel?

Two points about the words Jesus uses may be helpful here. The verb translated "troubled" is the one that was used in 5:4,7 of the superstitious tradition of an angel coming and "stirring up" the waters in the pool at Bethesda.[5] The disciples' emotions are understandably as churned up as those waters; yet Jesus assures his disciples that they do not need to be afraid. But the other important word is "heart": in biblical thinking the heart is not, as in our western way of thinking, primarily the seat of the emotions, but rather the seat of the will. It is with the heart that we make choices and decisions. So we do not need to debate whether or not Jesus is talking about what his disciples should or should not be "feeling"; what he is certainly saying is that whatever grounds they may have, humanly speaking, for feeling dismay, they should not allow this to deter them from continuing to follow and serve him in obedience. Jesus himself had set the example: in John 12:27 he had indeed said, "Now my heart is troubled, and what shall I say? 'Father, save me from this hour'?" Jesus was deeply disturbed at the prospect of what lay ahead of him, as, in a different way, the disciples also had reason to be. But he immediately continues: "No, it was for this very reason I came to this hour. Father, glorify your name!" Whatever his feelings may have been, Jesus chose to follow the will of the Father. The course of his life was determined, not by what he was feeling, but by what he knew to be the will of God; his emotions were as stirred up as the waters at Bethesda, but he did not allow his *heart* to continue to be stirred up—his will, his moral and spiritual decision-making faculties, remained focused on fulfilling the Father's purpose.

In a similar way, he challenges the disciples, though they may feel they have ample grounds for being troubled, not to allow those feelings to influence the decisions they make in their hearts. He is challenging them, as we shall see in a moment, to look to him in faith rather than to focus on their circumstances in fear. When we are troubled, the word of the Lord to us is not so much that we should not feel emotions, but rather that we

---

5. Verse 4—"From time to time an angel of the Lord would come down and stir up the waters. The first one into the pool after each such disturbance would be cured of whatever disease they had"—is almost certainly a later addition in the text of John, to explain the words of the crippled man in verse 7 ("Sir, . . . I have no one to help me into the pool when the water is stirred. While I am trying to get in, someone else goes down ahead of me"), which is why in many editions of the NIV it is quite correctly relegated to a footnote. The Bible is not saying that this idea that an angel stirs the waters is true; it is reporting what was a popularly held belief, but not endorsing it. And this superstition is typical of many religious traditions which reflect a mechanical and impersonal understanding of how spiritual things happen, almost, as it were, by a lottery ("the first one into the pool would be cured"); by contrast, Jesus' own way of ministering to people is always personal and pastoral.

should continue to focus on him despite our emotions, and never think that our emotions are a reason for not being able to trust him. Far from being a strange or even unfeeling command, Jesus' "do not let your hearts be troubled" is a very necessary word to our generation, in which people can frequently use their emotions as an excuse for the wrong choices they make.

"Trust In Me"

That brings us to Jesus' second command: "trust in me"[6] (14:1). The exact sense of the words about faith in God and in Jesus is notoriously ambiguous. The simple verb ("you believe") has in New Testament Greek the same form as the imperative ("believe!"): so is Jesus making one statement and giving one command ("You believe in God; believe also in me")?, or giving two commands ("Believe in God; and also believe in me")?, or making two statements ("You believe in God and you also believe in me")? In a sense it hardly matters, though if pushed I would suggest the first is perhaps the most meaningful; Jesus is saying in effect, I know that you trust in God: you need to have that same kind of trust in me when I say you do not need to be troubled despite what is about to happen. Be that as it may, what is beyond question is that Jesus says the answer to troubled hearts is not easier circumstances but faith. When we do not understand what is happening or seems to be about to happen ("Lord, where are you going?," 13:36; "Lord, why can't I follow you?," 13:37) Jesus says: trust me. If you are confident that I know what I am doing when you can understand it, then be just as confident when you can't; that is what will enable your hearts to remain untroubled.

"Obey My Commands"

Jesus tells his disciples a number of times in these chapters (14:15,21,23) to "obey" him; and he stresses that love and obedience go hand in hand. "If you love me, you will obey what I command." To say that we love Jesus whilst failing to obey his commands shows that our love is at best deficient; the love Jesus is looking for in his followers, and that which he inspires in them, is not an emotional love but an obedient love. If that is a command, it is also a very liberating assurance: it shows that to love Jesus does not mean that we have to try and work up lots of feelings towards him. This can be a real concern for the self-conscious Christian who frequently sees people all

---

6. The verb is of course the simple verb "believe"; the NIV translation rightly points out that such faith is about trusting Jesus personally.

around him in church who are clearly getting deeply involved in and emotionally stirred by their worship, whilst he himself, as he might say, "doesn't feel anything." Jesus' words here are a reassurance: love for me is not about what you feel but about how you live in obedience to my words.

The other side to this marriage of love and obedience is of course the fact that the obedience which we are called to demonstrate is not cold and impersonal—just doing as we're told—but needs to arise out of a will that wants to please Jesus because we love him. So if we ever suspect that our discipleship is becoming a bit routine, the answer is to spend time focusing again on Jesus, who he is and what he has done, and starting a regular practice of thanking and praising him, because the obedience that starts to flow out of that kind of devotion will be much closer to what Jesus asks of his disciples here in the upper room.

"Abide In Me"

The next command of Jesus is to "remain" (traditionally: "abide") in him (15:1–8). The well-known picture of the vine and the branches, and the teaching about bearing fruit for Jesus, stress the basis of all fruitful living and service—that we abide in him. Jesus does not tell us to bear fruit; he tells us to abide in him, and then promises that, as we do, we *will* bear fruit. As well as reflecting regularly and often on the person of Jesus, and consciously seeking to live our lives for him, Jesus mentions a number of specific ways in which we can abide in him. One is to feed continually on his Word: "If you remain in me and my words remain in you . . . " (verse 7); another is to practice regular obedience to Jesus: "If you obey my commands, you will remain in my love" (verse 10); a third is to persist in prayer: "ask whatever you wish" (verse 7).

"Love One Another"

But there is another aspect to abiding in Christ which is mentioned here, and which gives us a fifth command: "love each other as I have loved you" (15:12,17). The New Testament makes it abundantly clear that it is not only impossible but a contradiction in terms to think we can live in the love of Jesus unless we are at the same time living in relationships of love with other Christians. To remain in Christ is not merely a personal challenge but a corporate one. We should never forget that the commands in John 14–16—to trust in Jesus, obey him, abide in him, etc.—are all in the plural; Jesus is not speaking to Peter, James or Philip as individuals, but to his disciples as a group. An individual who chooses to keep himself at a distance from fellowship can no more live a fruitful Christian life than a sports fan can call himself a football player if he kicks a ball against the wall on his own in his back yard. By its very nature Christianity is a team game.

Furthermore, the nature of the love we are to have for one another is spelled out in the much quoted saying, "Greater love has no one than this, that he lay down his life for his friends" (verse 13), which makes specific Jesus' general principle that we love "as I have loved you." The love we are speaking of is love that puts the needs of others first, no matter what it costs us, that seeks to serve their deepest needs, and is willing to sacrifice our own good, our own comfort and convenience, and indeed, should it be necessary, our very lives, to that end. The world might say that is going a bit far; Jesus says it is walking the normal road of discipleship, as part of abiding in him.

"Testify about Me"

Jesus' sixth command is that his disciples must "testify" about him (15:27). After his resurrection he will commission his disciples to go out into the world as his witnesses; here he gives them a reminder that this was his purpose for them from the moment he chose and appointed them. But this call to witness follows on from Jesus' promise that the Holy Spirit will testify about him (verse 26); our witness to Jesus is only made possible because the Spirit himself bears witness in people's hearts to who Jesus is. We can tell people about Jesus, but only the Spirit can convict their hearts that what we share is true and that they need to respond to it in faith.

"Ask Me"

Finally, Jesus challenges his disciples to *pray*, in words that are very similar to a phrase in the Sermon on the Mount in Matthew: "Ask and you will receive" (16:24). Because Jesus is returning to the Father, we will have an advocate with God, one who can present the prayers that we bring in his name.

So although John says relatively little about the requirements of practical discipleship, he does give us, in this upper room discourse of Jesus, a good overview of the elements of the life of disciples: living in the peace of Jesus; trusting him; obeying his words out of a heart of love; remaining in him; loving one another in the fellowship of the church; telling the world about him; and seeking him in prayer.

Jesus, the Giver of the Spirit

Four times in this upper room discourse (14:16, 14:26, 15:26, 16:7) Jesus refers to the Holy Spirit as the "paraclete," translated in the NIV as "counselor." The Greek word *paráklētos* means literally "[one who is] called alongside"; it was sometimes used for a defense counselor or advocate in court, and more generally for someone who stood alongside you to help you. It was translated in the Authorized Version as "comforter," but if that is understood in the modern sense of one who consoles, it does not quite convey the sense of a "paraclete,"[7] though the Holy Spirit does no doubt bring such comfort to those who need it.

In 14:16 Jesus says that he will ask the Father to send "another counselor"; the word translated "another" means "another of the same kind" (as opposed to "other" in the sense of "different"); the Spirit is the same kind of advocate as Jesus has been. In 1 John 2:1 Jesus is called our *paráklētos* with the Father—translated in the NIV as "one who speaks to the Father in our defense"—because he represents us before the throne of God in heaven and pleads our case with the Father; as Hebrews 7:25 says, he always lives to intercede for us. And it is noticeable that all the ministries that in this upper room discourse are attributed to the Holy Spirit are elsewhere in John said to be done by Jesus: the Spirit will be with the disciples (14:16), as Jesus now is (14:25); he is the Spirit of truth (14:17), just as Jesus is the Truth (14:6); he will be in the disciples (14:17), and so, in a sense, will Jesus be (14:20, 15:4); he will teach the disciples (14:26), just as Jesus has been their teacher (7:14, 13:13); he will testify to Jesus (15:26), as did Jesus himself (8:14); he will convict of sin (16:8), just as Jesus does: the same verb that in 16:8 is translated as "convict" is used in 3:20 of how evil men refuse to come to the light of Jesus lest their sin be "exposed."

The Spirit will continue to be to the disciples, and he is to us, all that Jesus had been to the disciples during his three-year ministry, apart from his physical and visible presence. The Spirit can sometimes be thought of in rather vague and mystical terms, but the way that Jesus speaks here is much more practical: he will be to believers a friend, helper and strengthener. We should not perhaps focus too much on the specifically legal image of "advocate," but see the *paráklētos* as our Enabler; that may not be as elegant a

---

7. The English word "comfort" is derived from two Latin words, the intensifying prefix *com* + *fortis*, meaning "strong" (as in "fortify," "fortress," etc.), and so means literally "very strong": as a verb, it means "greatly to strengthen." In that original sense "comforter" is perfectly correct: the Spirit gives us strength; he is our Enabler, our Helper, our Equipper.

phrase as "counselor" or "comforter," but it captures the sense of what the Spirit is sent to do for us.

There are two significant points in Jesus' teaching about the *paráklētos* which are important for our doctrine of the Spirit. First, the Spirit is fully personal. In 14:26 Jesus calls him "the Holy Spirit," and in 15:26 "the Spirit of truth." In Greek, the word for "Spirit" (*pneûma*) is grammatically neuter, so according to the strict rules of grammar the following demonstrative pronouns which refer to him ("*he* will teach you . . . *he* will witness") should be neuter; but in both verses John in fact uses an emphatic masculine word (*ekeînos*) meaning "he." John breaks the rules of grammar in order to stress that the Spirit is not an "it" but a "he"; he is not an impersonal force or power, but the personal presence of God himself with us.[8] And second, the Spirit comes to make Jesus real to us. He will remind the disciples of Jesus (14:26), testify about Jesus (15:26), he will glorify Jesus and make Jesus known to them (16:14). The Spirit never distracts our attention away from Jesus and to himself: he only ever points to Jesus. It is sometimes said of those in the charismatic and Pentecostal tradition that they only ever go on and on about the Spirit. The criticism is perhaps not always fair, and the church as a whole needs to be regularly reminded that to expect the Spirit to be really and fruitfully working amongst us in the ways Jesus describes in John 14–16 should be the Christian norm; but it is true that the sign of someone in whom the Spirit of God is really at work is not that they are forever talking about the Spirit, but that they are focused on Jesus, that they have a deeper and more real appreciation of who Jesus is and what he has done, and that they live to glorify Jesus. It has rightly been said that the Holy Spirit's role is rather like that of effective spotlighting that is often placed round buildings like cathedrals; if the lighting is doing its job, people's attention should not be drawn to the lights: they should just see the cathedral better. The Holy Spirit comes to shine a spotlight on Jesus.

So Jesus, the leader of the new community of the Kingdom, is preparing his disciples for the fact that, when he has returned to heaven, they will not so much have to continue without him, like a business or a sports team whose manager resigns, but rather will be equipped by the Holy Spirit to continue to live and work in relationship with him.

---

8. The personality of the Spirit is also evident from the fact that many passages in the New Testament speak of the Spirit carrying out personal actions: e.g. he speaks (Acts 13:2), knows (1 Corinthians 2:11), makes moral judgments and choices (Acts 15:28), teaches (Luke 12:12), and can be grieved (Ephesians 4:30). Christians do not merely experience the Spirit as a power, but can relate to him as a person.

Jesus, the High Priest

In John 17 Jesus, having taught his disciples, goes on to pray for them. This is often called Jesus' "High Priestly prayer," because it shows us Jesus fulfilling one of the classic functions of a priest, namely to pray for the people. Jesus has, in the upper room, already assured Peter that he had prayed for him (Luke 22:32). Here he prays for all his followers.

As a point of interest, this is the only extended personal prayer of Jesus which is actually recorded in the Gospels. The only others are his brief prayers of thanks in Luke 10:21, and of agony in the Garden of Gethsemane. This prayer therefore gives us a uniquely fascinating insight into how Jesus spoke to the Father in prayer.

Jesus begins by praying for himself (verses 1–5). His prayer is that the Father will be glorified in what is about to happen to him, when he goes to the cross. In John's Gospel, language about Jesus' glory is always focused in his cross. When the time has come for Jesus to go to the cross, he says that the time has come for him to be glorified (12:23). The most "glorious" thing about Christ is not simply his sheer magnificence—unspeakably great though that is—but the way in which he redeems sinners by his own self-sacrifice on the cross. This is at once a paradox—the cross is the opposite of anything that would normally be thought of as "glorious"—and a model for our lives. The way we bring glory to God in the world is by faithfully taking up our cross and following Jesus, denying ourselves and serving the cause of his Kingdom, whatever the cost. Every time we pray or sing with enthusiasm that God would glorify his name through us, it is worth remembering that what we are asking God to do is to enable us to live worthily as suffering servants, to walk the way of the cross; that is above all how God is glorified in the lives of his people. And even in heaven, Jesus is glorified because he is "the Lamb who was slain" (Revelation 5:12); and he appears bearing the marks of his suffering (verse 6). As has been rightly said, the only man-made thing in heaven will be the scars in the hands and feet of Jesus; and they are the signs of his everlasting glory.

Jesus then turns to praying for his disciples (verses 6–19). Amongst much thanksgiving for them, and much of John's typically repetitive language about the inter-relationship between the Son and the Father, and his disciples and himself, he specifically prays for four things for them.

Protection

He prays for *protection* (verses 11,15), as his disciples continue to live in the world; though, as verse 15 points out, the one from whom they particularly need to be protected is the devil. The word translated as "protect" in these verses is simply the verb "keep," but amongst other senses it was used to mean "to guard" or "to keep safe"; it is the word used in Acts 16:23, where the Philippian jailer is told to guard Paul and Silas carefully. Jesus asks God the Father to stand guard over his people.

And he does so "by the power of your name" (verse 11). The phrase recalls verse 6, where, although the NIV translates as "I have revealed you to those whom you gave me," the wording is literally, "I have revealed *your name*." In biblical thinking names are not arbitrary labels but descriptions of character, so for Jesus to say that he has revealed his Father's name means that he has revealed God in his true character; and that in its turn teaches us that "protect them by the power of your name" means that God as he really is in himself watches over us, that he will make all the qualities of his own perfect character available to protect us.

Unity

He prays for *unity* (verses 11,23), that they may be one "as we are one." The church unity or ecumenical movement has rightly stressed that Jesus in this prayer prays for unity amongst all his followers. His phrase "as we are one," that is, as Jesus is one with God the Father, ought to warn us however that such unity cannot be achieved by changing structures or organizing committees; it is not a human or organizational unity, but a unity that comes from having a shared spiritual life. Having said that, the very fact that Jesus prays for unity suggests that he knows that it will not happen automatically. Paul tells us in Ephesians 4:3 to "*keep* the unity of the Spirit"; unity is not ours to create or to build, but it is ours to maintain. It is significant that the verb in verse 11 translated "that they may be one" does not mean "that they may *become* one," but rather "that they may *continue to be* one"; unity is not a future goal but a given fact. However, it must always be maintained: it will not maintain itself.

When we remember that Jesus is speaking in the context of the hostility of the world, from which the disciples will need to be protected, this prayer for unity becomes more focused: Jesus is praying that his people will continue to stand together in love and faith, whatever the world may throw at them. When groups are under pressure, it becomes easy for cracks to show and to start to become real divisions. That can be seen whenever a government party is doing badly in the opinion polls and there are murmurs of discontent in the nation and the media; before long there are likely to be similar murmurs on the back benches, and shortly after that on the front benches as well. Jesus prays that his people will be kept from being similarly divided, but will stand together in the face of opposition or difficulty.

Joy

He prays for *joy* (verse 13); indeed, for "the full measure of my joy." Joy is to be one of the key marks of the Spirit-filled community; and if anyone thinks that such joy is dependent on the absence of trouble, it is good to remember that Jesus spoke about the disciples being filled with "my" joy on the evening before he was to be crucified. In fact there is a remarkable paradox in John's use of this "joy"-language: until the upper room the word "joy" has been used in this Gospel only once, in 3:29, where John the Baptist speaks of his joy that Jesus has now appeared; but in the upper room,[9] where all the focus is on the imminence of the cross and the fact that Jesus will be leaving his disciples, the word occurs seven times (twice in 15:11, 16:20,21,22,24, and 17:13). Joy is the fruit of the atoning work of Christ on the cross. Professor Strachan has a good comment in his commentary on John:[10] "The joy of Jesus is the joy that arises from the sense of a finished work. It is a creative joy, like the joy of the artist. It produces a sense of unexhausted power for fresh creation. This joy in the heart of Jesus is both the joy of victory, and the sense of having brought his church into being."

---

9. By which I mean, in John 13–16. In the last verse of chapter 14 Jesus says, "Come now, let us leave"; some commentators have therefore suggested that Jesus and the disciples left the upper room at that point, and that and that the rest of this discourse from chapter 15 onwards (and the prayer in chapter 17) is given as they are walking towards the Kidron Valley, *en route* to Gethsemane: in fact it is sometimes suggested that the language about the vine and the branches at the beginning of chapter 15 was inspired by the fact that Jesus was walking past trees at the time; that is of course possible, though not necessary—Jesus was more than capable of using metaphors in his teaching without having to be prompted by actually seeing the things he uses as illustrations. The other possibility is that "Come now, let us leave" does not mean that they left the house at that moment, but that Jesus spoke the remaining words from 15:1 onwards as they were preparing to leave. It really does not matter greatly either way, and it is normal to refer to the whole of chapters 13–16 as "the upper room discourse."

10. Strachan, *Fourth Gospel*, 303.

Holiness

Finally, he prays for *holiness* (verse 17); "sanctify them by the truth." The phrase "by the truth" (literally, "in" the truth) does not simply mean that it is in the Bible that believers will be taught how to live a holy life, true though that is. The sense is rather what Jesus had earlier referred to as "*doing* the truth" (3:21; that is the literal translation: the NIV reads "whoever *lives by* the truth"). Disciples are not merely those who believe the truth, but those who "do the truth," who live the whole of their lives in accordance with the norms of God's Kingdom. The contrast in John 17 is with the world—the previous verse says "they are not of the world even as I am not of it"—and part of the significance of that multi-faceted phrase is that disciples of Jesus do not live according to the norms of the world, but according to the truth of God's Kingdom. Jesus prays that the Father will set the disciples apart—which is the literal meaning of "sanctify"—so that they can live *in* the truth, and so might, as we would say in modern English, live *out* the truth.

Having mentioned that Jesus prays for his disciples to be holy in the sense that they will live lives that are very different from the typical life of "the world," it is worth noting that one of the points of interest in the Great High Priestly prayer is to see the ways in which Jesus speaks of the relationship between the disciples and the world, and the different prepositions he uses.

- The Father gave the disciples to Jesus "out of" the world (verse 6): that speaks of God rescuing us from the world of sin. We did not start out by being different from or better than the rest of the world; we were, so to speak, in the same boat as the rest of the world, but God has now rescued us from it.

- Unlike Jesus, they will continue to live "in" the world (verse 11): that is the context in which they are to practice their discipleship. Jesus does not take us out of the world in order to help us to live differently: he gives us his Spirit to help us live differently whilst we are still in the midst of the world. These words clearly suggest that there will always be an element of vulnerability about Christians so long as they are still in this world, which is why Jesus prays for protection for them.

- They are not "of the world" (verse 14): they are no longer part of the secular world-order, they no longer derive their life and their resources from the world; rather they belong to the Kingdom of heaven. Though we live "in" the world, we do not belong "to" it; and that means, amongst other things, that we do not live in the same way that the world—including the respectable secular world, not just the wicked and immoral world—lives.

- Jesus does not ask for them to be taken "out of" the world (verse 15) in the sense of being enabled to live in a kind of spiritual "safe house"— the world is precisely where they are to discover what it means to live for Jesus. We are not merely stranded or abandoned in the world; we are here for a specific purpose.

- He sends them "into" the world (verse 18): that is their mission-field. Just as Christian life begins as God rescued us out of the world and brings us into his Kingdom, so it continues as Jesus sends us back into the world, but with a different life, a different purpose, and a different agenda.

Those four requests are a very helpful model for how we can pray for the church. Jesus does not pray for his church to be financially solvent, or to be enabled to run worthwhile programs, or even to grow in numbers; in the spirit of his earlier word, "Seek first the Kingdom of God and his righteousness, and all the rest will be added to you also," he prays instead for those spiritual qualities that will alone make the church fruitful in his service. And the four things for which he prays reflect four of the clauses in the Lord's Prayer; John does not include Jesus' teaching about the Lord's Prayer, but here in Jesus' great prayer for his disciples he shows us Christ himself practicing for us the same principles that he had taught them should shape how they prayed. The prayer for protection is clearly a parallel to the clause "lead us not into temptation, but deliver us from evil [or: from the Evil One]." The prayer for unity reflects the principle that Jesus adds as a vital corollary to the clause asking for forgiveness, which is traditionally translated as " . . . as we forgive those who trespass against us"; the fellowship of God's forgiven people needs to be marked by mutual grace and acceptance. The prayer for joy is in a similar spirit to the closing doxology of the Lord's Prayer, "for yours is the Kingdom and the power and the glory . . . "[11] And the prayer for holiness with which Jesus ends in John 17 is where he begins in the Lord's Prayer; "hallowed be your name" is not just a statement of worship, but a prayer that God's name might be hallowed—that is, honored as holy—through us and the way in which we live as his people.

---

11. The traditional wording of the doxology, "For yours is the Kingdom . . . ," is not part of the biblical text in most of the earliest manuscripts of Matthew or Luke. But it is entirely consistent with both the content and the spirit of the rest of the prayer; and it would be unthinkable in Jewish circles to end a prayer without a concluding statement of praise, not least because, without the doxology, the last word in the prayer would be "evil," which is not the note on which anyone would want to conclude!

Bearing in mind that Jesus prays this prayer immediately following his time in the upper room with his disciples, there is also a somewhat poignant side to the prayer which can in fact encourage us greatly. The disciples for whom Jesus is praying for these qualities have, in the upper room, displayed exactly the opposite characteristics. He prays for them to be protected from the evil one: but one of his original twelve had, whilst sitting round the table, succumbed to the prompting of the devil to go and betray Jesus (John 13:2,27). He prays for unity for disciples who, just minutes before, had been arguing about which of them was the greatest (Luke 22:24). He prays for joy for disciples who were "filled with grief" (John 16:6) because Jesus had said he would be leaving them. And he prays for sanctification for disciples who, despite their protestations, he knew were about to abandon and deny him.

That is why Jesus' prayer is so encouraging. It is easy, when we read or hear of great prayers for Christians to be holy, empowered by the Spirit, filled with grace and goodness, to see such a level of spirituality as simply beyond us; it would be like praying that a child who after his first piano lesson can just about find middle C on the keyboard will go on to give a performance of Beethoven's *Emperor* concerto that will carry off the first prize at an international piano competition. Jesus is not unrealistic, he has no naïve delusions about his disciples' own spiritual potential; yet this is how he prays for them. What is impossible for man is possible with God. Jesus is praying for things that he knows, despite all the frailties and fallibilities of human nature, are by the grace of God possible for his people.

And that includes us. Because the last part of Jesus' prayer (verses 20–26) goes beyond his present disciples, and embraces all who will come to faith through their message. For them—for us—Jesus prays for the same unity, and for the same vision of his own glory (verse 24). Jesus desires for believers in our generation the same blessings as those for which he prays for his own disciples. To desire and pray for less is not modesty, but limited vision. We may feel that, in our case, Jesus is having to work with extremely raw material; but, leaving aside the question of whether his immediate disciples were any less raw, if Jesus believes that his prayer can be fulfilled in us—and from the fact that he prayed as he did, we have surely to conclude that he does indeed believe that—then who are we to suggest that he was wrong?

8

The Suffering Servant

"The Son of Man is going to be betrayed into the hands of men"
(Matthew 17:22)

We now come to Gethsemane (Matthew 26:36–46//Mark 14:32–42//Luke 22:39–46), and to the betrayal and arrest (Matthew 26:47–56//Mark 14:43–52//Luke 22:47–53//John 18:2–12). In fulfillment of Isaiah's prophecy, Jesus suffers being "despised and rejected" (Isaiah 53:3).

The Garden of Gethsemane

The agony in the Garden, as Jesus wrestles with the knowledge of what is about to happen, torn between his human reluctance to have to face it and his total surrender to obey the Father's will, shows us, perhaps more clearly than any other part of the Gospel story, the true humanity of Jesus. There will be those who, very understandably, are reluctant to ascribe an emotion like fear to the Lord; but to avoid the term by using phrases like "his prayer reveals a natural human shrinking from the awful death that lay ahead of him"[1] seems to come very close to a distinction without a difference. What we can certainly say is that, even if we grant, as the biblical text surely demands, that Jesus was afraid of and appalled by what he would soon be going through, there was no element of sin in his struggle; though tempted in

---

1. Morris, *Luke*, 311.

every way as we are, he was and would remain without sin (Hebrews 4:15). To be afraid of doing what we are called to do for God is not in itself a sin; it is merely to be human. What would happen to Jesus was indeed utterly revolting, so there is no sin in being revolted by it. Jesus' temptation in the Garden was not to feel fear, but to allow that fear to cause him to abandon the path of obedience to the Father; and that temptation he successfully, albeit after a painful struggle, overcame. Those who similarly feel personally overwhelmed by or frightened of what their Christian duty requires of them can take great encouragement from knowing, first, that Jesus knew and fully sympathizes with exactly the same anguish, and second, that there is nothing wrong in feeling such emotions; they do not brand us as failures. There is a line in Samuel Crossman's classic hymn "My song is love unknown" which, I confess, I always found off-putting: "Yet cheerful he to suffering goes." "*Cheerful*?"—that does not seem to come close to reflecting the agony in the Garden. We can surely thank God that we do not follow a Savior who was able to breeze through pain without even letting it affect him, but rather one who entered fully into it, was deeply hurt by it, and can fully identify with the effect it has on suffering humanity today.

It should be said also that what caused Jesus such anguish in the Garden was not simply the fact that he would die, or even that he would die a very painful death. The history of the world is not short of examples of people who have faced death with remarkable courage, calmness and dignity; it would be wrong to think that Jesus is here, in terms of moral courage, falling short of what others, not least many persecuted Christians, have attained: "No servant is greater than his master" (John 15:20). What Jesus was going to face was not simply death; it was the fact that he would carry the sins of the whole world, and would in consequence be separated from the love of the Father, and bear the wrath of the Father; and as Tasker says, "Jesus is filled with anguish and dismay as he becomes fully conscious of the weight of the burden he is carrying as the Sin-bearer of mankind."[2]

The Garden of Gethsemane shows us two important things: first, it is, as much as the cross itself, a vivid reminder of the personal cost to Jesus of being the Savior of the world. Lesslie Newbigin has a very good comment on the contrast between the work of creation, in which God speaks a word and creation springs into being—"And God said, 'Let there be light,' and there was light" (Genesis 1:3)—and the agony in the Garden. "He wrestles in prayer. His sweat falls like great drops of blood. He cries out in agony . . . That is what it cost God to deal with man's sin. To create the heavens and

---

2. Tasker, *Matthew*, 248–249.

the earth costs him no labour, no anguish; to take away the sin of the world costs him his own life-blood."[3]

And second, the Garden of Gethsemane shows us the true nature of commitment to the will of God. Jesus did not find it easy, emotionally, psychologically, or even, dare we say, spiritually, to say "yes" to the Father's will. But he said it anyway. Even from a secular perspective, many would say that courage does not mean not feeling fear, but rather doing what we are required to do despite the fear. The same is true of commitment to the will of God: devotion does not mean that Christian commitment comes easily to us, but that we follow Christ despite how hard it sometimes feels. Again, some believers can lash themselves with quite unnecessary guilt in this area: they see around them examples of Christians who seem to take to Christian lifestyle and service like a duck to water, and assume that, because they themselves struggle even to take the first steps in that direction, they are clearly sinful, fleshly and unworthy disciples. They need to look again at Jesus in the Garden. There is no shame in struggle, or in being tempted to give up. And just as, in the midst of Jesus' appalling internal wrestling-match with the Father's will, "an angel from heaven appeared to him and strengthened him" (Luke 22:43), so we can be very sure that, far from condemning us for feeling the struggle, the Father is only too willing to give us the strength to come through it with our Christian integrity intact.

The key phrase that sums up this commitment to serve the Father, whatever it might cost, is Jesus' words, "Not my will but yours be done" (Luke 22:42), or "Not as I will but as you will" (Matthew 26:39//Mark 14:36). Jesus had said that he only ever did what the Father told him to do (John 5:19, 12:49). Here in the Garden he prays that he will be able to continue to do the same. It can in a sense be easy to say "your will be done" when God's will happens to coincide or at least overlap with our own—though in Jesus' case of course this was no mere coincidence: he had come into the world with the deliberate intention of doing the Father's will—but it is quite another matter when God's will runs counter to our own will or convenience or assumptions about what is best.

But that challenge also leads to another: we must never misconstrue "your will be done" as passive resignation. Jesus is not resignedly submitting to God's will, but actively embracing it. Passive resignation is a characteristic of a number of world religions—the word "Islam" is from the Arabic word for "surrender," and there can often be in both Islam and Hinduism an element of inevitability: whatever God's will might be is what will happen and we simply have to accept it, because there is nothing we can do to change

---

3. Newbigin, *Sin and Salvation*, 32.

it—and indeed in quite secular thinking, as epitomized in the song *que sera sera*.[4] But Christ calls his people, not merely to allow God's will to happen in a passive way, but actively and positively to *choose* to do the will of God. The process of growth in grace and obedience is well expressed in the words from the hymn,[5] "Until with thee I will one will to do or to endure"; in other words, to pray "Your will be done" means "Help me genuinely to want what you want, and then actively and positively to do it."

Jesus' repeated prayer, that the Father might, if possible, "let this cup pass from me," arises from an image that is used about fifteen times by the Old Testament prophets, namely "the cup of God's wrath" (first mentioned in Isaiah 51:17; it is sometimes called, as in Isaiah 51:22, a "cup that makes you stagger"). God's judgment against the sinful nations is portrayed as a cup of intoxicating wine which, when men drink it, makes them stagger and causes them to lose control: it will destroy them. In the passage in Isaiah 51, God is promising his people that the cup of his wrath that they are at present tasting will pass from them to their enemies. In the Garden, Jesus knew that he was called to drink the cup of God's wrath against sin; and on the cross, he drank that cup down to its very dregs. That is why Paul in 1 Corinthians 10:16 refers to the cup that is shared in the Lord's Supper as "the cup of blessing";[6] because Jesus drank the cup of God's wrath, we can drink from the cup of his blessing.

Jesus' pain and struggle in the Garden is compounded by another trial with which, sadly, many Christians can identify: the fact that he was left to face it, humanly speaking, on his own. The disciples, whom he asked to stay and pray with him, fell asleep. How true to life that is! Christian fellowship can be warm, rich and consistent until the time when we really need it; then suddenly it appears that no one is around. Jesus, the suffering Servant, suffers alone; and those who feel isolated in their struggles can take courage from the fact that, although it should not be that way, they are nonetheless following in the Master's footsteps. If we suffer with him, we will reign with him.

---

4. Or "Whatever will be will be"; it was written by Jay Livingston and Ray Evans, and is best known as sung by Doris Day in Alfred Hitchcock's 1956 film *The Man Who Knew Too Much*.

5. "Breathe on me, Breath of God," by Edwin Hatch (1835–89).

6. The NIV translates as "the cup of thanksgiving"; the word means both. We give thanks for the cup; and the cup represents to us the blessings with which we are blessed in Christ.

The Arrest

When we come to the arrest itself, there are a number of details that repay reflection. One is the kiss with which Judas betrayed the Lord. This was an agreed signal to the Jewish religious leaders (Matthew 26:48//Mark 14:44); it seems to suggest that Judas hoped that his role in the betrayal might remain a secret, so he had arranged a covert and apparently innocuous sign, a contemporary equivalent of which might be something like, "The first person I shake hands with when I rejoin the group—he's the one you should arrest." The fact that Judas betrayed Jesus with a kiss of course underlines the sheer awfulness of his treachery; but apart from the human poignancy of it, two other lessons are clear. One is the fact that outward signs of devotion may or may not be indicative of true and positive commitment; tragically, there have probably been in the course of history a number of parallels to Judas' kiss in the performance of outward demonstrations of piety—crossing oneself, genuflections, prayer postures, and in the more recent church hand-raising and enthusiastic clapping—whilst those performing them have in their hearts been set on courses of action which have been tantamount to betraying Jesus. That is not a reason to become cynical about all expressions of piety; it is however a reminder that we always need, as Paul says of our approach to the breaking of bread, to examine ourselves (1 Corinthians 11:28), to be sure that if we in any sense "kiss Jesus," that we do so with our hearts and not just our mouths.

That challenge becomes all the more urgent when we consider the second lesson that arises from the story of Judas' kiss, which is that Jesus clearly knows perfectly well what Judas is doing. Any hope that Judas may have entertained that his role in the arrest might remain a secret is dashed by Jesus' words of reproach to him: "Judas, are you betraying the Son of Man with a kiss?" (Luke 22:48). The Lord welcomes and indeed delights in the expressions of devotion and worship of his people; but he always sees through them to whatever is in our hearts, and it is the state of our hearts that decides whether or not he is pleased with our acts of piety. We should not find that a threat; God is never looking to find fault in a nit-picking way. In a prayer in his book *Thoughts in Solitude*, the Trappist monk Thomas Merton, acknowledging that he does not always know for sure whether or not he is doing the right thing, adds the lovely and encouraging phrase, "But I believe that the desire to please you does in fact please you."[7] Tragically, Judas was not looking to please Jesus. So long as we are, however inadequate

---

7. Merton, *Thoughts in Solitude*, 81.

our expressions of devotion and service, the Lord who sees the heart is pleased.

From the kiss we come to the swords. Jesus emphasizes that, even in a situation of such extreme peril, he will not allow his disciples to resort to the world's ways of attack as the best form of defense: here, swords. His disciples are only too willing to step in with swords to try to prevent the arrest—in all honesty a somewhat futile hope, in view of the large crowd that had come to take Jesus,[8] and indicative of a human principle of "going down fighting," which, although it can have a certain tragic nobility, has nothing in common with the biblical call to stand firm in the face of adversity—but Jesus says that they are to put their swords away (Matthew 26:52// John 18:11). No circumstances, however exceptional, can justify believers using secular tactics and seeking to fight against the evil of the world on the world's terms—and certainly never violent ones.[9] It is interesting, incidentally, that the same Peter who was, perhaps impulsively, prepared to take on an armed crowd including (John 18:3) "a detachment of soldiers" was only hours later too afraid of the consequences to admit before a servant girl that he was a follower of Jesus. It can require more moral and spiritual courage to confess that we believe in Christ as our Savior than to fight physically; but the Holy Spirit can instill such courage into all God's people, whether or not they appear in human terms to be physically tough.

Speaking of the swords brings us to the unfortunate servant of the high priest, whose name, John tells us (18:10), was Malchus. All the Gospels record that one of Jesus' companions—John says that it was Peter—lunged out with his sword and cut off the high priest's servant's ear[10] (Matthew

---

8. A crowd, incidentally, that, although it included, as John 18:3 tells us, some soldiers, was made up primarily of an angry mob stirred up and led by the Jewish religious authorities (Matthew 26:47//Mark 14:43). The so-called arrest of Jesus was more like the work of a lynch mob than a police action.

9. I do not propose here to discuss the thorny question of whether or under what circumstances it is right for Christians to join the armed forces and to take part in armed conflict, a subject on which Christians can legitimately have different views. What I do say is that the cause of the Kingdom of God and of the Gospel of Christ can never be advanced by force. "The weapons we fight with are not the weapons of the world" (2 Corinthians 10:4).

10. Matthew and Luke (in verse 51) both use the word *ōtíon*, which means the outer ear; Mark and John both use the diminutive *ōtárion*. This suggests that the injury was to the flesh of the outer ear, maybe even the lobe, rather than inflicting serious damage to the hearing organ. But Jesus still regards it as unacceptable for his people; it is not enough for Christians to dismiss or justify any level of violence by saying that mere flesh wounds do not really matter. What was wrong in Peter's action is not measured by the amount of injury he inflicted, but lies in the fact that he believed that it was appropriate to meet aggression with aggression.

26:51//Mark 14:47//Luke 22:50//John 18:10). Luke adds the fact that Jesus reached out and healed the man's ear (22:51). This is Jesus' last recorded healing miracle, and the fact that he performs it for one of the crowd that has come to arrest him is a remarkable demonstration of the fact that Jesus' (and our) ministry of love and compassion extends to those who oppose us, even whilst they are in the act of persecuting us. There are a number of stories from the persecuted church, for example in the countries of the former Soviet empire, of Christians imprisoned for their faith who prayed for, served the needs of and led to faith in Christ those who guarded and often tortured them. That is truly a model of God's will, rather than our own, being done.

There is however another way in which this healing of the servant's ear is especially poignant: Jesus' last healing miracle during his time on earth had to be performed in order to repair damage that his own people had inflicted. How often over the last two thousand years has the Lord had to do the same?

The Trial

From the Garden we come to the trial. Jesus is taken before Caiaphas, the Jewish high priest (Matthew 26:57//Mark 14:53//Luke 22:54), and, John says, first for a preliminary hearing before Annas, who was a previous high priest and Caiaphas' father-in-law (John 18:13-14,19-24).[11] Jesus appears before the Sanhedrin, the highest tribunal or council of the Jews[12] (Matthew 26:59-68//Mark 14:55-65//Luke 22:66-71//John 18:19-24), then before Pilate, the Roman governor of Judea (Matthew 27:1-2,11-14//Mark 15:1-5//Luke 23:1-6//John 18:28-38). Luke tells us that he was also seen by Herod (Luke 23:7-12), that is, Herod Antipas, the son of the Herod of the birth story. Pilate attempts to release Jesus, but, under pressure from the crowd, agrees to have him crucified (Matthew 27:15-26//Mark 15:6-15//Luke 23:13-25//John 18:38—19:16).

---

11. The "high priest" referred to in verse 19 is Annas, as verse 24 makes clear; there is some evidence that those who had once served as Jewish high priests, like American presidents, retained the title for life. Moreover, Annas had been deposed from the high priestly office by the Romans, and it may be that some Jews, who did not recognize the right of Rome to decide who was or was not a priest, still regarded Annas as the *real* high priest, whoever may have officially held the title.

12. The Sanhedrin was not simply, as is sometimes assumed, a religious body; it exercised civil, political and criminal jurisdiction as the Jewish "Supreme Court." It was because Israel's religious law was part of its constitution as a nation that it also regulated religious issues.

Jesus was, in effect, tried twice: once by the Jews (by Caiaphas, the high priest, and the Sanhedrin), and once by the Romans (by Pilate, the Roman governor). In John 18:31-32 Pilate tells the Jewish religious leaders to deal with Jesus themselves, but they say that they have no authority to impose the death penalty on their own people. Legally this was correct; the law was sometimes ignored—there had been a number of occasions on which the Jews had threatened to stone Jesus to death (John 8:59, 10:31) and in Acts 7:57-60 they actually kill Stephen by stoning—but although the Sanhedrin could pronounce the death sentence they were officially required to have the sentence ratified and carried out by the Roman governor. The dialogue in John 18:31-32 is significant at a number of levels: first, it makes clear to Pilate for the first time that what the Jews want is to have Jesus killed; up to now he has probably assumed that he is dealing with a minor religious dispute. Second, since the offense with which Jesus was charged was one which would be taken very seriously by the Romans—claiming to be the King of the Jews, which could be taken to mean one who would lead the Jews in opposition to Rome—it was obviously in the Jewish authorities' interests to let the Romans deal with Jesus; and having him crucified by the Romans would be a publicly humiliating end to one whom they had feared might attract a large following, and would cause his supporters to lose heart, as indeed happened to the disciples until they met with the risen Christ. But the main significance for John in the referral of Jesus' case to Pilate is not so much in the question of who was technically responsible for the death but in the manner in which it was imposed: as verse 32 says, "This happened so that the words Jesus had spoken indicating the kind of death he was going to die would be fulfilled." Jesus would not be stoned to death but crucified, which he had alluded to in saying that he would be "lifted up" (John 3:14, 8:28, 12:32) and had explicitly predicted in Matthew 20:19. If we ask why the manner of his death is important to Jesus, and to John in writing his Gospel, it is because of the principle given in Deuteronomy 21:22, that anyone who is put to death "and his body is hung on a tree" is under the curse of God.[13] In dying as he did for our sins, Jesus suffered the curse of God against sin; "Christ redeemed us from the curse of the law by becoming a curse for us" (Galatians 3:13). Caiaphas pressed for crucifixion because it was a humiliating and scandalous way to die; but in the purposes of God, it was not the physical barbarity nor the social disgrace of the cross that was

---

13. In the Old Testament criminals were not executed by being impaled "on a tree"; they were stoned to death, and the dead body was then often hung on a tree as a warning to others. It is on the basis of this verse in Deuteronomy that the cross is sometimes referred to as a "tree," both in the New Testament (Acts 5:30, 10:39, 13:29, 1 Peter 2:24) and in the history of Christian devotional language and hymnology.

the most significant, but the spiritual curse: Jesus, who had come into the world to bring us one blessing after another (John 1:16) himself became a curse, and so, in the wonderful phrase in Nehemiah 13:2, he "turned the curse into a blessing."

So the Jewish leaders send Jesus to the Roman authorities for sentencing when they decide that he deserves death. There is no doubt that the whole proceeding was illegal. The trial broke lots of rules of proper procedure. Under Jewish law the death sentence was not allowed to be pronounced until the day after the defendant had been convicted—but the Sanhedrin pronounce the sentence immediately on hearing Jesus' claim to be the Messiah (Matthew 26:64–66//Mark 14:62–64). A Roman court was not allowed to sit after dark on a capital charge—Jesus was tried in the middle of the night. It was established beyond doubt that the testimony of those who spoke against Jesus was wrong and that they contradicted each other (Mark 14:56), so Jesus should have been released—instead of which, he was sent to the Romans for sentencing. Pilate admitted that he could find no grounds to condemn Jesus (Luke 23:13–16), and the specific charge against Jesus that is mentioned in Luke 23:2, that Jesus opposed the payment of taxes to Caesar, is in blatant contradiction to what Jesus had explicitly said (in front of witnesses) to the very Pharisees and religious leaders who bring this accusation (Matthew 22:15–21); but Pilate still had him condemned to death. Just as Jesus in the Garden identified with those who struggle with the challenges of their calling, so in the courtroom he identifies with those who are the victims of corrupt justice.

In the trial before the Jewish council, the charge against Jesus was that he claimed to be the Messiah, the Son of God: in other words, blasphemy. In the trial before the Romans, it was that he claimed to be the King of the Jews: in other words, treason. Jesus, the Messiah—the King and Priest—was tried by a human priest and a human king (or at least, the governing representative of the king), and found guilty of claiming to be Priest and King.

It is significant that Jesus said nothing in his own defense. He fulfilled the prophecy of Isaiah 53:7 and was as silent before his accusers as a lamb before its shearers. 1 Peter 2:23 sees this as a model of how we should not retaliate if we are accused wrongly, but just commit ourselves to God. The only thing Jesus said in answer to the accusations made against him was that he admitted that he was the Son of God (Matthew 26:63–64//Mark 14:61–62). In 1 Timothy 6:13 Paul refers to the "good confession" that Jesus made before Pilate as a model of how Christians are to confess Jesus before the world; in the light of the way in which Jesus spoke at his trial only to confirm that he was indeed the Son of God, the lesson is that Christians should not get drawn into a tit-for-tat debate, and certainly not into self-justification or self-defense, but should simply affirm who Jesus is.

Apart from confirming that he is indeed the Son of God, Jesus is recorded by John as adding to his response in the affirmative to Pilate's question whether he is a king the comment, "For this I came into the world, to testify to the truth," which elicits from Pilate his famous retort "What is truth?" (John 18:37-38). It would be misleading to think that Pilate's question indicates any serious interest in the question of spiritual truth. The tone of his response—after which he immediately went out, suggesting that he was not sufficiently interested in his own question to wait long enough to hear if Jesus might have an answer to it—is much more probably to be understood as dismissive: "Truth?!—what are you talking to *me* about 'truth' for?" To a man like Pilate, living only in the world of *Realpolitik*, spiritual truth, or, as he would no doubt put it, "religion," is abstract and theoretical; as Tasker says, "[Pilate] is not of such a company [that is, of those who are of the truth and hear Jesus' voice]. He is satisfied with the imperfect and pragmatic judgments of earthly rulers, and he would equate belief in spiritual power with superstition. By asking *what is truth?*, he shows himself to be not *of the truth*."[14] The modern western world has more in common with Pilate that it might like to imagine; many people are not particularly interested in the question whether or not Christianity is *true*, but merely whether it would be helpful to them or might improve their lives. Pilate was probably concerned only with questions of power, control and—to judge from his willingness to please the crowd even though he thought they were wrong—popularity (or, as we would say today, his "image"); his dismissive question about truth suggests that he believed that, for someone in his position, truth was a luxury that he could not afford. But Jesus knows not only that truth matters, but that, far from being abstract and theoretical, it is the only thing that can ever set people free (John 8:32) and make them holy (17:17). The Christian church needs to avoid the temptation to try and "sell" Christian faith by appealing to the things the world values; we offer to the world Jesus who is the truth and the Gospel that is the truth. Oliver Barclay said that "the Christian faith is to be believed primarily because it happens to be true. We do not believe because it is comforting, increases psychological health or international peace, or seems to us attractive and pleasant for any other reason."[15] Of course having faith will in many ways improve our lives, but it can do so only because it is *true*; we always need to be aware of the danger of offering faith as a means to another desirable end rather than

---

14. Tasker, *John*, 202.
15. Barclay, O., *Reasons for Faith*, 7.

as truth in itself. The fact that the world may sometimes, in the spirit of Pilate, say "Don't talk to me about what you say is 'true'!" should not deflect us from telling people the truth about Jesus. And the example of Pilate is an obvious warning to all Christians: faced with a choice between doing what he felt was right (releasing Jesus) and pleasing the crowd, he chose to please the crowd. It is a sobering reflection that, because of that lack of moral backbone, his name is forever commemorated in the clause in the creed, "crucified under Pontius Pilate"; it would be better to have been completely forgotten than to be remembered in that way. Pilate is a terrible example of the man who chooses expediency rather than truth, doing what will make him, if not exactly popular, at least less unpopular, rather than what is right.

The Suffering

Before the crucifixion itself, two other things happen to Jesus following the trial. One is that he is flogged (Matthew 27:26//Mark 15:15//John 19:1). This appears to have been part of Pilate's plan to get away without having to have Jesus crucified; he seems to have hoped that, once the Jewish religious leaders saw that Jesus had been severely beaten, they would be satisfied. It is not easy to know quite how to assess Pilate's behavior: on the one hand, he clearly and repeatedly affirms that Jesus is innocent (Matthew 27:23//Mark 15:14//Luke 23:22, Luke 23:4//John 18:38, Luke 23:14, John 19:4, 19:6), and seems to want to set him free (Matthew 27:17–18//Mark 15:9–10, Luke 23:16,20,22, John 19:12). On the other hand it is hard to see any moral virtue in that desire, in view of the fact that his way of seeking to achieve it is to have Jesus severely flogged, and then, when he sees that he is not going to persuade the Jewish leaders to let him release Jesus, he capitulates and hands him over to them with a pathetic attempt to save face by pleading that he is not responsible for Jesus' death (Matthew 27:24). It is likely that his reluctance to co-operate with the Jewish leaders was not the result of any positive sense of sympathy with Jesus, but arose from his well-documented hatred of the Jews, and his desire to insult and oppose them at every opportunity.[16] Pilate's dilemma seems to have had less to do with seeking to arrive at a just

---

16. When the emperor Tiberias appointed him governor of Judea in AD 26, his first action was to do what no previous governor had done and send soldiers into Jerusalem bearing standards with images of the emperor, a move which, in the holy city of Jerusalem, could not but cause deep offense. On another occasion he took money from the temple in Jerusalem to pay for the building of a new aqueduct, and when this led to protests and demonstrations in Jerusalem, he ordered his soldiers to beat the crowds into submission. Luke 13:1 alludes in passing to a time when he had had some Galilean Jews killed as they were offering sacrifices at the temple.

verdict in Jesus' case and more with being torn between being on the one hand loath to be seen to be supportive of the despised Jews and on the other desperate to avoid anything that might damage his reputation in the eyes of the emperor; John 19:12 tells us that what finally caused him to make up his mind and have Jesus executed was the hint from the Jews that to be seen to sympathize with Jesus would make him "no friend of Caesar." In the face of that possibility any vestiges of moral qualms he might have had about condemning an innocent man disappeared.

But whatever may have been Pilate's motivation, the fact that Jesus suffered a terrible flogging—an ordeal which was known to be sufficient in itself to kill some prisoners—shows us another way in which Jesus identifies fully with suffering humanity. The victim of physical abuse or torture can find in Jesus a Savior who is, as Isaiah 53:3 puts it, "familiar with" his particular experience of suffering, one who stood where he stands. The second-century BC Roman playwright Terence said, "I am a man; I consider nothing that is human alien to me";[17] that is even more wonderfully true of the man Christ Jesus, who endured all that belongs to our humanity, and in particular the worst results of the sinfulness of fallen humanity. The physical flogging he endured was part of that.

But alongside the physical there is also the psychological: Jesus is not only flogged but also mocked. This is part of what had been prophesied about Christ, that he would be "*despised* and rejected" (Isaiah 53:3). The soldiers' treatment of Jesus included public humiliation ("they spit in his face," Matthew 26:67) and physical abuse (they "took the staff and struck him on the head again and again," Matthew 27:30); but it also included spiritual mockery: having blindfolded Jesus, they hit him repeatedly whilst taunting him, "Prophesy to us, Christ. Who hit you?" (Matthew 26:67-68//Luke 22:64): in other words, "So, you say you are a prophet?—alright then, show us how good a prophet you are! Tell us which one of us it was who hit you!" And they not only poked fun at his prophethood, but also at his kingship: they dressed him in a purple robe—probably a discarded and quite likely faded soldier's mantle,—put a crown of thorns on his head, a reed in his hand as a parody of a scepter, and indulged in some horse-play, bowing down to him with exaggerated exclamations of "Hail, King of the Jews!" (Matthew 27:28-30//Mark 15:16-19//John 19:2-3).

In our own day we are only too used to seeing or hearing Jesus made the butt of comedians' jokes, and his person and status parodied and travestied, and Christians have often responded to such appalling blasphemies by protests, demonstrations and denunciations of those responsible; that

---

17. *PDQ*, 392.

notoriously happened on the release in 1978 of the Monty Python film *The Life of Brian*, with consequences which, despite the undoubtedly genuine and righteous intentions of the outraged protesters, reflected very little credit on the cause of Christ,[18] and it has happened many times since. To those who would insist that we cannot simply remain silent in the face of such a terrible abuse of the Lord, it is perhaps worth pointing out that Jesus did: he uttered not one word of complaint or moral protest about the way he was treated. Our missionary task is not to defend Jesus against those who would insult him—he will vindicate himself in his own time—but to win sinners to faith, and to start by disapproving of the fact that they are sinners will not make that any easier.

In saying that, I have no desire to minimize the dreadfulness and the sheer evil of the mockery; and of course we find it deeply troubling and offensive to see our Savior abused. But to protest about it does not seem to me to be in the spirit of the New Testament. Why should we be surprised that the unbelieving world does not hold Jesus in reverence? Our task is to share the truth of who Jesus is, and to help people to repent and believe in him, rather than to be deeply offended about the fact that they do not at this stage believe. When cynics are converted to Christ, they will revere him; denouncing them for not revering him before they are converted will not contribute positively to their coming to salvation. The fact that Jesus is mocked and parodied in our society—that the tradition of at least speaking of him with respect has largely died out—is no doubt a sign of appalling spiritual decline, but it shows that we live in the same kind of society as that of the first century, where the same happened; we should remember the remarkable impact that the Gospel had in that society, and that the same Gospel can do the same again in our own irreverent culture.

The reassurance for the Christian is that all the mockery in the world will not prevent the Kingdom from coming. The soldiers may have parodied Jesus' Kingship; but one day they will see it in its reality. And we should never forget that at least one of the soldiers—the centurion who stood at the cross—came to realize who Jesus was when he saw him die (Matthew 27:54//Mark 15:39//Luke 23:47). As we proclaim Christ crucified, the cross can do its own work of convicting those who have previously despised and rejected him.

Everything that Jesus went through from his arrest onwards shows him going through the worst things that can happen to people in the world. His

---

18. Some irate Christians made the classic mistake of publicly denouncing the content of the film, whilst having to admit when asked that they had not seen it, which hardly lent their objections credibility.

suffering was holistic. He suffered *physically*—that is obvious and scarcely needs further comment. He suffered *socially*: he was the victim of an unfair trial and was wrongly condemned. All the people and institutions that he should have been able to rely on abandoned him one by one. His own friends let him down and deserted him. The law let him down and wrongly condemned him. The "church" (the official Jewish religion) let him down and plotted against him. The common people let him down—the people whom he had served and healed cried "Crucify him!" He suffered *emotionally*, both in the humiliation of the mockery he underwent, and in the sense of complete isolation on the cross. He suffered *psychologically*: the pain in his body was compounded by the pain in his soul, as expressed in what is usually called the "cry of dereliction," "My God, my God, why . . . ?" Most mysteriously of all, he suffered *spiritually*; having been abandoned by every other person and agency that could and should have been there to support him, he was finally abandoned by God himself—at the end Jesus had to cry out, "My God, my God, why have you forsaken me?!" (Mark 15:34)—and he dies bearing the pain and the punishment of the sins of the world.

The fact that Jesus' suffering was holistic gives us the reassurance that his salvation is also holistic, that he can bring renewal and grace to every part of our lives, physically, emotionally, socially, psychologically, spiritually. The whole of Jesus' life was sacrificed to save the whole of our lives.

Jesus identified fully with the suffering of humanity; he has been through the worst that can happen to people, including feeling forsaken by God. That is why he can help us now when we go through the struggles and injustices of life. The German poet Friedrich Hölderlin wrote a poem called *The Song of Fate*, the first two stanzas of which depict the blessed and comfortable life of "the gods" up in heaven: "You walk around up there in the light on soft ground . . . glistening divine breezes gently touch you like the fingers of a harpist stroking sacred strings . . . the heavenly ones, untouched by fate, breathe like sleeping infants . . . " The third stanza then turns to the state of things in the human world: "Suffering people plummet headlong from hour to hour, hurled like water from precipice to precipice down through the years into uncertainty."[19] Though most people would not express it quite so poetically—and it sounds much better in the original German—an idea not far removed from that is in many minds: it is all very well for God, living up in heaven where everything is nice and trouble-free; but we are down here suffering what Hamlet called "the slings and arrows of outrageous fortune." What does God know about what we have to put up with?

---

19. My translation. I have aimed at fairly literal accuracy rather than lyrical quality!

The answer is, everything, because he has been through it. Whatever cruelty, injustice or pain the world may throw at us, it has thrown at the Son of God himself. Jesus is the one who at the end of the ages will return to judge the world; here, he is judged by the world. Contrary to what many people seem to think, God does not have to answer to us; we will answer to him. Yet even if he did have to answer to us, he could do it; God the Son himself has suffered the worst of the consequences of living in a fallen and sinful world—including even the experience of feeling totally abandoned by God himself—whilst himself having contributed absolutely nothing to its fallenness and sinfulness. Such a one is more than fully qualified to be both our Savior and our Judge.

9

The Crucified Savior

"There they crucified him" (Luke 23:33)

And so we come at last to the account of the crucifixion and death (Matthew 27:32–50//Mark 15:21–37//Luke 23:26–46//John 19:16–30). Before we come to the significance of the cross, there are two small points of factual detail which can usefully be clarified.

- In traditional devotional language the place of Jesus' crucifixion is often called "Calvary"; that word is found only in the Authorized Version's translation of Luke 23:33, and the only other Bible translation known to me that uses it is the (not very common) *New Life Version*: all others, including all the best known and most widely used translations, read simply "the [place of the] Skull" (Matthew 27:33// Mark 15:22//Luke 23:33//John 19:17). The Greek word so translated is *kraníon*, the normal word for "skull," from which we get our English word "cranium"; and "Calvary" was an English version of the Latin word for "skull," *calvaria*. All the Gospels apart from Luke give the Aramaic name *gûlgûltâ* ("Golgotha": the Greek spelling of the name dropped the second "l"), meaning "skull"; the most likely reason for the name is that it was a regular place of execution, or possibly that it was a hill shaped somewhat like a skull.

- There has been over the years some quite unnecessary dispute about the actual form or shape of the cross on which Jesus died, and some groups have argued vehemently against the traditional image and language of a "cross." It is true that the Greek New Testament word for "cross," *staurós*, originally meant simply an upright stake, and came to be used for any kind of wooden structure on which a criminal was executed. The Romans used a variety of forms of "cross": the simplest was an upright post, on which the criminal was tied or impaled; another was in the form of a capital T; a third was literally cross-shaped, like an X; and another was in the form which very early came to be associated with the Lord's death, †. The only clue in the text of the Gospels that might suggest it was this fourth "cross" shape on which Christ died is the reference to the charge against him being nailed "above his head" (Matthew 27:37), which would imply the top part above the cross-piece. But when all is said and done, the actual shape of the cross is irrelevant—what matters is the fact that Christ died for our sins—and I see no reason to object to the traditional word "cross," which is as accurate a translation of *staurós* as any; those who argue that the conventional † is probably not the form of cross on which Christ died often seem to do so, not out of any interest in historical accuracy, but simply out of a desire to dissociate themselves from the historical tradition of the church.

In the Catholic tradition of the church, the approach to the passion story often focuses on the contemplation of and meditation on the actual physical suffering of Jesus, as depicted in the "stations of the cross," the stages in the story of Jesus' suffering culminating in the death itself, and recently very graphically in Mel Gibson's remarkable film *The Passion of the Christ*. In the Bible, by contrast, the crucifixion narratives do not stress particularly the physical agony of Jesus. It is not ignored or passed over, but it is not dwelt on at great length, partly perhaps because the Gospel writers did not need to; it is significant that the tradition of emphasizing the sheer goriness of the death started to develop only after the practice of crucifixion had been abandoned. But the Gospels' emphasis is on other things.

For example, they emphasize *other aspects of the suffering*, including the injustice of his trial; Jesus' being rejected and abandoned by his friends; his isolation; ultimately, his being cut off from the love of God (Matthew 27:46//Mark 15:34). Maurice Gaugel says, "It is not without significance that the earliest account of the Passion has not attempted (as it would have been easy to do) to emphasize the physical torture which Jesus endured, while it has retained so accurate and precise a recollection of his spiritual agony."[1] Jesus suffered in many ways, physically, mentally, personally,

---

1. Gaugel, *Life of Jesus*, 541.

emotionally and spiritually; and just as the saving grace that he offers to us is holistic—he brings newness of life to minds, bodies, emotions, souls and in fact to whole people—so the atoning agony that he went through to make that grace available was "holistic"; the whole of the person of Jesus suffered to redeem the whole of my person.

They also emphasize the fact that *Jesus was affirmed to be innocent*, by Pilate (Matthew 27:23//Mark 15:14//Luke 23:4), the centurion (Luke 23:47), and by the dying criminal on the next cross (Luke 23:41). Just as a lamb offered as a sacrifice under the Old Testament law had to be spotless and without blemish in order to be acceptable to God, so the Lamb of God, if he is to take away the sins of the world, must himself be morally and spiritually without blemish. His judge, his executioner and his fellow-prisoner affirm him to be that.

Apart from the obvious roles of the Jewish leaders in betraying Jesus and the Romans in carrying out the execution, the Bible narratives indicate in one particular symbolic way *the powers that rejected and condemned him*. The charge against him ("The King of the Jews") was posted above his head in Aramaic, Latin and Greek (John 19:20). Aramaic, a dialect related to Hebrew, was the language of (Jewish) religion; Latin was the language of politics and diplomacy; Greek was the language of culture and philosophy. This world's religion, politics and culture all combined to condemn Jesus.

There have been many attempts over the last two thousand years to incorporate Christianity into the political and cultural life of Western Europe. Just focusing for now on the "Greek" aspect of his condemnation, that of culture, there is a long-standing tradition in western art of depicting the person of Christ, especially in painting—there is scarcely a major artist of the last five hundred years who has not painted pictures of Christ, from Leonardo da Vinci and Titian to El Greco and Salvadore Dali—and music, ranging from the great passions of J. S. Bach to the *Seven Last Words from the Cross* by contemporary Scottish composer James Macmillan. Speaking as a music lover, I would never want the world to be without Bach's *St John Passion* or Handel's *Messiah*, and there is no doubt that those works, as well as many others, were expressions of deeply-held faith and devotion on the part of their composers, and that they can glorify the Lord. But there is a real danger that Jesus comes to be seen as one of the themes of western art and culture, rather than as he is, the eternal Son of God, who is sovereign over all. The fact that religion, politics and culture were all involved in nailing Jesus to the cross must warn us against the dangers of thinking of Christianity as subsumed under the general heading of "cultural life," in the way that the teaching of what used to be known as "R.E." is in some schools now treated as part of the general area of "humanities." Cultural Christianity may entertain and edify people artistically, but it cannot save them from sin; for that, we all need to lay aside any political agendas, philosophical positions or artistic tastes and preferences, and come simply to Christ crucified, as revealed in the Bible.

Some people might think that, when Pilate wrote "the King of the Jews" above Jesus, he was saying something positive—that he was endorsing Jesus. It is far more likely that he wanted to humiliate and intimidate the Jews. That is why he refused to amend the wording of his charge (John 19:21–22): to say that Jesus *claimed* to be king would be an insult to Jesus, implying that he had delusions of grandeur; but to label him as king would be to say to the Jews: "This is *your* king—and look at what I can do to him!" Pilate is warning the Jews not to set themselves up as any kind of authority in opposition to Rome; this is what will happen to them if they do. This reminds us that being a Christian is a humbling thing—even in one sense a humiliating thing. We identify ourselves with a publicly disgraced Jesus; as Paul says in Galatians 6:14, "May I never boast except in the cross of our Lord Jesus Christ." There can be a tendency in our own day to water down the shame of the cross, by presenting all the aspects of Jesus that everyone will admire and approve of. And it is unfortunate that people's concept of the cross can be shaped more by attractive jewelry and ornate and artistic gold crosses in churches than by the historical reality of the crucifixion. Even if crucifixion is not seen as the social shame that it was in Jesus' day, we must never forget that all the things that the cross is about—sin and judgment, rejection, saying "no" to the world and "yes" to God's Kingdom, whatever it costs us in terms of popularity or social advance—are still things that are the cost of salvation; they are the reason that the apostle Paul spoke of the "stumbling block" (or "scandal," or "offense") of the cross (1 Corinthians 1:23, Galatians 5:11); and they are what we are saying we will willingly and uncomplainingly accept every time sing, in the words of the old hymn, "Beneath the cross of Jesus I fain would take my stand."[2]

There is no doubt about the medical reality of the death; Mark 15:44–45 points out that Pilate specifically asked the centurion to confirm a second time that Jesus really was dead. In John 19:32–35 John typically uses language that is heavy with symbolic meaning. What he records when he describes the flow of blood and water from the side of Jesus is a physical fact, and is in the light of current medical knowledge (not available to John) evidence that Jesus had actually died. Dr Samuel Houghton of Dublin University has written, with regard to the physical causes of Jesus' death,

---

2. By Elizabeth Clephane (1830–69). The old-fashioned word "fain" means "gladly" or "willingly."

"A copious flow of blood, succeeded by a copious flow of water ... would occur in a crucified person who had died upon the cross from rupture of the heart."[3] But for John, the words are almost certainly intended to convey more than that. The phrase in verse 30, that Jesus "gave up his spirit," is literally, "he breathed out spirit." That of course means that he died—he "breathed his last." But, in keeping with John's regular use of simple words with spiritual meanings, it carries the underlying sense that from the death of Jesus comes the gift of new life through the Spirit. There is a flow of blood; the blood which cleanses us from all sin, and atones for our guilt. And there is also a flow of water; we are purified and washed because Jesus died.[4]

The Seven Last Words

Much has been made, rightly, of the famous series of the "seven last words from the cross"; they have been celebrated in music, most notably by Haydn, and have frequently been taken as the basis for a series of sermons. Between them, they give us an all-round summary of the work of the cross and its effects for us. I am here listing the seven words in the order in which they are usually assumed, from hints in the Gospels, to have occurred,[5] except that I am treating "Father, into your hands I commit my spirit" as the sixth, and "It is finished!" as the seventh and last word: Luke records "Father, into your hands ... ," and John "It is finished!," and each says that "When he had said this ... "/"With that ... ," Jesus died (Luke 23:46, John 19:30). And it is after all the content and significance of the words that are important, not their precise order.

The Word of Pardon

"Father, forgive them, for they do not know what they are doing" (Luke 23:34). The cross makes available to us the forgiveness of God. Jesus' words "for they do not know what they are doing" do not mean that there could

---

3. Quoted in McDowell, *New Evidence*, 224–225.

4. Commentators who hold a more sacramental theology often see in the flow of blood and water a picture of the two great sacraments: water as a sign of baptism, and blood as central to Holy Communion with its focus on the blood of Christ. That seems to me a classic case of making the symbol more important than the reality symbolized: what happened at the cross is not a sign of the sacraments; rather, baptism and the Lord's Supper are signs of the central reality of the death of Christ on the cross, which alone secures our salvation.

5. See, e.g., *NBD*, 1083–4, and Hendriksen, *John*, 433.

have been no forgiveness for his executioners if they *had* known what they were doing: the blood of Christ can purify us from *all* sin (1 John 1:7). The Old Testament laws of atoning sacrifices covered only unintentional sins; under the old covenant, there was no forgiveness for persistent deliberate and willful sin, so when John says that the blood of Jesus cleanses from "*all* sin," he is saying that the death of Jesus achieves far more than any Old Testament sacrifice ever could. That point is made repeatedly in the letter to the Hebrews:

> "The former regulation [that is, the Old Testament priestly laws] is set aside because it was weak and useless (for the law made nothing perfect), and a better hope is introduced . . . " (7:18–19); " . . . the gifts and sacrifices being offered [in the Old Testament temple] were not able to clear [literally: to make perfect] the conscience of the worshiper. They are only a matter of food and drink and various ceremonial washings [and] external regulations . . . " (9:9–10); "Day after day every priest . . . offers the same sacrifices, which can never take away sins. But when [Jesus] had offered for all time one sacrifice for sins, he sat down at the right hand of God . . . , because by one sacrifice he has made perfect forever those who are being made holy" (10:11–14).

The death of Jesus can bring complete forgiveness for sins that could never be forgiven under the regulations of the old covenant.

That does not mean that forgiveness is now automatic or universal. The same letter to the Hebrews makes it clear that those who continue to oppose the truth, who persist in sin and refuse to repent, or who, having professed faith, then turn away from Christ and consistently refuse to return to him, can face only judgment and the wrath of God (10:26–27). But the cross of Christ can achieve what the Old Testament sacrificial laws could never achieve—as Paul says in Acts 13:39, "Through him [that is, Jesus] everyone who believes is justified from everything you could not be justified from by the law of Moses,"—namely that all sins, including deliberate, repeated or heinous sins, can be forgiven on the basis of faith in the blood of Jesus, if people repent of them.

So Jesus' words, "they do not know what they are doing" do not mean that only unwitting sins can be forgiven: all sins can, through repentance and faith. But also, it is very important to understand that the fact that those putting Jesus to death did not fully understand what they were doing, or, more precisely, to whom they were doing it, does not mean that it is any less a sin needing forgiveness. Ignorance is not an excuse for sin; nor is it the grounds for forgiveness. All people, including Jesus' murderers, can be forgiven because Christ shed his blood, not because of any plea that "I didn't know what I was doing!"; and in fact, even assuming that the plea is true, the moral blindness that it implies is part of the very fallenness from which Jesus redeems us. What the cross makes freely available is the forgiveness of God, not the opportunity to plead mitigating circumstances.

The Word of Promise

The second word is a firm promise: "Today you will be with me in Paradise" (Luke 23:43). All who turn to Jesus will live eternally with him. "Paradise" has come to be a vague word which most people assume means more or less the same as heaven. It is derived from a Persian word meaning a walled garden or a beautiful park. When the Old Testament was translated into Greek, the Greek version of the word, *parádeisos*, was used for the "Garden" of Eden in Genesis 2 and 3. In later Jewish thinking it had come to be used in two particular ways that developed in the period between the Testaments. Because of its use to refer to the Garden of Eden, it came to be seen as a word for the state of original blessedness before the fall—from that later developed also the idea that such a state of blessedness and peace would be restored when the Messiah came. And second, it came to be used for the state of blessing into which the souls of the righteous enter at death. That is clearly the background to Jesus' words here to the criminal. What Jesus is referring to here is not "heaven"—that is, the eternal life in the new heavens and the new earth, in a resurrection body—but to the fact that those who are saved will, immediately after death, live spiritually with the Lord. As Paul says in Philippians 1:23, "I desire to depart and be with Christ, which is better by far."

The word "today" is seen as a problem by many people, as it seems to run counter to the teaching of Peter that, after death, Jesus went to the place of death, to Hades;[6] 1 Peter 3:18–20 say that he went and preached to "the spirits in prison," which is usually assumed to mean the departed spirits

---

6. *Hádēs* is the Greek name for the "underworld," or the world of the dead; it is more or less the equivalent in Greek thinking of the Jewish understanding of *sheôl*, which is mentioned many times in the Old Testament. It does *not* mean "hell," the place of final punishment for the unredeemed, and in fact it is thought of less as a place than as a *state*: the state or fact of being dead. It is always described as a bleak, colorless, hopeless existence; and it came to be seen as the "waiting-room of hell," the state of existence after death of those whose final destination would be condemnation and exclusion from God's heaven. The word is used ten times in the New Testament, and with one exception (Luke 16:23) it does not mean "hell," but death, the fact and the power of death.

of those from the Old Testament era who had died and were in Hades. If Hades may be regarded as the waiting room of hell, then paradise is the waiting room of heaven. So if Jesus went to Hades, it is often asked, how can he promise the criminal that he will be "with me in paradise"? In fact this need not be a serious problem. First, we do not really understand exactly what happened after Jesus' death, which by its very nature must be for us a profound mystery; we are told, and we therefore accept, that he went and ministered to the souls in prison. But that does not mean that he was not also with the righteous departed in paradise; we need to be very wary of saying dogmatically what Jesus in his spirit after death could or could not do. If Jesus could say to this man that he would experience being with Jesus in paradise, then we can be sure that he would experience being with Jesus in paradise. In any case, Jesus is not speaking this word in order to teach us all about *he* will do in the period between his death and resurrection—he is making *this man* a promise about what will happen to *him*, that he will be with Jesus in paradise.

Furthermore, Jesus' words are a response to the man's request in verse 42, "Jesus, remember me when you come into your Kingdom." It is fascinating that Jesus, as well as granting the spirit of the man's request, both endorses what he says and gently corrects it. The criminal's plea to Jesus clearly assumes that whatever "salvation" or blessing he might hope for after death, he will not experience it until the end of history, when the final consummation of God's Kingdom takes place. But Jesus says, in effect, I can do more for you than that. Yes, you will be part of that final Kingdom, when I return in glory to raise the dead and to bring about the new heavens and the new earth. But you don't actually have to wait till then; even before that, you will experience my blessing and my peace after death. "Today"—from the moment you die physically—you will be with me in spirit in paradise.

That is a word for all of us who believe in Jesus. The resurrection body and the new heavens and the new earth are still some time in the future—how far, we do not know. But from the moment we die, we will be conscious of being in paradise, in the immediate presence of the Lord. Whatever we may not fully understand about the nature of paradise, or its relation to what we conventionally call "heaven," we can at least be confident of two things: that it means being with Jesus; and that it will be, as Paul said in Philippians 1:23, "better by far."

It is worth pondering the question, what was it in the words and the attitude of the repentant criminal that led Jesus to make this remarkable promise? There are three aspects of what he says that represent the basic ingredients of faith: first, he recognized his own sin and that he deserved judgment ("We are punished justly, for we are getting what our deeds deserve," verse 41); second, he recognized the righteousness of Jesus (" . . . but this man has done nothing wrong," verse 41); and third, he appealed to Jesus for help ("Jesus, remember me when you come into your Kingdom," verse 42). This account clearly shows that the Lord finds that an adequate faith to which he can respond with the promise of salvation.

But although it is an adequate faith, it would be misleading to regard it as a normative faith. On the basis of this story of the penitent criminal, we can be assured that "deathbed conversions" can be a true basis for eternal salvation; but to treat it as demonstrating that such things as baptism ("After all, the penitent thief wasn't baptized!") or commitment to devoted discipleship are unnecessary or "optional extras" is a hideous distortion of Scripture. For those who turn to Christ immediately before death, the penitent criminal's profession of conversion is indeed a valid model; but for those who continue to live as believers in this world for many years it is an inadequate model: other things are called for if we are to respond to Jesus' call to follow him in a holistic way. That does not detract from the greatness of the promise Jesus made; but it affirms that the assurance of a place in his heavenly Kingdom is normally the foundation on which a life of ongoing discipleship can and should be built.

The Word of Provision

"Dear woman, here is your son . . . here is your mother" (John 19:26–27). Mary will not be left alone, but will be provided for by John. The cross provides for our needs, especially for new, secure relationships, both with God and with fellow-believers in the church. Because of the cross, the believer is never alone. Jesus had told his disciples (Mark 10:29–30) that none of those who give up worldly security for the sake of following him "will fail to receive a hundred times as much in this present age: homes, brothers, sisters, mothers, children . . . ," and he is almost certainly referring to the fellowship of the church. Even if your human family disowns you because of your allegiance to Christ, you will always have your church family. Family language is used a great deal about the church in the New Testament, not just in specific references to the church as the "family" (or "household") of God, such as Galatians 6:10, Ephesians 2:19, 1 Timothy 3:15 and 1 Peter 4:17, but also in the numerous references—about 230 times in the New Testament—to fellow-Christians as "brothers."[7] And lest anyone feel that the church might be a poor substitute for one's own flesh and blood—though

---

7. Modern Bible translations, including more recent editions of the NIV, often translate this, quite properly, as "brothers and sisters."

it is something of an indictment of the church if it is—it is worth reflecting for a moment on the question why Jesus entrusted his mother to John, who was not a blood relative; after all, Mary and Joseph had other younger sons, and the responsibility for looking after Mary should surely have fallen to them.[8] But Jesus wants to commend Mary into the care of the believing family rather than the blood-related family; and at this stage his own brothers were not, so far as we know, believers. He does not regard the fellowship of the disciples as a second-best or makeshift family, to be put up with if we don't have the real thing. To Jesus, Christian fellowship *is* the real thing. It is the church's responsibility to be so open to the grace that flows from the cross that we become precisely that.

The Word of Punishment

"My God, my God, why have you forsaken me?" (Matthew 27:46//Mark 15:34). On the cross, Jesus is suffering the punishment that sin brings, of being cut off from God, on our behalf. Of all the seven last words, this one presents us with what is probably the most profound mystery; here, more than anywhere else, we have the sense that we are treading on holy ground. How can God be abandoned by God? How is it possible for the Son of God, the one who is in very nature God, to be cut off from God? With this word, even more than the others, there is a limit to how much we can hope to understand with our minds. This much we can however say: the penalty for sin, the very essence of hell, is separation from God; Isaiah had already said "Your iniquities have separated you from your God" (Isaiah 59:2), and Paul speaks of eternal punishment in terms of being "shut out from the presence of the Lord" (2 Thessalonians 1:9). On the cross, Jesus experienced, not merely physical pain and death, but the spiritual punishment of hell itself: not the place, but the experience of being separated from God. It is worth noting that this separation from the presence of God is just one of the ways in which Jesus, on the cross, experienced what is said in the New Testament to be the state of existence in hell. Hell is often referred to as a place of utter darkness (Matthew 8:12, 22:13, 25:30); and there was darkness over the land whilst Jesus was on the cross (Matthew 27:45//Mark 15:33). In Jesus' parable of the rich man and Lazarus, the rich man, as he is tormented in Hades,

---

8. From the fact that Joseph is not mentioned after the incident with the twelve-year-old Jesus at the temple in Luke 2, that whenever Mary appears in Jesus' adult ministry she is on her own, and that Jesus here takes responsibility to ensure that his mother is provided for, it is to be assumed that Joseph had died at some point before Jesus began his public ministry.

cries out for a drop of water to cool his tongue because of his agony in the fire (Luke 16:24); on the cross, Jesus cried out "I thirst."

On the cross Jesus drank the cup of God's wrath, so that we might not have to. Our society has coined a phrase to describe anyone who has been through any time of hardship and pain, that they "have been to hell and back." Whilst never wanting to minimize or make light of anyone's suffering, such language can only trivialize our understanding of what hell really is; but in Jesus crucified we have one who truly has on our behalf "been to hell"—and who has also come back to share his salvation with us.

The Word of Pain

Jesus' next word, "I am thirsty" (John 19:28), reveals the depths of his sufferings for us; he enters fully into our human experience of pain and deprivation. There is of course a remarkable paradox here: the one who gives the water of life, which a man may drink and never thirst again (John 4:14), must himself become thirsty in order to make that living water available. "Though he was rich, yet for your sakes he became poor, so that you through his poverty might become rich" (2 Corinthians 8:9). The fact that Jesus' pain was real gives us the assurance that his redemption is also real.

The Word of Peace

"Father, into your hands I commit my spirit" (Luke 23:46). Jesus is able to entrust his life to the Father, and surrender completely to his will. These words were used as part of Jewish evening prayer; a Jewish child might well be taught to pray them every night on going to bed. For us, because of the cross, death can be as peaceful as going to bed at night.

This word is taken from Psalm 31:5. The other word from the cross which is based on the Psalms is from Psalm 22:1; one is a cry of anguish ("My God, my God, why . . . ?"), the other is a calm expression of faith ("Father, into your hands . . . "). The cross models the whole of Christian life; sometimes we find ourselves saying "My God, why . . . ?," at other times we can say "Father, into your hands . . . " There is a mystery in this—but both are real. In Acts 12, we read that James was beheaded, but Peter was miraculously rescued from prison. Why?—we don't know! Sometimes it can seem that God allows us to go through anguish ("My God, my God, why . . . ?!"); at other times, there is the deepest of peace in the darkest of circumstances ("Father, into your hands . . . "). Jesus went through both. And we might be going through the darkest suffering, but we can still know that our spirit is in our Father's hands.

The Word of Payment

And so we come to the last great word from the cross: "It is finished" (John 19:30). There are many "famous last words": they range from the merely well-known (Nelson's "Kiss me, Hardy"), to the amusing (Viscount Palmerston, "Die, my dear doctor?; why, that's the last thing I shall do!"), to the poignant (Edith Cavell, "Patriotism is not enough"). But these words of Jesus are the greatest "last words" in the world. "It is finished" is in the Greek New Testament just one word; it is the word that would be stamped across a bill that was fully paid. The same verb is used twice in that way in the New Testament, both to do with paying taxes: in Matthew 17:24, "the collectors of the two-drachma tax came to Peter and asked, 'Doesn't your teacher *pay* the temple tax?,'" and in Romans 13:6 Paul writes, "This is also why you *pay* taxes, for the authorities are God's servants . . . " Jesus cries out from the cross, "Paid!" This is the word of full and final payment. The debt of our sins is not ignored, or swept aside—nor is it simply canceled—it is paid by Jesus in his death.

In the light of that wonderful Gospel truth, there is a remarkable irony in the very next verse, John 19:31—"It was the day of Preparation." The day on which Jesus died was the day of preparation for a great religious festival to symbolize a salvation that Jesus has just won and paid for fully. There are sadly many people in today's religious society who in a similar way are working to prepare for something that has already been perfectly fulfilled; trying hard, by good works and religious rituals, to accomplish something about which Jesus has already cried out "It is accomplished!"; hoping to be able to do enough to pay for their acceptance in heaven, although Jesus has already exclaimed "It is paid for in full!"

It is not just what Jesus said, it is also how he said it. Matthew (27:50) and Mark (15:37), although they do not record the words, do mention that Jesus cried out one more time, and they both say it was "in a loud voice,"[9] like a great shout of triumph: "I've done it!" "I've paid for all sin once and for all!" This is a cry, not of defeat or despair, but of victory. "Finished" does not mean "done for" ("I've had it!") but "completed," "accomplished," "consummated," "perfected." It is not a moan of defeat, nor a sigh of resignation; it is

---

9. Mark 15:34 is translated in the NIV as "with a loud cry," but the phrase this translates does not mean "cry" in the sense of "lament"; in fact Mark uses the same phrase as Matthew, namely *phōnē megálē* ("[in a] loud voice").

a cry of triumph, as Jesus recognizes that he has now fully accomplished the work that he came to do. Jesus' last word from the cross is a cry of victory. In Britain, one of the best known sporting quotations must be the words spoken by Kenneth Wolstenholm in the closing seconds of his commentary on the 1966 World Cup final: "They think it's all over . . . it is now!" In a similar way Jesus cries out from the cross, "They think *I'm* finished with— but I'm telling you that *it*—sin, death, hell—*it* is now!" All that Jesus had come into the world to do is done; all that needed to be achieved for sin to be atoned for and the Kingdom of heaven opened to all believers has been achieved. "Mission accomplished!" Human work and achievement is never in that way complete; every political leader leaves office knowing how much more remains to be done that was not done: Cecil Rhodes' last words were, "So little done, so much to do." But Jesus has perfectly fulfilled his mission, his life's work: salvation is achieved forever. It is finished.

Signs at the Cross

The first three Gospel writers all stress the darkness over the land for three hours (Matthew 27:45//Mark 15:33//Luke 23:44–45)—from the sixth hour to the ninth hour means, in our terms, from mid-day to 3.00 p.m. I take the darkness to be a historical fact, and that it is to be understood as a supernatural miracle, rather than merely some anomalous meteorological phenomenon, such as an eclipse or a sirocco wind. Luke 23:45 adds the phrase "for the sun *stopped shining*," and the verb used is the Greek verb *ekleípō*, which gives us our English word "eclipse"; but Luke obviously does not mean that the sun was "eclipsed" in the normal astronomical sense: this occurred at Passover time, when the moon was full, making a solar eclipse impossible. *Ekleípō* was often used in a general, non-technical way, just as "eclipse" is in English, and in the two other places where it occurs in Luke it is used in a metaphorical sense, of money running out ("when it *is gone*," 16:9) and of Jesus' praying that Peter's faith will not "fail" (22:32). Some ancient writers and historians are said to have alluded to the fact of a strange and unaccountable darkness around the time of the crucifixion: Tertullian (*c.* 160–*c.* 225), writing to people in the Roman empire, says of the darkness at noonday over the cross that this miracle "is related in your own annals and preserved in your archives to this day";[10] and both Origen (*c.* 185–*c.* 254) and Julius Africanus (*c.* 160–*c.* 240) refer to a statement by the historian Phlegon (born *c.* 80 AD) mentioning that "during the time

---

10. Quoted in Hendriksen, *Matthew*, 970.

of Tiberias Caesar an eclipse of the sun occurred during the full moon."[11] But the lessons we can learn from the darkness do not depend on whether these secondary references, interesting though they are, can be proved to be reliable; they arise from the fact that the Bible records that God caused darkness to cover the land.

This darkness is obviously deeply significant, in a number of ways. It symbolizes the terrible evil that was going on, as men crucified the Son of God. It represents the darkness of God's judgment on sin and evil, which was being visited on the person of Jesus. It reminds us of the darkness before creation (Genesis 1:2): at the cross, God is about to bring about the beginning of a new creation. It recalls the darkness before the exodus (Exodus 10:21–23); the last of the plagues on Egypt was a plague of darkness over the land, and was immediately followed by the death of the firstborn and the Israelites' leaving Egypt. In the same way, this darkness over the cross was immediately followed by the death of God's "firstborn," and led to freedom for all who are in the slavery of sin. Finally, the Bible says that, before the great Day of the Lord, the appearance of the sun will be turned to darkness (e.g. Joel 2:31). The darkness of the cross is a foreshadowing of that final darkness; what is happening at the cross is a pre-figuring of the Last Day, when God will come to judge all the earth.

Matthew records the supernatural signs that occurred at the moment Jesus died: the curtain in the temple was torn in two, there was an earthquake, and some of the people of God who had died were raised to life (Matthew 27:51–52); Mark and Luke also record the curtain being torn in two. These phenomena symbolize the effects and achievements of Jesus' death. The curtain separated off the Most Holy Place in the temple, where no one could go except the High Priest once a year. It represented the fact that sinful men are excluded from the presence of a holy God. When Jesus died, that curtain was torn open—the way into God's presence is now open, we can approach him without fear or restraint (Hebrews 10:19–20). And, significantly, the curtain was torn "from top to bottom"—from God's end, so to speak. This work of opening the way into God's presence is not man's work, but God's. The death of Jesus brings forgiveness and access to God.

The earthquake shows that the death of Jesus will, ultimately, affect the whole created order; God will shake the whole cosmos before the final establishment of the new heavens and the new earth (Haggai 2:6). Jesus' cross will bring about a new creation. And the "small-scale" resurrection of some of the Old Testament saints prefigures the final resurrection of all

---

11. McDowell, *New Evidence*, 123.

God's people, which Jesus' death has made possible. The death of Jesus will bring resurrection to eternal life.

The centurion at the cross declares that Jesus is "the Son of God" (Mark 15:39). In the context of Mark's Gospel, this verse is very significant. Jesus is called "the Son of God" four times in Mark. Once is in the opening verse, as part of Mark's heading to his book. In 1:11 and 9:7 the voice of the Father is heard speaking from heaven, saying that Jesus is his Son. But here in 15:39 is the first time that Jesus is declared to be the Son of God by another human being. And it is significant that it takes place at the cross. The wording of this verse is very important: "When the centurion . . . heard his cry and saw how he died, he said, 'Surely this man was the Son of God.'" It is only when we see the cross of Jesus that we can make sense of who he is. We don't understand Jesus until we see the cross.[12]

The Stumbling-block of the Cross

As we have said, the apostle Paul described the message of the cross as an offense or a stumbling-block—literally, a "scandal"—to many (1 Corinthians 1:23); and in our own day it has become offensive and the object of attack and disdain for one particular reason. The cross is often rejected, and those who make it the focus of their faith are despised, because of its barbarous cruelty; and, it is claimed, a God who can be satisfied only by such a vile and inhuman sacrifice is not a worthy object of worship.

We could, I suppose, point out the irony that an age which has produced weapons of mass destruction and widespread ethnic cleansing, and which seems quite prepared to allow multiple acts of murder and torture to be seen in graphic detail in films on general release, should take moral exception to one historical case of execution. Be that as it may, the objection, though in a sense understandable, misses the point of the message of the cross, in at least three ways.

---

12. In Luke 23:47 the centurion is recorded as saying, "Surely this was a righteous man." But the difference from Matthew's and Mark's wording ("This was the Son of God") is in fact not very significant. First, Luke precedes the words by saying that "The centurion . . . praised God and said . . . ": what is said about Jesus is described as a declaration of praise to God. Second, whether or not the words the centurion actually spoke were a combination of Matthew//Mark's and Luke's recorded sayings, or whether the words of Matthew//Mark and/or Luke are paraphrases of the original statement, the spirit of what is being affirmed is the same, bearing in mind that the speaker was not a Jew and did not share the understanding of God that the Gospel writers had. Plummer paraphrases Luke's saying as, "He was a good man, and quite right in calling God his Father." (Plummer, *Luke*, 539.)

1. It fails to recognize the importance of the Trinity. The one who suffered on the cross is himself God the eternal Son. God is not removed from the horrors of the cross; the God whose wrath is satisfied at the cross is not an impassive onlooker watching an innocent third party suffer. God himself comes into our world in the incarnation of Jesus, and himself suffers on the cross; he is, in the striking phrase which forms the title of a book by Jürgen Moltmann, *The Crucified God*. God is not remote from the suffering of the cross; he is personally enduring it. Such suffering undoubtedly happens in our world: it shouldn't, but it does. In Christ, God himself has entered into the suffering of our world, and himself stands with those who are on the receiving end of its cruelty.

2. It fails to recognize the fact of human responsibility. Crucifixion is a work of man. It was the Jews who betrayed Jesus and the Romans who killed him; and it would be naïve in the extreme to assume that our own age would have treated him any better. The cross is the most striking instance of what is often called "man's inhumanity to man." The barbarism of the cross is the barbarism of people who can treat a man—any man, let alone the Son of God—in such a way.

    It is a grotesque travesty of the message of the cross to suggest that God approves of or takes any pleasure in the suffering inflicted by people on other people, including the suffering inflicted on Jesus at the cross. However necessary it was to have sin atoned for, the cruelty of the cross is man's cruelty; it does not mean that God is cruel. At the end of Charles Dickens' *A Tale of Two Cities* Sydney Carton allows himself to be executed in the place of the French aristocrat Charles Darnay; his famous last words begin, "It is a far, far better thing that I do than I have ever done." He was right; but to call his execution "a far, far better thing" is not to approve of the guillotine or to deny the evil of what happened following the French Revolution. It was Carton's willing self-sacrifice to save another that was "far better," not the manner in which the revolutionaries inflicted death on him. The same is true of Jesus' crucifixion.

3. It fails to recognize the seriousness of sin. One of the things that the Christian is called to accept by faith is that the atoning work of the cross was necessary. If sin were a less extreme need, then a less extreme way of dealing with it might have sufficed. One of the worst effects of sin is that it blinds us to the very seriousness of sin, just as some forms of addiction can so weaken their victim's will-power and his ability to make proper choices that they can blind the addict to the

very seriousness of what he is doing to himself and rob him of the will to do anything to repair the damage. Extreme cases call for extreme remedies; and we need to trust that if God thinks that the death of his Son was the extreme remedy that was necessary if our sins were to be forgiven—and he clearly does—then he is right; and if we do not see exactly how right he is, that is our failure to understand the seriousness of sin, rather than a valid criticism of the extreme remedy applied.

The Burial

Jesus was buried in a tomb belonging to "Joseph of Arimathea, a prominent member of the [Jewish religious] council" (Mark 15:43). Joseph is described in the Gospels as a rich man (Matthew 27:57), a good and upright man (Luke 23:50), one who was looking for the Kingdom of God (Mark 15:43, Luke 15:51), and a secret disciple of Jesus (John 19:38).[13] That Jesus was buried in the tomb of a wealthy man has always been understood, in my view rightly, as a fulfillment of the prophecy of Isaiah 53:9 that the suffering servant would be buried with "the rich," though none of the Gospels actually mention this Scripture in the account of the burial.

John's account of the burial includes one point of interest: that Joseph was assisted in the preparation of the body for burial by Nicodemus, "the man who earlier had visited Jesus at night" (19:39). Both Joseph and Nicodemus were secret disciples of Jesus; but now that Jesus has died, and there is therefore (they would assume) no further advantage to be gained from being known as his followers, they both come out of the closet and openly profess their allegiance to Jesus. This contrasts significantly with Jesus' "official" disciples who, when the crowd came to arrest him, all ran away. We should perhaps not be too hard on the disciples, given the frightening and bewildering circumstances, and after Pentecost they all proved their worth as bold witnesses for the Lord; but it is interesting, and reflects our experience today, that the cross, which can cause some who would profess religious allegiance to disappear shamefacedly into the background, can also challenge others to renewed and more public commitment.

---

13. Many additional stories and legends have grown up around the figure of Joseph, including that he traveled to Britain and became the first keeper of the so-called Holy Grail (the cup which, according to Arthurian legend, was used by Christ at the Last Supper). What we know about him is summarized above; and, as with the Wise Men at the beginning of Jesus' story, we need to distinguish biblical fact from legendary accretions.

The suggestion is sometimes made that the Gospels simply give us the story of the cross; the theological significance of it is found in the letters, especially of Paul. Of course the Gospels are above all a narrative, whilst the letters focus on doctrine; but it is not true that the Gospels contain no theological message about the cross, and it is emphatically not true that Paul in his letters has foisted onto the straightforward narrative a theology that does not arise from the story itself. Jesus had spoken about his forthcoming death in terms of giving "his life as a ransom for many" (Mark 10:45), and the word "ransom" is a word full of theological significance, being connected with the verb "to redeem": a ransom is a redemption-price. At the Last Supper, Jesus said that his death would bring about "the new covenant in my blood" (Luke 22:20), blood which is "poured out for many for the forgiveness of sins" (Matthew 26:28). John, as we have seen, speaks in typically symbolic language of the water that poured from the ruptured side of Jesus; in the light of the frequent use throughout his Gospel of "water" as a metaphor for the gift of new spiritual life, it is impossible to deny that John is not only narrating an event but also communicating a theology. To drive a wedge between the story of the cross and the Christian Gospel of its significance and achievement is to separate what God has joined. All four Gospels spell out what Paul summarized in 1 Corinthians 15:3, that "Christ died for our sins," a Gospel that is a historical story ("Christ died") with a spiritual significance ("for our sins"). To keep the story but deny, ignore or downplay its redemptive significance is as meaningless as to hold on to the theology of redemption but to forget that it was only made possible by the fact that Jesus died. If we want to find a proper summary of the fact and the significance of the cross, apart from the words of the Bible itself, we are not likely ever to improve on Cecil Frances Alexander's lines, "He died that we might be forgiven, he died to make us good; that we might go at last to heaven, saved by his precious blood."

10

The Risen Christ

"He is not here; he has risen" (Matthew 28:6)

The last week of Jesus' ministry, leading up to the cross, as we have seen, shows Jesus fulfilling all the roles that the expected Messiah had to fulfill; and it is important for the Christian, if he or she is to live an all-round Christian life, to respond to Jesus as King, Judge, teacher, Lord, prophet, Lamb of God, suffering Servant, leader, High Priest and Savior. Christians can often use phrases like "Jesus is everything to me!" That is a wonderful confession; but it is to be hoped that it means, not just "I love him with all my heart," but also "Everything that Jesus is, all the roles that he fulfills, I want him to be for me in my own life"; in other words, that it is not only a subjective devotional statement about our response to Jesus, but an objective doctrinal statement about who Jesus *is*.

But there is one more vital thing that Jesus is. The Gospel story does not end at the cross, but with an empty tomb, a risen conqueror and a living Lord.

Cross and Resurrection

The question is sometimes asked, which is more important, more central to Christian life and faith: the cross or the resurrection? It is frankly an absurd question; one might as well ask which wing of a plane is more important to its flying. Clearly, without both wings the plane is never even going to get off the ground, much less take anyone anywhere. Sadly, there are some within the tradition of the church who do not seem to have understood with equal clarity that unless our faith is focused in Jesus who died for our sins *and* rose again for our justification (Romans 4:25), our faith will never take off and our lives will not be going anywhere. The heart of our faith is and must always be, as the liturgical exclamation has it, that "Christ has died, Christ is risen, Christ will come again!" The return of our Lord in the future is indeed a vital part of core Christian faith; but as we look at the final chapters of the Gospels (Matthew 28, Mark 16, Luke 24, John 20–21), it is with the cross and resurrection that we are mainly concerned; and we start with a confusion that can sometimes be found about the relationship between the two.

We sometimes hear Christians talk as though the cross is the bad news, and the resurrection is the story of how God turned defeat into victory and brought about an unexpected happy ending after all. That is *not* how the New Testament handles the story of the cross. The resurrection does not undo or reverse the defeat of the cross; it publicizes the victory of the cross. Paul said that he gloried in the cross (Galatians 6:14), not in the fact that the resurrection had obliterated the horror of the cross; the message about Christ crucified is not, as it may seem to "those who are perishing," about weakness which was (thankfully!) overcome by the power of the resurrection, but rather is itself "the power of God" (1 Corinthians 1:18).

The cross is the place of victory; it was there that Jesus, by his blood, triumphed over sin, death and the devil. If we think of the cross in terms of defeat later redeemed by the resurrection, we miss the whole glorious paradox of the Gospel; the cross itself, with all its apparent—and of course, in a sense, actual—squalor and weakness, is nonetheless the place of redemption, the triumph of salvation over sin, of good over evil, of God over the devil. The message of Christ crucified and risen is not a message of "bad news—good news." The cross is good news, the fact that Christ died for our sins is good news; which is why the church was in fact showing biblical wisdom when it called the anniversary of the day on which Jesus died "Good" Friday.

Evangelicals can sometimes be accused of appearing unmoved by the sufferings of Jesus; whilst those in the Catholic tradition of the church tend to respond to the passion of our Lord in a spirit of profound meditation on the pain and agony of Jesus, and a desire to weep with his suffering, evangelicals, it is said, focus solely on the positive achievements of the cross, on redemption, forgiveness and the finished work of salvation; so whilst a Catholic will weep because Jesus died, an evangelical will shout "Hallelujah!" because Jesus died. Of course this is a gross over-simplification:

the evangelical tradition affords many outstanding examples of devotional meditation on the cross, not least in its tradition of hymn-writing, perhaps most famously represented in Isaac Watts' "When I survey the wondrous cross," but continuing into our own day by many of the best-known contemporary worship leaders, like Graham Kendrick and Stuart Townend; and we all need to face with a sense of sobriety and penitence the fact that it was our sins that made the cross necessary. But there is no doubt that the New Testament as a whole does not lament the awfulness of the cross, but rather proclaims the triumph of the cross. All the songs that celebrate the victory and achievement of the cross, from centuries-old classics like "In the cross of Christ I glory" or "It is a thing most wonderful" through to the best of contemporary evangelical worship, are not ignoring or making light of the suffering of Christ, and must never be sung as though they were; but they stand fully in the tradition of positive and grateful affirmation of the finished work of Christ that springs from the New Testament itself.

So what of the resurrection? If the cross is not the bad news that is turned into good news by the resurrection, what is the distinctive message of the fact that Christ rose on the third day?

The first thing we need to say is that the resurrection is affirmed in the Gospels, and is accepted by Christians, as just as much a physical fact of history as the cross. The Gospel records go out of their way to emphasize the physical reality of the risen Christ. In Luke 24:36–43 the disciples thought at first that they were seeing some kind of ghost; Jesus invites them to touch him, and, when even that does not seem to convince them, eats a piece of fish in their presence. In John 20 Thomas, having declared that he would not believe that Christ could be risen unless he saw with his own eyes the wounds in his hands and side, is confronted by the Lord, who invites him to "reach out your hand and put it into my side" (verse 27); and in the next chapter, Jesus is found cooking breakfast for his disciples on the beach, and eating with them (21:9–15). The pseudo-theological view that the resurrection is a metaphor ("in some sense the life of Jesus continues with us through his teaching") or a symbolic way of saying that Jesus, although dead, was alive spiritually in heaven, or understands it as a subjective psychological experience of the disciples ("they 'felt' as though Jesus was still with them, which encouraged them") is just as much an expression of downright unbelief as the skepticism that simply regards it as fictitious nonsense. A physical cross followed by a metaphorical resurrection would be the most terrible of anti-climaxes, unworthy even of a second-rate storyteller, let alone the living God.

This is perhaps the place to make explicit a principle that underlies everything in this book: that the Bible is the objective and normative statement of Christian truth. Some people will say that the reason why they believe as they do that Jesus rose from the dead is on the subjective grounds that they have personally experienced the reality of Jesus' new life affecting them, in other words, that Jesus is personally alive in their experience, or, as the popular evangelical phrase has it, that "he lives in my heart." It is true that real Christian faith always means a life-changing relationship with the risen Lord, but that personal experience, precious though it is, cannot in itself be the grounds of our assurance of the truth; if truth is defined by what I experience, what status does that truth have in the face of those who say they have had no such experience?; or, for that matter, in those times when we ourselves are less conscious of Jesus' risen presence with us, when we do not "feel" that he is there?

We believe that Jesus rose from the dead because the Bible says he did. Jesus himself said, "Your Word is truth" (John 17:17). For the Christian believer, truth is defined by what the text of the Bible itself says, not by whatever subjective gloss or "spin" this or that reader may want to put on what the Bible says. In our day we can seriously abuse the notion of "interpretation" to mean that truth is defined by what I choose to think of what the Bible says, rather than by what it actually says. By all the normal criteria of literary judgment, the text of Scripture is quite clearly describing the resurrection of Jesus as a physical fact; so anyone who says that his "interpretation" of the resurrection is to see it as a metaphor referring to the ongoing influence of Jesus' ideas and teaching is in fact saying that he does not believe the Bible. The question of whether or not something in the Bible is or is not a metaphor has to be decided on the basis of what the text is to be understood as saying on its own terms, not of whatever theological or philosophical assumptions we bring to our reading of the text; those who are unwilling to believe that something the Bible asserts is true cannot take refuge behind the argument that they believe it, but "in a metaphorical way." The account of Jesus' resurrection appearances to the disciples is clearly presented as the historical narrative of a physical event; that leads to the quite separate question of whether we believe that what the text is narrating is true. Ultimately, that is the challenge that lies at the heart of any theological dispute or controversy: do we believe what the Bible says or not? Do we allow the Bible itself to shape how we think, or do we allow how we think—the attitudes, assumptions and general world-view that we have derived from the culture in which we live—to shape the way in which we choose to respond to the Bible?

The reason many modern readers, including a number of theologians of the liberal school, are skeptical about the idea that Jesus physically rose from the dead is that such an understanding of resurrection does not fit into the prevailing western world-view. They are quite right: it doesn't. In fact the resurrection cannot be accommodated into any existing world-view. But it can and does in itself provide the basis of a biblical world-view; and it is quite possible to hold a completely consistent and rational world-view which takes as its starting point the fact that God raised Jesus from the dead. To try and slot the resurrection into any other world-view is rather like trying to fit a significant piece from one jig-saw puzzle into a different picture, and getting very frustrated or disillusioned because it will not fit properly. So people can end up throwing the piece away ("I don't believe in the resurrection anymore, because it doesn't seem to make sense") or so trimming and re-shaping the piece to fit into the gap we have left for it in our own picture that it is no longer recognizable for what it is ("The way I've come to see the resurrection is . . . ").

What the Bible does is to give us a different jig-saw frame from that of the secular culture in which we live. And the central piece in that picture—the vital piece that perfectly fits into God's biblical frame—is the resurrection of Jesus. Part of what is involved in conversion to Christ must always be to jettison the world-view with which we have grown up and replace it with a new biblical world-view; or, as Paul puts it in Romans 12:2, "to be transformed by the renewing of [our] mind," that is, of our "mind-set" or "world-view." What will never work is to try and fit the resurrection into our existing mind-set. Jesus said that the new wine of God's Kingdom needs to be kept in new wine-skins; old wine-skins won't be able to contain it (Matthew 9:17//Mark 2:22//Luke 5:37–38). He was specifically referring to the "old wine-skins" of established Jewish religious practice; but the same is true of any existing or inherited world-view or religious tradition. The new wine of Jesus' resurrection life can only be kept in the new wine-skin of a biblical mind-set.

So the resurrection is presented as a physical fact, as a biblical truth, and thirdly, as an essential doctrine. In Romans 10:9 Paul says that "if you confess with your mouth, 'Jesus is Lord,' and believe in your heart that God raised him from the dead, you will be saved." Here is an explicit statement of the irreducible minimum of faith, the basis of salvation: the belief in and confession of the Lordship of Christ and the resurrection of Christ.[1] What defines the Christian is not holding some view or other of Jesus, but the

---

1. The phrases "confess *with your mouth*" and "believe *in your heart*" also make the vital point that, for faith to be real, what we do and say outwardly must be the same as what we believe inwardly. Faith that saves can never be the faith that professes one thing but harbors quite different thoughts and values in our hearts; nor, on the other hand, beliefs in our heart that never find their way to being professed and lived out in ways that others can see.

faith that Jesus is Lord and that he rose from the dead; a statement like "I'm a Christian, but I don't believe in the resurrection" is simply a contradiction in terms, and displays a complete misunderstanding of what being a Christian means. It is a form of what we might call the "Humpty-Dumpty" use of words: in Lewis Carroll's *Through the Looking-Glass*, Humpty-Dumpty says to Alice, "When *I* use a word, it means just what I choose it to mean." Many people want to choose that the word "Christian" should mean "holding a general traditional religious and moral view which has something or other to do with Jesus"; but the New Testament has a much more specific understanding, central to which is the conviction that he is Lord and the assurance that he rose from the dead.

Not only is the resurrection essential to the Christian faith we profess, it is also central to the Gospel we proclaim. In the book of Acts, the resurrection was at the heart of the message the apostles preached. Every evangelistic sermon in Acts, whatever else it does or does not contain, always reaches its climax in the declaration that God raised Jesus from the dead (e.g. 2:31–32, 3:15, 4:10, 5:30, 10:40, 13:30–37, 17:31); and in the light of passages like 4:33 ("With great power the apostles continued to testify to the resurrection of the Lord Jesus") and 17:18 ("Paul was preaching the good news about Jesus and the resurrection") it is hardly going too far to say that, for the apostles, to preach the Gospel meant to preach that Christ was risen from the dead.

That should lead us to reflect on how we preach the Gospel in our own day. A lot of Gospel preaching in the modern western church tends to focus more on expounding doctrinal truths—about forgiveness, justification by faith, the atoning work of Christ—than it does on telling people that God raised Jesus from the dead. If it be argued that in today's materialistic and cynical society people will not accept the simple story of the resurrection, it is worth pointing out that the society into which the apostles first proclaimed the good news was capable of being just as cynical and dismissive as our own ("When they heard about the resurrection . . . some of them sneered . . . " Acts 17:32), but that the apostles still told people that Jesus had been raised from the dead. Maybe we need to rediscover both the simplicity of the Gospel, and also—which is perhaps the real challenge—our own confidence in the power of the Gospel story to impact people; is the tendency to proclaim the Gospel by expounding the doctrine of salvation in a way we hope will appeal to people perhaps a form of seeking to make the Gospel sound more sophisticated? It is worth remembering that the word "Gospel" means "good news," and that "news" means telling people what has happened: the Gospel is not good advice, or interesting ideas, or profound theories, or helpful principles—it is the *news*, the story, that Jesus died and rose again from the dead.

That leads to two further inter-related thoughts. The first concerns again the balance between cross and resurrection: the apostles throughout the book of Acts proclaimed the resurrection as the heart of their message, yet when Paul is summarizing his message in 1 Corinthians 1:23 he says "we preach Christ crucified." But this is not intended to mean "crucified as opposed to risen"; Paul is contrasting the simple story of Christ with the sophisticated philosophical discussions that were so popular in Greek society, not one part of the story of Christ with another, and is stressing that we do not preach the Gospel by philosophizing about Christianity, but simply by telling people about Jesus. Second, this reaffirms that, when it came to preaching the Gospel, the apostles did not, as is so often the norm these days, present people with the doctrines of salvation and atonement through the cross; they told people that Jesus was crucified but that God raised him from the dead. Nowhere in the evangelistic messages in Acts is there any exposition of the atoning work of the cross; the nearest we come to it is in Peter's words in 5:31, that "God exalted [Jesus] to his own right hand as Prince and Savior, that he might give repentance and forgiveness of sins to Israel," and even here forgiveness is spoken of as the gift made available by the risen and exalted Christ. Elsewhere the crucifixion is spoken of as a fact but its redemptive significance is not developed in the apostolic preaching of the Gospel; it is in the letters, written to those who had become Christians, that we find the doctrinal teaching about forgiveness, justification and atonement, as Paul instructs believers about the new status in which they live as those justified by the blood of Christ. But when the early church preached the good news to unbelievers, they said that Christ had been put to death, but God had raised him to life.

That does not have to mean that preaching the Gospel by speaking of the atoning and redemptive achievements of the cross is wrong; but maybe we need to have more confidence that telling people that God raised Jesus from the dead can challenge them to faith. The truth about atonement and redemption is part of the teaching that we give to new converts; but in the book of Acts, the Gospel message is the story that Jesus died and rose again. It was simply telling that story—backed up of course by the radically new quality of life that the believers lived in the power of the Holy Spirit, and also by the works of power which the Spirit enabled them to do to confirm the reality of the message—that so dramatically impacted the first-century world. Is it perhaps the absence of that radical lifestyle and spiritual power that has led the modern western church to feel that simply telling the *story* of the resurrection is somehow inadequate, and to evangelize instead by teaching in more depth the biblical doctrines about the *significance* of Jesus' atoning work? The New Testament church told the story of the cross and resurrection; it was the quality of life they lived in the power of the Holy Spirit that convinced their hearers of the significance of that story.

New Creation

The resurrection is such an absolutely and utterly unique event that it can be thought of only as an act of new creation. Just as in the beginning God created the heavens and the earth, and time, space and matter were formed out of nothing, so in the early hours of the first Easter morning God brought about the beginning of a new creation when he raised his Son to new life. That is part of the significance of the fact that Jesus rose from the dead on a Sunday morning. In our western thinking, regarding as we do Saturday and Sunday as the week-end, we tend to think of Monday as the first day of the new week; but in the Bible Sunday is the first day of the week. Jesus rose from the dead on day one of a new week, the first day of God's new creation.

God raised Jesus to new life, he did not merely restore him to his old life. Just as in the incarnation the life of the eternal Son of God was united with a normal, frail human body—a body that was part of the original "old creation" and therefore, like it, subject to frailty and mortality—so in the resurrection the life of the eternal Son was united with a new glorified and imperishable body that is part of the new creation. The promise of the Scriptures is that there will one day be "new heavens and a new earth," a completely new creation without the curse of the present order of nature: without pain, decay, death or corruption of any kind, physical, moral, social or spiritual. The resurrection body of Jesus is, so to speak, the first physical part of that new creation to come into being; and the words of Paul in 1 Corinthians 15:42-44, though he is speaking primarily of the future resurrection body that we shall receive, are of course supremely true of the resurrection body of Jesus, which is the firstfruits of that future resurrection: "The body that is sown is perishable, it is raised imperishable; it is sown in dishonor, it is raised in glory; it is sown in weakness, it is raised in power; it is sown a natural body, it is raised a spiritual body."[2]

That is the biblical significance of the cross and resurrection. The cross achieved the victory over all that had damaged and cursed the old creation;

---

2. By "a spiritual body" Paul does *not* mean "incorporeal"; "spiritual" is the opposite, not of "physical" or "tangible," but of "natural." The intended contrast is between our "normal" bodies, which are part of this present order of creation, and the future resurrection body, which will be part of and perfectly suited to God's heavenly Kingdom.

the resurrection initiates the new creation. The cross purifies us from the sin of the old life; the resurrection makes available a new kind of life into which we can enter by faith. The cross makes a new beginning possible; the resurrection makes it real.

The fact that Jesus' resurrection was to a life that is part of God's glorious new creation is reflected in one recurring feature of the resurrection narratives in the Gospels: the fact that Jesus is still clearly Jesus—his disciples could see that it really was their Master himself—and yet he is somehow different. He is often not immediately recognized (Luke 24:16, John 20:14, 21:4); he can pass through locked doors (John 20:19); he can be in Emmaus, then disappear from sight, and by the time the two disciples in Emmaus have run back to Jerusalem, a distance of about seven miles, Jesus has already been seen there by Peter (Luke 24:31,33–34). Jesus rose, not with his previous human body restored, but with a new, heavenly, glorious body, such as we will have in heaven, a body that is not limited by the same laws of physics as our present bodies. Having in the incarnation laid aside his heavenly glory, he lived for thirty-three years in this normal human world in a normal human body; but he then spent forty days living in this ordinary human world in a glorious heavenly body. Even during Jesus' three-year ministry, the miraculous power of the Father could on occasions enable him to transcend the normal limitations of earthly physics—he could walk on water, he was seen transfigured—but those were rare exceptions to the "normal" human life of Jesus, and hints that Jesus was more than a mere man. But that heavenly transcendence over the constraints of physical life in this world, which in Jesus' human incarnation was the exception, was in his risen body—and will be in our resurrection bodies—the norm.

There is however one aspect of Jesus' incarnate, human body that remains and is still visible in his new glorified body, namely the wounds that are the marks of his suffering: the scars left by the nails in his hands and feet and by the spear thrust into his side. The hymn "Crown him with many crowns" calls them "those wounds, yet visible above, in beauty glorified"; and Revelation 5:6 speaks of Jesus, as he appears surrounded and worshiped by the heavenly host, as "a Lamb looking as if it had been slain." Here is a remarkable mystery: the only thing that will in any sense be an imperfection or blemish in the whole of heaven will be the wounds in the glorified body of Jesus. All believers will be raised, we are told, with perfected resurrection bodies that will have nothing of the imperfections and frailties of the bodies in which they lived on earth, but Jesus alone will bear for eternity the marks of the cross. That is surely an enduring reminder that it is the cross alone that made heaven possible, and that the achievements of his death will be eternally effective; if "by his wounds we are healed" (Isaiah 53:5), then the fact that his wounds are everlasting is a sign that our healing is also everlasting.

The Significance of the Resurrection

That the resurrection of Jesus is the beginning of God's new creation is the key to the New Testament's theology of resurrection. Within that general overall theme, we can identify a number of other specific truths from the ways in which the resurrection was preached in the early church, starting with the fact that it is *the vindication of who Jesus is.* Paul begins his letter to the Romans by saying that Jesus "was declared with power to be the Son of God by his resurrection from the dead" (Romans 1:4). During his ministry Jesus had made many explicit, and many more implicit, claims to deity; the Pharisees recognized these claims for what they were and condemned them, for example when they accused him of blasphemy, saying (John 10:33), "You, a mere man, claim to be God." The resurrection is the vindication of those claims.[3] If Jesus had been "a mere man," albeit an outstandingly good man, he would have remained in the tomb: when they die, good men, as well as bad men, stay dead. The fact that Jesus rose in a different way demonstrates that he is more than a godly man; that he is the man who is God.

It also shows that *Jesus' atoning death has been accepted by God the Father* as an all-sufficient payment for sin. The resurrection demonstrates that when Jesus cried out "It is finished!"—all sin has been paid for once and for all—he was right. A convicted criminal who is sentenced to a fine or an indefinite term in prison cannot be released from prison until the fine is paid. When his family and friends see him walking about the streets, they can rightly conclude, assuming he has not staged a prison break, that the fine has been paid.

There are no prison breaks from Hades. Jesus' death was a sacrifice of atonement; and the resurrection demonstrates that God has accepted his death as a completely and eternally sufficient payment for all sin. If 0.00001

---

3. Note that I say "vindication" rather than "proof." To say that the resurrection "proves" that Jesus was the Son of God is not so much right or wrong as unhelpful; in a sense it does, or at least it offers a very powerful case for affirming the deity of Christ. But the language of "proof" is from the outset treating God as though he were a scientific theorem to be discussed, rather than a person to be encountered. Christian faith is a covenant relationship with a personal Lord and Savior, not assenting to a theological theory ("Jesus rose from the dead; *ergo*, he is the Son of God. Q.E.D."). A scientifically-minded gentleman who had challenged me to "prove" that God was real was most put out when I invited him to "prove" that his wife was real; he said, in effect, "You can't treat my wife like a theory!" He was right, you can't; nor should we treat God as one.

percent of sin had remained unatoned for by Jesus' death, he could not have been raised from the dead; as Jesus himself said, speaking of the need to put right any damaged relationships with one another, the unrepentant and unforgiving prisoner "will not get out until [he has] paid the last penny" (Matthew 5:26). That Jesus was released from the prison cell of death publicizes the good news that the last penny has been paid: all that is or could ever be necessary for sinners to be set free from the penalty of sin has been accomplished by Jesus on the cross.

Third, it demonstrates that *death is defeated*. Death was, and still is, the great enemy, what Paul calls "the last enemy to be destroyed" (1 Corinthians 15:26). Whatever real and valuable improvements and enrichments to human life people may accomplish, death remains the great unbeatable enemy, the hurdle at which all human achievement falls. However many diseases we find cures for, people will still die of something; however many world problems we solve, those who live in the world will still die; no matter how many arguments we win, death will always have the last word; no matter how many of the ills of life a person may succeed in avoiding, he cannot indefinitely postpone his encounter with death. George Bernard Shaw said that the ultimate statistic was that "one out of one dies."[4]

Until Jesus, that is. On the cross he fought death in single combat and won; he went fifteen rounds with death and, when it appeared that death was winning on points, landed the knock-out blow—by dying. The resurrection declares that death is now a defeated enemy. I once heard the great American preacher Tony Campolo say, in the context of preaching about the battles we sometimes have to face in Christian life, "But don't worry. I've read the last chapter of the book, and guess what: we win!"

That brings us to another great lesson: the New Testament presents the resurrection of Christ as *the pattern and guarantee of our own resurrection* at the end of the age. Because he has risen, we will rise; "We eagerly await a Savior from [heaven], the Lord Jesus Christ, who . . . will transform our lowly bodies so that they will be like his glorious body" (Philippians 3:20–21). The fact that Jesus rose is the assurance that our future hope is not vague and theoretical. It was the late Magnus Magnusson who popularized the phrase, when he chaired the quiz program *Mastermind*, "I've started, so I'll finish." Even more assuredly, God himself might well say, "With the resurrection of my Son in a new glorified body, I've started; so you can be quite certain that, with all who believe in him, I'll finish."

---

4. Quoted in Blanchard, *Gathered Gold*, 60.

Telling the Story

Mary Magdalen was the first witness of Jesus' resurrection (Matthew 28:1,8–9, John 20:10–18). This is remarkable, and shows Jesus overturning the social norms of his day. Women had no right to give evidence in court, and their testimony was regarded as invalid. But Jesus tells Mary to go and witness to the disciples that he is risen. Moreover, Mary was a woman with a very bad past (Mark 16:9). It is a further sign of the grace of Jesus that this woman was allowed to be the first to see him alive. And, without wishing to read too much into this, and without over-simplifying a complex and controversial issue, the word that Jesus uses to Mary and the other woman in Matthew 28:10, which is translated in the NIV simply as "go and *tell* my brothers . . . ," is the formal word for proclamation or heralding, the same word that Paul uses in Acts 26:20, when he says "I *preached* that they should repent and turn to God," and which John uses in his first letter about "proclaiming" the Word of life (1 John 1:2–3). The issue of women's ministry is far from simple, even within the Bible, let alone within denominational traditions; but those who would exclude women from any kind of "word ministry" ("The Bible says women can't preach: end of issue!") need to find a place in their thinking for this radical challenge from Jesus to two women, making them the first commissioned heralds of his resurrection.

Matthew 28:11–15 tells how the Roman authorities tried to concoct a story to explain the disappearance of Jesus' body, the first of many attempts through history to come up with an alternative to the resurrection. Even if we grant that it calls for faith to believe that Jesus rose, this Roman story, like most subsequent attempts to explain away the resurrection, takes far more faith of a much more gullible kind. It is frankly a ridiculous and impossible story, for at least two reasons. First, if the guards were asleep, how did they know it was the disciples who came and "stole" the body? And second, we know that the stone was very large (Mark 16:4); it was quite normal for stones in the entrances of tombs to be so big that they could take anything from ten to fifteen men to move them. So how did the disciples succeed in moving it without waking the guards who were a few yards away?

The unbeliever might well reply to my assertion that such attempts to explain away the resurrection are "ridiculous" by saying that, in his view, the idea that Jesus rose from the dead is ridiculous. I dare say; but what we are talking about are two fundamentally different ways of thinking about what is or is not possible, not two different opinions based on the same premise. The person who simply does not believe that miracles happen, or who does not believe in God, will of course dismiss the story of the resurrection. But if one grants, even hypothetically, that God can work miracles, there is nothing inherently improbable about the resurrection story; and within the world-view that accepts faith in God and the possibility of miracles, the resurrection is not only possible but it is entirely consistent with the rest of the Bible's account of who Jesus is. The unbeliever is however arguing from the assumption that miracles do not happen, and that all things must therefore in principle be explicable on the basis of what naturally and normally happens in this material world. On the basis of a biblical world-view, the resurrection story makes sense; on the basis of a naturalistic world-view, the authorities' naturalistic explanation simply does not hold water. "Natural" explanations have to make sense in natural terms; theirs doesn't.

That raises an important point about how Christians present the story of the resurrection. There have been many excellent books which argue on rational and logical grounds the case for believing that Jesus rose. The old classics, Sir Norman Anderson's booklet *The Evidence for the Resurrection* and Michael Green's *The Day Death Died*, are still hard to beat; and many more recent works have presented a strong case for saying that, by all historical criteria, believing that Jesus rose fits the known facts far better than any of the so-called alternative explanations. There is of course a great value in demonstrating to a skeptical age that Christians do not have to abandon intelligent thinking in order to embrace belief in the resurrection; and yet the fact remains that no one in the Bible who was originally skeptical about the account of the resurrection was ever convinced and persuaded to believe on the strength of argument. The apostles never presented an apologetic for the resurrection: they simply said that God had raised Jesus from the dead. Some mocked (Acts 17:32), but when they did, the apostles did not try to defend the resurrection by reason. Thomas is the classic example of the materialistic skeptic: he would not believe anything unless he saw it with his own eyes; Thomas could have stepped into the New Testament straight from out of the late twentieth and early twenty-first centuries. What changed him was not that the other disciples argued sufficiently convincingly, but that he met the risen Jesus himself.

Let us by all means make the best use we can of logical historical apologetics; but the mission of the church is not to persuade people to accept the belief that Jesus rose from the dead. It is entirely possible for people to believe that the resurrection happened and yet still to be living under the judgment of sin, just as it is entirely possible to believe that a cure for a fatal disease has been discovered, and yet still to be suffering from it. What saves the terminally ill patient is not merely believing that a cure exists, but personally receiving treatment. And what brings new life and the full assurance of faith is not coming to the conclusion that the resurrection-story makes sense after all, but being personally touched by the new life of the risen

Christ. That can only ever come about as the Holy Spirit works through our proclamation of the Gospel of Christ crucified and risen, and opens people's hearts to respond to the message in repentance and faith.

One of the things that makes it impossible to claim, as many a cynic will, that the biblical accounts of the resurrection stories are mere fables is the down-to-earth realism of the disciples' reactions to the news of the resurrection, and then to actually meeting the risen Christ. Those who see Jesus risen invariably react with confusion ("Trembling and bewildered," Mark 16:8), fear ("The women hurried away . . . , afraid . . . ," Matthew 28:8; "They were startled and frightened . . . ," Luke 24:37) or, especially, doubt (" . . . they worshiped him, but some doubted," Matthew 28:17; "[Jesus] rebuked them for their lack of faith and their stubborn refusal to believe," Mark 16:14; "They did not believe the women, because their words seemed to them like nonsense," Luke 24:11); and very often with a confused mass of conflicting emotions ("afraid yet filled with joy," Matthew 28:8; "they still did not believe it because of joy and amazement," Luke 24:41). It is only after the initial shock of meeting with the risen Christ has worn off that those natural human feelings turn into joy and confident faith. Christians should not be distressed or frustrated when people react to the message of the Gospel with similar incredulity; all that suggests is that we are living in the same world as the disciples in the New Testament. The risen Christ still has the same power to turn unbelief into faith, fear into joy and confusion into assurance.

And once the reality of Christ's resurrection has truly touched the disciples, it is quite natural that it should lead to an explosion of sheer joy. We have already seen how such joy was a central thread in the birth story, as recounted in Luke 1 and 2, and we have also commented on the fact that in some church circles joy can be misunderstood, disapproved of and dismissed as superficial "happy-clappiness." In fairness, it is often the lively and charismatic churches that are partly responsible for such a hostile reaction, if their expressions of joy seem to be mainly about young people enjoying themselves and modeling church praise on the secular disco culture. But there is also in our society a suspicion of joy; I have heard the comment made about Christians, "What's wrong with all you lot?—you're always so *happy!*" The newspaper columnist Bernard Levin wrote a book called *Enthusiasms*, in which he talked about the various things that he was unashamedly enthusiastic about; and he said in his introduction, "We live in a querulous age; more, we live in an age in which it is argued that to be happy is frivolous, and expecting to be happy positively childish. To be passionate in a cause provokes widespread embarrassment . . . We live in a world which not only fears and distrusts joy, but which goes far towards denying its existence."[5] And that mistrust of joy can lead, in religious circles, to a skepticism about a church atmosphere of rejoicing and celebration.

The Bible as a whole, but in particular the fact of the resurrection, clearly establishes joy as real and normal. Because Christ is risen, the disciples rejoiced; and those who encounter his risen life today will invariably be as overjoyed as John tells us the original apostles were when they saw the Lord (20:20). There are few things more tragically inappropriate than the tendency in some church circles to discuss the doctrine of the resurrection in a cool and objective way, or to debate theories about the significance of this or that recorded resurrection appearance, but to remain apparently untouched by the sheer joy of the fact that Christ is risen. Joyless Christianity should be as much of a contradiction in terms as a gloomy wedding.

But because joy is often misunderstood, a few things need saying about it. First, the disciples' joy when they saw the risen Lord was not merely—except perhaps for the first few minutes—the personal relief that Jesus was with them again, that they had not lost him after all. It went far deeper than that; it was the eruption of celebration that comes following a great victory. As football fans break out in cheering and singing when their team wins the cup final, as a political candidate's supporters go wild with delight when he wins the election, so Jesus' disciples burst out into what 1 Peter 1:8 calls "an inexpressible and glorious joy" when they realized that sin and death were defeated once and for all. The resurrection gives Christian joy its real and reliable basis; that joy is not naïve optimism, a determination to look at the sordid and pain-ridden world through rose-colored spectacles, or a childish and desperate hope that, if we ignore problems for long enough, they might just go away. To rejoice is to appreciate what is true, that Jesus has defeated all the powers of evil, and that we can now share in his victory. Joy can be real because the victory of the cross and resurrection are real.

From that follows another vital characteristic of Christian joy: Paul tells us to "rejoice in the Lord always" (Philippians 4:4). The call to rejoice is so much at the heart of any genuine faith that Paul repeats it: "I will say it again: rejoice!" But we must never forget the key phrase "rejoice *in the Lord*." Christian joy is not about enjoying ourselves or having fun; it is about celebrating Jesus. To rejoice in the Lord is to show our true understanding of who he actually is and what he has actually achieved. If, following an exhilarating performance of a Beethoven symphony the audience bursts into rapturous applause, it is a sign that they have appreciated how great the music really is. But if there is a member of the audience who remains unmoved, or gives one or two nominal claps then lapses into stony silence,

---

5. Levin, *Enthusiasms*, 1,8.

those around him are almost certainly justified in drawing the inference that he simply doesn't understand or appreciate great music.

That is a very great loss; but it is as nothing compared to the loss suffered by those who simply don't see what Jesus has done for us. And that loss may be being suffered, not only by those who tut-tut at modern noisy worship, but also by some of those who engage in it, but simply because they find it fun to dance around in church. The flesh can clap and dance; but the Holy Spirit enables us truly to rejoice "in the Lord."

It is because our rejoicing is "in the Lord" that Paul can urge Christians to rejoice in the Lord "always." The lives of Christians will often go through the same ups and downs as anybody else's, so if our rejoicing is dependent on our circumstances, we will not be able to rejoice "always": we will rejoice when things are going well, but not when circumstances are against us. But Jesus is always risen; he is always the Lord who has conquered death; so those whose rejoicing is truly "in the Lord" will be able to rejoice "always," as did Paul and Silas when they were in chains in prison (Acts 16:25). If we cannot rejoice when circumstances are against us, we would do well to reflect on how much our previous rejoicing was actually "in the Lord"; our circumstances may have changed, but the Lord hasn't.

There are some who see joy and peace as opposites, or as options that we can choose between: "Your church is into being joyful, but I like a church with a peaceful atmosphere." But it is a false opposition. John 20:19–20 says not only that the disciples were "overjoyed" when they saw Jesus, but that Jesus also said to them "Peace be with you." The fruit of the Spirit is love, joy, peace. God has not given us the choice of a joyful Spirit or a peaceful one, depending on which suits our temperament more. Joy in the Lord and peace with the Lord are equally key characteristics of Christian life. F. F. Bruce quotes the wonderful line of "an old Scots preacher," "peace is joy resting; joy is peace dancing."[6]

But an even more seriously false opposition is between different ideas about or styles of worship; there are those who think that worship should be all joy and celebration and others who will say they prefer worship to be reverent, quiet, focusing on the holiness of God. Again, they are not alternatives. Reverent holiness and joyful celebration are the two sides of the same praise-coin; but lively charismatics can be just as dismissive of those who want to kneel quietly in church as those who like a more sedate atmosphere can be of hand-raising and lively music. Yet again, man is separating what God has joined. Psalm 95 is our model. Both verses 1 and 6 invite us to "come"; verse 1 says "Come, let us sing for joy to the Lord; let us shout aloud

---

6. Bruce, *Romans*, 120.

to the Rock of our salvation"; then verse 6 says, "Come, let us bow down in worship, let us kneel before the Lord our Maker." I will take seriously as spiritual worship the insistence of those who urge us to shout and sing when I see that there are also times when they kneel and bow down; and *vice versa*. Revelation 4 and 5 give us a glorious picture of the worship of heaven, for which all our worship on earth is merely the preparation—the "tuning-up" to get us ready to join in the great heavenly symphony. And what we read of there is endless singing—giving glory, honor and thanks to God (4:9), bursting out into a "new song"[7] (5:9), singing in a loud voice (5:12)—and also reverent worship: the elders "fall down before him who sits on the throne and worship him" (4:10), they fall down before the Lamb (5:8), and at the chorus of praise from every creature in heaven and on earth they "fell down and worshiped" (5:14). It is not only right to sing "Christ is risen: hallelujah!," it is a sign that we have really taken on board what it means that he is risen. But it is equally right that we worship him in reverent holiness, because that is the sign that we have truly grasped who the risen Christ actually is.

The Four-fold Commission

In all four Gospels the risen Christ commissions his disciples to go and bring the Gospel to the world. Those in the classic evangelical tradition of the church are very familiar with the last verses of Matthew's Gospel, which are regularly referred to, quite properly, as the "Great Commission." But it is as always far more helpful, if we are to be not only all-round Christians but also all-round witnesses, to set the various forms of commissioning alongside each other. For once, let us start with John: "As the Father has sent me, I am sending you" (20:21). The most basic thing that arises out of those words is the reminder that the church's mission is Jesus' mission continued; we can be sent into the world in no other way, and with no other agenda, than that with which Jesus was sent by the Father. Jesus was of course sent, as we see throughout his ministry from Galilee onwards, both to proclaim

---

7. The phrase in Revelation 5 about singing "a new song" is often terribly misapplied by those who think it means that we should only sing songs that have been recently written. I appreciate the best of modern worship songs as much as anybody, and they constitute at least 90 percent of my church's repertoire of worship; but what entitles a song to be described as "a new song" in the sense of Revelation 5 is nothing to do with its date of composition; it means any song that celebrates the new thing that God has accomplished in Christ. Charles Wesley's "O for a thousand tongues to sing" is a new song; whatever is number one in this week's charts isn't.

the Kingdom in words and to demonstrate the Kingdom in works. As Jesus said at the end of his parable of the Good Samaritan, "Go and do likewise."

That word of commission is accompanied by two very important actions of Jesus, which together need to be held in proper balance. First, "he showed them his hands and his side" (verse 20). When Luke records that Jesus showed his disciples his hands and feet (Luke 24:39) it was with the intention of confirming to them his identity, convincing them that it really was he: they were not imagining it. The wounds certainly do that; but for John they have a different significance. Jesus is going to send his disciples into the world just as he was sent into the world; the marks of the cross are a vivid reminder to the disciples of what it can mean to be sent. This is what it cost Jesus to be sent; now he will send them: so are they willing to be sent? Are they ready to pay the price necessary for being sent as he was sent?

But then there is a second action: "he breathed on them and said, 'Receive the Holy Spirit'" (verse 22). Though they are sent to walk the way of the suffering servant, they are not sent out vulnerable and exposed, with no resources or defenses. They are sent with the Holy Spirit.[8] Those two actions need to be held together; there are too many Christians who seem to believe that the anointing of the Holy Spirit comes in order to ensure that we do not face opposition or hardship, or at least that, if we do, we will always come through it unscathed: in effect, that the Spirit equips us for mission without cost. That is simply not true. Spirit-anointed servants will still display in their lives the marks of suffering servants, just as Jesus, the anointed One, did; we are sent in the same way as he was sent.

It is worth remembering in this context what the New Testament speaks of as the marks of an apostle. There are essentially two: Paul says in 2 Corinthians 12:12 that "the things that mark an apostle [are] signs, wonders and miracles"; but he also regularly refers to suffering for Christ as the hallmark of a true apostle. In fact, whenever Paul's right to be called an apostle was questioned, as it often was, he invariably responded by speaking

---

8. I see no conflict or contradiction between this breathing out of the Spirit in John 20 and the pouring out of the Spirit on the Day of Pentecost. This immediate imparting of the Spirit from the risen Jesus is accompanied by a promise of a further experience of power (Luke 24:49), which will be fulfilled in Acts 2:1–4. The breathing out of the Spirit in John 20 seems to be an imparting of the new *life* of the Spirit: the verb "breathed on them" (literally, "breathed *in* [them]") recalls Genesis 2:7, where God breathes into the nostrils of the man he had formed from the ground, and the man became a living being. The outpouring of the Spirit in Acts 2 is clearly about the imparting of the *power* of the Spirit; in Luke 24:49 Jesus had spoken of the promised outpouring of the Spirit at Pentecost as the disciples being "clothed with power." Whilst new life and missionary empowering are inter-connected, and we do not drive a wedge between them, they are not the same thing; the Spirit comes to give new birth when we believe in the crucified and risen Christ, and he empowers us for mission in the imparting of gifts for service.

of how much he has suffered for Jesus (1 Corinthians 4:9-13, 2 Corinthians 4:8-11). We hear a lot about the marks of apostolic ministry these days, but normally in terms of the working of miracles; it is as though modern believers are happy for Jesus to breathe his Spirit into them, but rather less happy for him to show them his hands and his side and to remind them that this is what it means to be apostolic. The New Testament apostles were called to suffer for their Lord, as well as—not instead of—being equipped with the power of the Spirit to do the works of the Lord.

If John's commission focuses on the *spirit* in which we are sent, Mark's speaks of the immediate *task* with which we are sent: "Go into all the world and preach the good news to all creation" (16:15). He too tells us that works will accompany words—"these signs will accompany those who believe..." —but the heart of the commission is clear: preach the Gospel. All the good works in the world, valuable though they are and genuine signs of the compassionate heart of God though they are, will not bring sinners into an experience of God's salvation: only the Gospel will do that. Christian mission is rightly holistic—we feed the hungry, provide medical care, education, and whatever else is required to address human need—but unless at its heart there is the communication in words of the Gospel message that Christ died for our sins, and the invitation to "believe in the Lord Jesus, and you will be saved" (Acts 16:31), it is not the mission of Jesus. Compassionate care without Gospel proclamation is like a doctor with a beautifully warm and consoling bed-side manner, but who never actually addresses his patients' medical problems or offers any treatment.

Luke's commission stresses further the specific *content* of the message to be proclaimed: "repentance and forgiveness of sins" (Luke 24:47). At the heart of the Gospel message is the forgiveness of sins. No matter what else Jesus is—the healer of sickness, the bringer of peace, the befriender of the outcast—we do not begin to grow in the life of his Kingdom unless and until we receive him as the one who has atoned for and can now forgive all our sins. Forgiveness is *the* great human need. It is the great need, first, because it is the one from which all people, without exception, suffer. Jesus fed the hungry; however, not everyone is hungry—but everyone is a sinner needing forgiveness. Jesus healed the sick; however, not everyone is sick— but everyone is a sinner needing forgiveness. Jesus comforted the poor; however, not everyone is poor—but everyone is a sinner needing forgiveness. Jesus welcomed the outcast; however, not everyone is an outcast—but everyone is a sinner needing forgiveness. And it is the great need because of the consequences if it remains unaddressed. Being poor will not keep me out of heaven—but being unforgiven would. Being uneducated will not keep me out of heaven—but being unforgiven would. Being handicapped, or disadvantaged, or unemployed will not keep me out of heaven—but being unforgiven would.

And Jesus alone can address the need for forgiveness. When the doctor in Act Five of *Macbeth* watches Lady Macbeth sleep-walking, he sees her, clearly plagued with guilt, trying to wash her hands of the stain of her crime in conspiring to have Banquo murdered, but aware that "all the perfumes of Arabia will not sweeten this little hand." The doctor ruefully comments, "This disease is beyond my practice." So it is; but it is not beyond Christ's. The medical profession can help us live with or recover from illness, but they cannot forgive our sins. The social services can try to support needy families, but cannot forgive their sins. Schools and colleges can educate people and help them to get qualifications, but they cannot forgive their sins. Relief agencies can feed the hungry and house the homeless, but they cannot forgive their sins.

But Jesus can. And we are commissioned to go into all the world and tell people that. Which brings us to Matthew 28:19–20. We are to "make disciples of all nations, baptizing them . . . and teaching them . . . " If John shows us the spirit of Jesus' mission, Mark its task and Luke its content, then Matthew shows us its *process*. Jesus deliberately uses the word "disciples"; he does not commission us to call for decisions, or even to make converts, but to make disciples.

"Make disciples of" is actually the simple verb, "*disciple* all the nations." Whilst the noun "disciples" is used over two hundred times as a term for Christians, the verb "to disciple" is used in only three other places in the New Testament. In Matthew 13:52, Jesus speaks of the teacher of the law who has also "been instructed" about the Kingdom of God (literally: "every teacher-of-the-law discipled to the Kingdom of heaven"). The tense of "discipled" is the Greek aorist, which speaks of an event that happened and was completed in the past, whether at a specific point in time or over a period of time: whilst there is of course an ongoing process of being taught about the life and faith of God's new Kingdom, there is also a sense in which someone who has, like the teacher of the law whom Jesus is here describing, been taught the principles of living the life of God's new spiritual Kingdom can be said to have "been discipled." The same tense is used in Matthew 27:57 where we are told about Joseph of Arimathea "who had himself become a disciple of Jesus" (literally: "who also himself *was discipled* to Jesus"): that means that, at some point in the last three years, had become one of those who had decided to follow Jesus and learn from him. In Acts 14:21 we read of Paul and Barnabas that "they preached the good news in that city and won a large number of disciples" (literally: "evangelizing that city [= Derbe] and having discipled many"): that speaks of the fact that many people responded to the apostles' Gospel preaching ("evangelizing") by deciding to become Christians and embark on a life of discipleship.

From these other uses of the verb "disciple" in the Bible, we learn a number of truths.

1. People need to be "discipled" by someone else; no one can disciple themselves. The teachers of the law, and Joseph of Arimathea, are people who "have *been* discipled." Of course God in his sovereignty can reveal himself to someone in a way that leads to a changed life without any human intervention—as he did to Saul of Tarsus on the Damascus Road—but the process of becoming a disciple requires that people submit themselves to the process of being taught by others. There are self-taught musicians, self-taught artists, self-taught tennis players—but there are no self-taught disciples.[9]

2. Being discipled always starts as a response to the Gospel. In Derbe Paul and Barnabas preached the Gospel to the city and discipled many; in other words, they proclaimed the message about Jesus to all and sundry, and it was the people who specifically responded to that message who were discipled, that is, they were taught how to live in the light of the Gospel to which they had responded. The first step on the road of discipleship is to believe in Jesus as Savior; discipleship itself then begins, as we are taught how to start to follow Jesus as Lord.

3. The fact that all occurrences of the verb "disciple" apart from in Matthew 28 are in the aorist tense, the tense of actions completed in the past, is significant. As we said, Christian discipleship obviously includes an element of ongoing—indeed, life-long—learning, and no believer ever reaches the point where they have nothing more to learn. On the other hand, discipleship is not open-ended: those past tenses (aorists) indicate that to be "discipled" means that someone, having been taught what it means to live for Jesus' Kingdom, has chosen to commit him- or herself to that life. Actually learning to live it, and getting better at living it, will be a life-long process; but to have decided

---

9. It might be argued that the apostle Paul learned Christian truth directly from God, without having any human teachers, as he says in Galatians 1:11–24. True; but those who would justify their refusal to submit to the teaching of Christian leaders by saying that Paul didn't need it are not only being somewhat presumptuous—they are not the apostle Paul!—but are forgetting that Paul himself urges Christians to submit to those who instruct them in the Lord (1 Corinthians 16:15–16, Galatians 6:6, 1 Thessalonians 5:12–13; see also Hebrews 13:17, which is not by Paul but is just as much part of God's authoritative Word). Paul was an exception, as he himself says (1 Corinthians 15:8), but modern believers are not at liberty simply to decide that they too will be exceptions.

to embark on that lifestyle, and to become a follower of Jesus, is to have been "discipled." At some point, the person learning to drive will take their driving test. If they pass, they can from that moment on legitimately be called a driver. That does not mean that their driving skills will not continue to improve over the years—they certainly should—but that they are now qualified drivers. In a similar way, the person who, as part of having been encouraged to trust in Jesus as Savior, has also been taught the spiritual principles of what it means to live for God's Kingdom, and has committed him- or herself to start to live by those principles, can be said to have "been discipled," even though they will for the rest of their lives grow in experience and, by the grace of God, get better at serving Christ and living the Christian life.

4. The saying about the teacher of the law who has been discipled (Matthew 13:52) reminds us that becoming a disciple will in principle always involve our learning to think and live on a different basis. The teacher of the law would know a great deal about the Old Testament scriptures and the Law of Moses; but the new life of God's Kingdom in Christ goes beyond that religious tradition, and calls for a willingness to let God do new things: as Jesus said elsewhere, the "new wine" of God's spiritual Kingdom cannot be contained or confined within the "old wineskins" of traditional Jewish teaching and practice (Matthew 9:17//Mark 2:22//Luke 5:37–38).[10] Becoming a disciple involves more than adding Christian faith to the life and worldview one already has: it means accepting that our lives as disciples are to be lived on a different basis, that of God's Kingdom. The person who has seen *that* can in a real sense be said to have "been discipled."

Returning to Matthew 28:19, Jesus' words "make disciples . . . baptizing them . . . and teaching them . . . " show that there are two equally important parts to disciple-making. There is the initial step of becoming a Christian, which he refers to in the call to baptize in the name of the Father, the Son and the Holy Spirit. Baptism in the New Testament is always linked with and the expression of repentance towards God and faith in Jesus: James Denney

---

10. Luke's version of this saying adds the phrase (verse 39) "And no one after drinking the old wine wants the new, for he says, 'The old is better!'" We need not take "no one" too literally: some people clearly *did* respond positively to the new wine of the Gospel. Jesus' words are an ironic comment on the attitude of those who refuse to consider the Gospel because they are so settled in their religious traditions that they do not believe they need anything else. It is unfortunately still the case that some of the people who are most resistant to the Gospel of new life in Christ are those who are staunch upholders of established religion: they can greatly value the old wineskins of tradition without apparently being aware that they have no new wine in them.

rightly said that in the New Testament "baptism and faith are but the outside and the inside of the same thing."[11] That then leads to the ongoing process of being taught to obey all that Jesus said to his disciples. It is sometimes said that Jesus in the "Great Commission" tells us to do three things: [1] disciple people, which means lead them to faith; [2] baptize them, which incorporates them into the church; and [3] teach them, which is about learning to serve Christ. That is not how the sentence is to be construed: Jesus is not telling us to do three things, but one thing—to disciple people—which he then describes as involving the two elements of conversion or initiation (baptism) and teaching; the only imperative (that is, command) is "disciple": "baptizing" and "teaching" are participles, not commands: they introduce explanatory clauses which clarify what "to disciple" means. To reduce "disciple people" to meaning simply "encourage them to come to faith" misses the vital truth that part of the challenge of the Gospel itself is the call to follow Jesus as disciples; to drive a wedge between believing and committing oneself to learn how to follow Jesus is a distortion of the Gospel. Mission does not end when a person decides to accept the salvation of Christ. As Sir Winston Churchill famously said in a rather different context, "This is not the end. It is not even the beginning of the end. But it is perhaps the end of the beginning." Jesus is looking, not for those who merely make a good beginning, but for those who grow from that beginning into mature and all-round disciples. Evangelistic head-hunting ("We had four people make decisions last Sunday!") seems to imply a rather different understanding of the missionary task of the church from that of Jesus.

Throughout this section, I have on a number of occasions used the word "commission" to describe the missionary challenges which the risen Jesus gave his disciples; and the words at the end of Matthew's Gospel in particular are conventionally referred to in the evangelical church tradition as "the Great Commission." It is worth pointing out, first, that the word "commission" is never actually used in the Bible itself to refer to the call to mission,[12] and second, that for some people it can have very misleading connotations, which can seriously distort their understanding of what mission is. People often seem to think of Jesus' "commission" as the fact that he gives us orders: if we think in military terms, the assumption is often that Jesus is our commanding officer, and he gives his soldiers their marching

---

11. Denney, *Death of Christ*, 185.

12. The NIV translates Paul's words in Colossians 1:25 as "the commission God gave me"; but the Greek word Paul uses, *oikonómia*, is not, like "commission," a military metaphor, but rather a domestic one: it means the responsibility of being a steward, one who manages a household.

orders which they are duty-bound to carry out. But that is not what "commissioning" means. To be "commissioned" means to be given authority; it is newly-trained officers who have the privilege of being "commissioned." The typical wording of a certificate of commissioning for an officer in the Royal Navy Reserve, the volunteer branch of the Navy, begins: "Elizabeth the Second, by the grace of God of the United Kingdom of Great Britain and Northern Ireland, and of her other realms and territories Queen, Head of the Commonwealth, Defender of the Faith, Lord High Admiral. To our trusty and well beloved *[name]*: Greeting: We, reposing especial trust and confidence in your loyalty, courage and good conduct, do by these presents constitute and appoint you to be an officer in our Royal Naval Reserve . . . "

That is commissioning. If we think of Jesus' "commission" as simply the fact that he tells us what to do, and so we do it, we miss the wonderful privilege that being "commissioned" by Jesus implies. Of course, unlike a naval officer, who has undergone strict training and has had to pass rigorous tests, we are not "commissioned" on the basis of any personal qualities or attainments: we are enrolled in the service of Jesus' Kingdom by sheer grace. But just as a commissioned officer, though he is still of course under the authority of his superiors, is also given authority, so Jesus "gave [his twelve apostles] authority to drive out impure spirits and to heal every disease and sickness" (Matthew 10:1). Those who serve the Kingdom of Jesus in the spirit of the New Testament are not those who see themselves as simply "under orders"—press-ganged into religious service—but rather those who appreciate what a tremendous privilege it is to have been commissioned to serve Jesus, our heavenly Commander-in-Chief, and to have been given the authority to speak and to act in his name.

The Ascension[13]

The Gospel story does not in fact end with the resurrection of Jesus, but with his ascension to heaven forty days later. Luke describes the ascension in the closing verses of his Gospel (24:50–52); the so-called "longer ending" of Mark[14] mentions it more briefly (16:19). Luke of course also repeats

---

13. I am greatly indebted for some of the thinking behind this section to David Pawson's excellent little book, *Where Is Jesus Now?*, which is a much-needed fresh look at the ascension.

14. Verses 9–20 of Mark 16 are usually assumed, almost certainly correctly, to be a later addition to the text of the Gospel. In my view that in no way affects their status as part of the inspired Word of God; the fact that they may be by another hand than Mark's is irrelevant—other books in the Bible have multiple authorship, such as the Psalms, and one book in the New Testament (Hebrews) is anonymous, but that does

the account of the ascension in more detail at the start of Acts,[15] and we will make some reference to that longer account in what follows. But the description of the ascension at the end of Luke makes it part of the story of the Gospels.

During the forty days between the resurrection and the ascension Jesus did a number of things; but one vital thing that he was doing was to prepare his disciples for his ascension, for the fact that he would not always be with them physically and present to their senses. That is partly the reason for his sudden "appearances"—he can simply appear with them through locked doors (John 20:19,26)—and his "disappearances," as when he simply vanishes before their sight (Luke 24:31). He can show Thomas that he knows exactly what Thomas said about needing to see his wounds, even though he was not physically present when Thomas said it (John 20:25–27). Acts 1:3 says that Jesus "appeared" to his disciples, which suggests that he was simply there and then not there; and he appeared on "occasions" (Acts 1:4). He is getting his disciples used to his invisible presence.

The ascension is a neglected truth—it has been called "the Cinderella of the creed"—and for many people a puzzling or even embarrassing one. That we often do not quite know what to make of it is largely due to two things: pious language, and scientific difficulties. The church has adopted a pious form of evangelical language which talks about Jesus living in our hearts, and evangelists call on people to invite Jesus into their lives.[16] All of this seems to be saying that Jesus is somehow still with us here. So language about his departing in the ascension seems strange to us. Moreover, it confuses people; they will ask: "You say Jesus lives in your heart (whatever that means!); but you also say that he reigns in heaven—so where is he actually?"

But the biggest problem with the ascension is scientific. It can seem to imply a flat earth and a "three-story universe," with the earth in the middle, hell as a kind of basement, and heaven as "up there" somewhere, rather like the penthouse suite of the cosmos; this seems embarrassing and ridiculous in an age of astronomy and space travel. These days it is generally, almost

---

not invalidate them as part of God's Word.

15. The fact that Luke describes the ascension at the end of his Gospel and again at the beginning of Acts shows that the ascension is *both* the end of Jesus' earthly ministry *and* the premise, the launching-pad, for the ministry of the church.

16. I am never happy with clichés like "inviting Jesus into your heart," for three reasons. [1] It is not a biblical phrase; and it is always best to stick to the things Scripture actually says. [2] Talking about the "heart" can, in western thinking, imply something to do with the emotions, and we need to avoid implying that a response to Jesus that is primarily emotional will lead to a real change of life. [3] It is obviously a metaphor, and so might unwittingly send the signal that whatever we might *say* happens when people respond to Jesus, it is actually just a figure of speech, and has no objective reality to it.

universally, assumed that the writers of the Bible believed in that kind of very primitive cosmology; and to many that invalidates anything the Bible has to say about the world, and in particular rules out taking the account of the ascension seriously. Such a judgment is unnecessary: whether or not the biblical writers actually believed in a flat earth and a three-story universe—and it is not as certain as is sometimes claimed that they necessarily did,—the language used in the Bible is not intended to be read as scientific but as either "popular" or laymen's language or as poetic imagery. When biblical writers, for example, speak of "the ends of the earth"—a phrase that occurs forty-five times in the Bible—there is no need to accuse them of teaching *as a doctrine* that the earth is flat; many of the places where the phrase is used clearly mean little more than "a long way away" (e.g. "she [= the Queen of Sheba] came from the ends of the earth to listen to Solomon's wisdom," Matthew 12:42//Luke 11:31), and we are quite capable of using similar non-scientific language today: when people who want to say that something is very widespread describe it as having spread to "every corner of the world," there is no need to assume that what they are affirming must be wrong on the grounds that, since we know the world to be a circular globe, it clearly doesn't have "corners"; and for that matter we still regularly talk about "sunrise," even though that, if pressed scientifically, would imply a geocentric view of the solar system—the sun, the pedant would insist, does not "rise"; rather, the earth revolves round it. Yes, of course it does; but we all know what people mean when they use the everyday language of "sunrise," and there is no need to read into that phrase that they actually believe that the sun revolves round the earth. In the same way, the language of the Bible about God's heaven being "above" the earth is never intended to teach a physical cosmology, but is using similar popular and non-technical language to teach his sovereign rule over all creation, in the same way that our own language speaks of a monarch reigning "over" his or her people. And even if the cultures in which the Bible was written did have a simple "three-story" view of the universe, the doctrine of the ascension is in no way tied to or dependent on that kind of primitive cosmology.[17]

17. Christians who are keen to defend the scientific accuracy of the Bible have often seized on the wording of Isaiah 40:22, which says of God that "he sits enthroned above the circle of the earth," as evidence that Scripture teaches that the earth is a globe. That is in all honesty reading far more into the text than is justified. The language of Isaiah is poetic, not scientific; and "circle" is probably referring simply to the horizon. But the same is true of conventional expressions, such as "the pillars of the earth" (Job 9:6, Psalm 75:3) or "the foundations of the earth" (1 Samuel 2:8, Psalm 102:25, Isaiah 48:13), which are often claimed by those who would debunk the Bible to imply a biblical doctrine of a flat earth: these are just as much poetic and figurative expressions as the old saying that "it's love that makes the world go round," and to try and read into them a

What the ascension is about is a spiritual reality rather than a cosmological journey. But "spiritual" does not mean non-historical; the language about the ascension is certainly not to be dismissed as merely mythical. It is presented as a historical event, which was witnessed by the disciples. In the account of the ascension in Acts 1:9-11 there are five references to "seeing": "Before their very eyes," verse 9; "A cloud hid him from their sight," verse 9; "They were looking intently up into the sky," verse 10; "Why do you stand here looking into the sky?," verse 11; ". . . in the same way you have seen him go into heaven," verse 11. The ascension, Luke stresses, is a historical event which the apostles witnessed.

So what is the ascension about? It is Jesus' departure from earth, from this life and this world. Just as Jesus had a unique entry into this life (the virgin birth), so he had a unique departure from it (the ascension).[18] It was fitting that Jesus should have a unique way of leaving this world; after all, everything about him was unique.

We need to understand the ascension as, in some ways, Jesus' return-journey to the Father. He had come into this world from the heavenly realms, and he now returns to those heavenly realms. In John's Gospel, Jesus speaks eight times about his having "come down from heaven" (as well as over twenty times about his having been sent into this world from God)—a classic example is 6:38, "I have come down from heaven not to do my will but to do the will of him who sent me"—but he also speaks eleven times about his returning to the Father or back to heaven: "I know where I came from and where I am going" (8:14), "I came from the Father and entered the world; now I am leaving the world and going back to the Father" (16:28). There is a parallel between Jesus' incarnation—his "descending" into human life—and his ascension at the end.

---

specific cosmology ignores the nature of poetic writing. Nothing in the Bible explicitly teaches or implies a doctrine of a flat earth, or for that matter a round one; and to wrest biblical phrases out of their context in an attempt to prove that Scripture either supports or contradicts modern scientific theories is not only a waste of time, but is likely to result in a failure to grasp what the Bible is actually saying.

18. Strictly speaking, not absolutely unique: Enoch (Genesis 5:24) and Elijah (2 Kings 2:11-12) both passed from this world into the presence of God without experiencing death. Jesus' ascension was different in nature and significance from their translation into heaven: Jesus had already been raised with a resurrection body that belonged to the "new creation," whereas Enoch and Elijah passed from this world in their "ordinary" bodies; and, most importantly, Jesus was exalted to sit on the throne of heaven, not merely translated to the life of heaven. But the instances of Enoch and Elijah are certainly foreshadowings of Jesus' greater ascension, just as the miraculous births in the Old Testament to mothers unable to conceive, like Sarah, were foreshadowings of the greater miracle of the virgin birth.

The incarnation is not primarily a move from one *place* to another, but a spiritual translation from one *state* to another: "The Word became flesh" (John 1:14), the Son took "the very nature [or, perhaps more correctly, "the form," as in the NIV footnote] of a servant" (Philippians 2:7). The repeated language about Jesus coming "down" from heaven does not have to imply a crudely physical and vertical descent; it is a metaphor to refer to the change of status involved in Jesus' becoming human, from glory and exaltation to humility and ordinariness. The same is true in reverse of the ascension. It is not primarily to be thought of as a move from one place (the earth) to another place (heaven?), but as a translation from the state of being part of this material world into the state of returning to the "spiritual world." The very first verse of the Bible tells us that "in the beginning God created the heavens and the earth." The phrase "the heavens" at its simplest means simply the sky, outer space. But there is almost certainly another sense: "the heavens and the earth" probably indicates the spiritual world and the material world; that is, the spiritual dimension that co-exists with the physical, but which is not normally seen. There is a spiritual world, where God lives, where the angels serve, where spiritual principalities and powers of evil operate. We cannot locate that world in a place with borders; it is a different level of existence—the spiritual realm or dimension to life—and it can co-exist in the same "space" as our human world, but is normally unseen.

Science cannot discover "the heavenly realms" as a "place"; the Hubble telescope will never locate "heaven." That is not because the spiritual world is beyond the reach of the human senses, but rather because God alone controls the audible and visible revelation of the heavenly realm. There are times when people see the spiritual realities that are normally invisible; in 2 Kings 6:15–17 Elisha's servant's eyes were opened to the reality of that spiritual world, and he saw what Elisha already knew was there, the chariots of the armies of heaven. In the New Testament, people sometimes see the heavenly realms: Stephen did in Acts 7:56, when he saw heaven opened and the Son of Man standing at the right hand of God; Paul did in 2 Corinthians 12:1–4, when he was transported before the very throne of God and heard "inexpressible things." Very particularly, John did in the book of Revelation. Some of the most frequent biblical instances of the inter-relationship between "heaven" and "earth" are encounters with angels. When angels appear, they are not to be thought of as traveling from another place to come to earth; rather, they are all around us already, but we do not normally see them, because they live in that spiritual realm or dimension. What happens when an angel "appears" is that God enables them to become, for a short time, visible and audible.

So the spiritual world of God's "heaven" co-exists with our human world. And in becoming a human being, Jesus became part of the human world; he stepped out of one realm, the dimension of spiritual life and reality, into the other, the human world. Then, in the ascension, he returned to the spiritual realm of God's heavenly reign.

The idea of a "parallel universe" is of course one that has been picked up by a lot of science fiction and fantasy writers. In C. S. Lewis' stories, you step through a wardrobe in the human world and are suddenly in the different realm of Narnia, which seems to co-exist in the same space, yet is a world of its own. The most recent popular example is of course the "Harry Potter" tales; by walking through a brick wall in an ordinary English railway station, you step into the magical world of Hogwarts. That parallel world is there all the time—but you don't see it unless you are intended to be part of it.

There are two ways we can think about the fact that this idea is popular in fiction. Some people will say, "You see! This Christian idea of a 'spiritual realm' is simply another example of popular fantasy-stories—Christianity is just another version of science fiction." But there is another possibility, namely that the idea of a "parallel world" has gripped the human imagination and is so widespread precisely because there really is one. It is not science fiction, but spiritual fact. The science fiction ideas are a fantasy version of something that actually exists in reality—the spiritual world of God's heaven.

Be that as it may, in the ascension Jesus stepped back into the spiritual world. From the perspective of this world, he certainly ascended—literally "rose." But that does not mean that we are to think of God's heaven as somewhere in outer space. What we call "outer space" is part of this physical world. Jesus "ascended"—was translated—from this material universe into the spiritual realm of God's Kingdom.

That is part of the significance of the clouds that were seen at the ascension (Acts 1:9). They are not simply to do with Jesus rising to the level in the earth's atmosphere where the clouds are: you can do that in an airplane. That is not the same thing as the ascension. But in the Bible clouds are often a sign and symbol of the glory of God. So, in the ascension, Jesus stepped out of the human world back into the spiritual realm from which he had come.

So what is the significance of the ascension?

The Heavenly Jesus

It is the final evidence that Jesus belongs to the heavenly realms. He had said he did; his works had demonstrated that he did; his character certainly suggested that he did. But the ascension clearly confirms it—Jesus is returning to the heavenly realms which are his true home.

The Exalted Jesus

It is the grounds for the glorification of Jesus as the exalted Lord. The New Testament church focused not just on the historical event of the ascension, but on the fact of the exaltation of Jesus to the throne of heaven. Paul wrote in Philippians 2:9–10, "Therefore God exalted him to the highest place and gave him the name that is above every name, that at the name of Jesus every knee should bow . . . " The word is literally "God 'hyper-exalted' him." Jesus, the ascended Lord, is worshiped as enthroned and crowned; the writer to the Hebrews says (2:9), "But we see Jesus, who was made a little lower than the angels, now crowned with glory and honor . . . "

Revelation 5 is the ascension seen, so to speak, from heaven's perspective. Luke 24 and Acts 1 show us Jesus as he leaves earth; Revelation 5 shows us Jesus, if we may so put it, as he arrives back in heaven. And what awaits him there is worship: "Then I . . . heard the voice of many angels, numbering thousands upon thousands, and ten thousand times ten thousand. They encircled the throne and the living creatures and the elders. In a loud voice they sang: 'Worthy is the Lamb, who was slain, to receive power and wealth and wisdom and strength and honor and glory and praise!'" (verses 11–12). The father in Jesus' "prodigal son" parable organized a party for his lost son when he returned; but with no disrespect intended towards that fictional father's skills as a host, even the greatest earthly celebration could not begin to compare with the heavenly Father's "Welcome home!" party for his Son.

The Spirit of Jesus

It marks the start of Jesus' heavenly ministry. We are very familiar with Jesus' ministry on earth: his Kingdom ministry of words and works, his atoning ministry on the cross and in the resurrection. But that is not the end of Jesus' ministry. We speak, rightly, of the "finished work" of the cross; and Jesus cried out before his death, "It is finished!" But what that means is that the work of atoning for sins is finished. The penalty for sins has been fully and finally paid, and nothing else need ever be done for sin to be forgiven.

But all-round Christian life needs more. The cross saves us from the penalty of sin; but it is the ascended Christ who delivers us from the power of sin. It is from his position as the exalted Lord of heaven that Jesus pours out his Holy Spirit on his people. The Bible speaks of two baptisms: baptism in water and baptism in the Holy Spirit. We might equally well describe them as the baptism that we perform on earth and the baptism that Jesus pours out from heaven. Water baptism makes us acceptable to God; Jesus' baptism makes us effective for God. Water baptism deals with our status as sinners; Jesus' baptism equips us for our service as disciples. Water baptism makes us clean before God; Jesus' baptism makes us useful to God.

And that baptism in the Holy Spirit depends on Jesus' ascension back to the Father. He had said to his disciples in the upper room, "It is for your good that I am going away. Unless I go away, the Counselor will not come to you; but if I go, I will send him to you" (John 16:7).

The High-Priestly Jesus

Moreover, Jesus ascends back to the Father so that he might represent us there as our Great High Priest. He is our perfect representative before God. "We have a Great High Priest who has gone through the heavens, Jesus the Son of God . . . [Christ] entered heaven itself, now to appear for us in God's presence" (Hebrews 4:14, 9:24). Whenever the Father looks at us, he sees us through Christ; and Jesus' finished work of atonement on the cross means that the Father can look on us with absolute acceptance and unreserved love.

That is why, as Hebrews 7:25 says, "he is able to save completely those who come to God through him, because he always lives to intercede for them." This permanent intercession does not mean that God is again and again inclined to look on us with disfavor and judgment, so Jesus needs again and again to intervene and persuade him to change his mind; rather, it speaks of the fact that the Father always looks on us as those who sins have for ever been atoned for by his Son's death on the cross, and that he never sees or thinks of us in any way other than as those who have been made unreservedly acceptable to him. The central point of Hebrews 7:23–25 is that Jesus, unlike the Old Testament priests, lives forever; and because his own life is eternal, the effectiveness of the salvation from sin that he achieved on the cross is equally eternal. F. F. Bruce summarizes this section of Hebrews very well in his commentary: "His once completed self-offering is utterly acceptable and efficacious; his contact with the Father is immediate and unbroken; his priestly ministry on his people's behalf is never-ending; and therefore the salvation which he secures to them is absolute."[19]

We rightly stress that Jesus' work of salvation was accomplished once and for all at the cross, and that nothing ever needs to be added to the atoning sacrifice which he perfectly offered there. Jesus' heavenly ministry does not *add* anything to his historical work of atonement; his eternal priesthood however does mean that, day by day and moment by moment, he *applies* his salvation to our lives; because Jesus is alive for ever, the Christian's salvation is as fresh and new each day as it was when Jesus first declared on the cross that "it is finished!"

The Reigning Jesus

And the ascension means that Jesus has entered upon his reign as King of kings and Lord of lords. Isaiah 9:6 had said that "the government will be on his shoulders"; we might reverently add that, now that Jesus has accomplished his earthly ministry and ascended back to heaven, the government *is* on his shoulders. Jesus now rules and reigns in the heavenlies; the ascension was his great coronation. The Old Testament verse that is by far the most frequently cited in the New Testament is Psalm 110:1. It is quoted over twenty times: "The Lord says to my lord, 'Sit at my right hand until I make your enemies a footstool for your feet.'" For the New Testament writers, the most fundamental fact about Jesus was that he reigned at God's right hand, and would continue to do so until all opposition to God's Kingdom was finally and permanently overcome.

It is right that we learn from Jesus' earthly ministry, and that the heart of our Gospel message is what Jesus achieved here amongst us when he died and rose again. But the Jesus whom we now serve and in whom we now believe is the ascended and exalted Lord of heaven. We need unashamedly to focus, not on earth, but on heaven. Many people today are afraid of being thought "so heavenly minded that they're no earthly use." But in fact the reverse is far more common in the western church: we can be so earthly minded that we're no heavenly use. Paul urges the Colossians, and us, not to be like that: "Since, then, you have been raised with Christ, set your hearts on things above, where Christ is seated at the right hand of God. Set your minds on things above, not on earthly things. For you died, and your life is now hidden with Christ in God" (Colossians 3:1–3). The focus of biblical faith is not that Jesus comes to help us in our earthly lives, but that he draws us into his

---

19. Bruce, *Hebrews*, 155.

heavenly life. We need rescuing from a too-domesticated view of Jesus and our life in him. The ascension, both the event and its significance, can help us to see Jesus as he is *now*; that is the Jesus whom we serve.

Moreover, the ascension reminds us of the sheer greatness—the "bigness"—of Jesus. One of the results of talking about "inviting Jesus into your heart" and having Jesus "living in your heart" is that it necessarily makes Jesus seem smaller than us. But the New Testament emphasis is not on the fact that Jesus is in me, but that I am in Christ. He is not only bigger than us, but infinitely bigger—he is exalted above all things. A church with a cozy, domesticated little Jesus will not impact the world with great power. The Jesus who was preached by the New Testament apostles was thought and spoken of in a way "which implies such dimensions as any theist would ascribe to God himself,"[20] or, as the old Sunday School hymn put it, as one who really did have the whole world in his hands.

The Jesus of the Gospels does not merely mean the man who walked the dusty roads of Palestine. Thank God he did that; and we rightly receive all that we can from his earthly ministry, and we live in the light of his atoning work. But the Gospel story concludes with Jesus as the Lord who is ascended, exalted, seated at the right hand of the Father. That is the Jesus we are to believe in, to preach, and to follow. There has been a lot of talk over the last century or so of "rediscovering the real Jesus"; unfortunately what that almost always means is stripping away from the biblical record of Jesus everything that makes him supremely real, to leave us with a purely secular first-century traveling preacher. But the ascended and glorified Jesus who reigns for ever and ever as King of kings and Lord of lords—that is Jesus as he really is. He does not need to be "rediscovered" by secular scholars; but he can be truly "discovered" by hungry souls, by all who seek him with all their heart.

---

20. Moule, *Origin of Christology*, 7.

Bibliography

Anderson, Norman. *The Evidence for the Resurrection*. London: Inter-Varsity Press, 1950.
Asimov, Isaac. *The Stars in their Courses*. First UK edition, London: White Lion, 1974.
Barclay, Oliver R. *Reasons for Faith*. London: Inter-Varsity Press, 1974.
Barclay, William. *The Gospel of Matthew*, vol. 1, Matthew 1–10. *The Daily Study Bible*, Edinburgh: Saint Andrew, 1956.
Blanchard, John. *Gathered Gold*. Welwyn, Hertfordshire, UK: Evangelical Press, 1984.
Brown, Colin (ed.). *The New International Dictionary of New Testament Theology*. English edition, 4 vols., Grand Rapids, Michigan: Zondervan, 1978.
Briggs, Charles A. *Theological Symbolics*. Edinburgh: T. and T. Clark, 1914.
Brown, Raymond E. *The Birth of the Messiah: a commentary on the infancy narratives in Matthew and Luke*. London: Geoffrey Chapman, 1977.
Bruce, F. F. *The Epistle of Paul to the Romans: an Introduction and Commentary*. London: Tyndale, 1963.
———. *The Epistle to the Hebrews*, in the *New International Commentary on the New Testament* series. Grand Rapids, Michigan: Wm. B. Eerdmans, 1964.
Carson, D. A. *Collected Writings on Scripture*. Nottingham, UK: Apollos/Inter-Varsity Press, 2010.
Davies, Horton. *Worship and Theology in England*, vol. 2 (1603–90). Princeton University Press, 1975.
Denney, James. *The Death of Christ*. London: Hodder and Stoughton, third edition, 1903.
Forsyth, P. T. *The Person and Place of Jesus Christ*. London: Independent Press, 1909.
Gaugel, Maurice. *The Life of Jesus*. London: George Allen and Unwin, 1958.
Green, Michael. *The Day Death Died*. Leicester, UK: Inter-Varsity Press, 1982.
———. *Matthew for Today*. London: Hodder and Stoughton, 1988.
Hendriksen, William. *New Testament Commentary: John*. Edinburgh: The Banner of Truth Trust, 1976.
———. *New Testament Commentary: Matthew*. Edinburgh: The Banner of Truth Trust, 1973.
Hill, David. *The New Century Bible Commentary: The Gospel of Matthew*. Grand Rapids, Michigan: Wm. B. Eerdmans, and London: Marshall, Morgan and Scott, 1972.
Hunter, A. M. *Introducing New Testament Theology*. London: Student Christian Movement, 1957.
Keller, Tim. *The Reason for God*. New York: Dutton Penguin, 2008.

Levin, Bernard. *Enthusiasms*. London: Coronet, Hodder and Stoughton, 1985.
Lewis, C. S. *First and Second Things: Essays on Theology and Ethics*, edited by Walter Hooper. London: Collins Fount Paperbacks, 1985.
———. *Mere Christianity*. London: Collins Fount Paperbacks, 1955.
———. *Timeless at Heart: Essays on Theology*, edited by Walter Hooper. London: Collins Fount Paperbacks, 1987.
Mandryk, Jason (ed.). *Operation World*. Seventh edition, Colorado Springs: WEC International/Biblica, 2010.
Marshall, I. Howard. *The Gospel of Luke*. Exeter, UK: Paternoster, 1978.
McDowell, Josh. *The New Evidence That Demands A Verdict*. Nashville: Thomas Nelson, 1999.
Merton, Thomas. *Thoughts in Solitude*. Tunbridge Wells, Kent, UK: Burns and Oates, 1975.
Moltmann, Jürgen. *The Crucified God*. New York: Harper and Row, 1974.
Morris, Leon. *The Gospel According to John* in the New International Commentary on the New Testament series. Grand Rapids, Michigan: Wm. B. Eerdmans, 1971.
———. *Luke, an Introduction and Commentary*. Tyndale New Testament Commentaries, Leicester, UK: Inter-Varsity Press, 1974,1980.
Moule, C. F. D. *The Origin of Christology*. Cambridge University Press, 1977.
Nee, Watchman. *The Normal Christian Life*. Eastbourne, UK: Kingsway, 1961.
Newbigin, Lesslie. *Sin and Salvation*. London: Student Christian Movement, 1956.
Pawson, David. *Where Is Jesus Now?* Eastbourne, UK: Kingsway, 2001.
Plummer, Alfred. *The Gospel According to Luke*. International Critical Commentary, Edinburgh: T. and T. Clark, 1928.
Rolph, C. H. (ed.). *Does Pornography Matter?* London: Routledge and Kegan Paul, 1961.
Shedd, William. *A History of Christian Doctrine*. New York: Charles Scribner and Sons, 1888.
Smith, Michael. *From Christ to Constantine*. Leicester, UK: Inter-Varsity Press, 1971.
Strachan, R. H. *The Fourth Gospel: its Significance and Environment*. London: Student Christian Movement, 1941.
Strobel, Lee. *The Case for Christ*. Grand Rapids, Michigan: Zondervan, 1998.
———. *The Case for a Creator*. Grand Rapids, Michigan: Zondervan, 2004.
———. *The Case for Faith*. Grand Rapids, Michigan: Zondervan, 2000.
Tasker, R. V. G. *The Gospel According to St John, an Introduction and Commentary*. London: Tyndale, 1960.
———. *The Gospel According to St Matthew, an Introduction and Commentary*. London: Tyndale, London, 1961.

www.ingramcontent.com/pod-product-compliance
Lightning Source LLC
Chambersburg PA
CBHW062028220426
43662CB00010B/1515